W9-CFZ-103

The World
and a
Very Small Place
in Africa

Kevin Reilly, Series Editor

The World and a Very Small Place in Africa

Donald R. Wright

M.E. Sharpe

Armonk, New York
London, England

Copyright © 1997 by M. E. Sharpe, Inc.

All rights reserved. No part of this book may be reproduced in any form
without written permission from the publisher, M. E. Sharpe, Inc.,
80 Business Park Drive, Armonk, New York 10504.

Library of Congress Cataloging-in-Publication Data

Wright, Donald R.
The world and a very small place in Africa / Donald R. Wright
p. cm. — (Sources and studies in world history)
Includes bibliographical references and index.
ISBN 1-56324-959-6. —ISBN 1-56324-960-X (pbk.)
1. Niumi (Kingdom)—Relations. I. Title. II. Series.
DT532.23.W75   1997
966.3—dc21
96-44139
CIP
r96

Printed in the United States of America

The paper used in this publication meets the minimum requirements of
American National Standard for Information Sciences—
Permanence of Paper for Printed Library Materials,
ANSI Z 39.48-1984.

BM (c)   10   9   8   7   6   5   4   3   2   1
BM (p)   10   9   8   7   6   5   4   3   2   1

For George Brooks

CONTENTS

LIST OF MAPS

FOREWORD

This is a refreshing, engaging approach to both African history and world history. Donald Wright gives us a history of Niumi, in Senegambia, West Africa, that is unabashedly local history. Niumi never constituted more than four hundred square miles, and most of its inhabitants have always lived in a much smaller area along the northern coast of the Gambia River and the Atlantic coast.

Wright does not distract us with events upriver or in the dry sahel of Senegal; nor does he turn local history into the regional history of Sudanic kingdoms or the Atlantic diaspora. But precisely because the author rivets our attention on such a "very small place," he enables us to know it in great detail.

Small places, especially African small places, have never stood for world history in the past. Earlier generations of historians writing from the vantage point of the imperial metropolis often entertained the conceit that "localities" like London stood for the world—as microcosms, motors, or models.

Donald Wright finds a more fitting paradigm of world history in the "world-systems" theory of Immanuel Wallerstein. Wallerstein has argued over the past twenty-five years that the development of a modern capitalist "world system" has benefited the developed countries at the expense of the colonized and exploited "periphery." Wright accepts this model but carefully avoids two pitfalls—ignoring precapitalist systems and understating the degree to which people on the periphery participate in the shaping of their own destinies.

Wright shows how Niumi from 1000 to 1450 was drawn into a "restructuring world system" in which the great forces of Islam and Sudanic kingdoms had only a minor impact on the local salt trade and fisheries. Similarly, after 1450, the emerging Atlantic plantation system and slave trade, far from victimizing the people of Niumi, offered them opportunities and increased political stability. But between 1600 and 1800, Wright argues, Niumi did not change as much as it did between 1800 and 1850, when it was increasingly incorporated into the world capitalist system, as a producer of agricultural staples, especially peanuts, for industrializing countries. As a result, the declining global price of peanuts had more bearing on

Niumi's twentieth century than the political vicissitudes of colonialism and its aftermath.

Even in telling the story of Niumi's twentieth-century dependence on world wars and global markets, however, Wright gives local actors center stage. We meet, for example, World War II veteran Jerre Manneh, whose great-great-grandfather, the *mansa*, sold the British their first permanent settlement on the river in 1816. We are introduced to Lamin Sowe, another veteran who fought in Burma and now grows mangoes and petitions the government for a pension that was promised long ago. And we visit Alhaji Karamo Njie, a village Imam, who recalls the names and stories of many of those who have long since gone. It is quite a cast.

Kevin Reilly

PREFACE

This is a book of African history inspired by my study and teaching of world history, or a book of world history inspired by my study and teaching of African history. I am still not sure which. Maybe that is good. It is a history of the Gambia River state of Niumi over the past seven or eight centuries with an emphasis on how the state's widening world, and especially its dealings with world systems, affected the lives of the people living there down through the years. But more of this in the introduction. I simply wish to convey here that in addition to standard elements of economic, social, and political history, I have tried to keep in focus some of the topics brought out in recent scholarship in world and African history—such things as cross-cultural influences, environmental and biological issues, and matters pertaining to women. Given the nature of the available evidence, this was not always easy.

Because world history, with its breadth and growing theoretical basis, and African history, with its grounding in African cultures unfamiliar to most American readers, can be complicated and confusing (to an author as well as a reader), I have attempted to keep theoretical discussions simple (or at least subtle) and to a minimum, and I have used words in foreign languages, especially Mandinka, only when I believed it necessary to do so. Persons who want more detailed discussions of world-systems theory, for example, or wish to know the Mandinka words for various terms used in the book, will need to look further. I have attempted to guide such looking in the citations.

I wish to make two points for the sake of honesty and clarity. First, although Mandinka-speaking Africans always referred to the state along the north bank of the Gambia River's estuary as Niumi, not everyone did. For a long time it was called "Barra" in the creolized trade language of the river, and between the seventeenth and nineteenth centuries British and French records use "Barra" or "Bar" more frequently than "Niumi" to refer to the state or its ruler. In quotations from these records and published sources based on these records, I have changed "Barra" to "Niumi," simply to avoid obvious confusion and continual inclusion of [*sic*] in quotations. Second, the official name of the modern West African country is The Republic of The Gambia, and it is properly referred to as The Gambia, with both words capitalized. Before 1965, the British referred to their Gambia River colony as the Gambia (or, officially, the Gambia Colony and Protectorate), without capitalizing the article. I keep this distinction in the text.

A long list of people and institutions—far more than I can recognize here—have lent assistance across my career of study and teaching of African and world history, but some have been especially helpful in my preparation of this book. Marilou Wright first heard my ideas about it. She has always been my first and best critic. Sharon Steadman taught me a great deal about current thinking on world systems and provided useful sources and regular encouragement. Dr. John Thornton read the entire manuscript and made useful comments from a perspective of both world and African history. Several people in The Gambia—Executive Director B.K. Sidibe, Abdoulie Bayo, Patience Sonko-Godwin, and Moro Komah of the National Council of Arts and Culture; Gidom Mballow and Honore Kujabi of the National Records Service—provided help and encouragement before and during a research visit there in 1996. I was fortunate to have encountered Dr. Christopher Schwabe, Project Director of a Health Sector Requirement Study for The Gambia, on my flight to Banjul. Chris has provided me with much information relating to the situation in The Gambia in recent years, and he and Hendrick Baeyens went out of their way to be helpful during my stay there. The staffs in the Public Record Office in Kew Gardens, the Memorial Library of Cortland College, and libraries at Cornell, Binghamton, and Syracuse Universities assisted me at various stages of my work. Dr. David L. Miller took my map sketches, which were real sow's ears, and turned them into the silk purses that appear in the text. And I am grateful to the State University of New York and its College at Cortland for the sabbatical leave that allowed me to work full-time on this project and the Faculty Research Grant that helped support my travel for research in The Gambia and the United Kingdom.

The men and women of Niumi hold a special place in my heart and mind. They have welcomed me into their villages and homes at different times over the past twenty-two years, and almost without exception they have been warm, friendly, open, and forthcoming. Most recently, Jerre Manneh, Imam Ibrahim Njie, and Lamin Sowe spent several hours talking to me about their lives and Niumi's recent history. Would that I could do more for all of them than write about their plight.

Finally, I will forever be indebted to my mentor at Indiana University, Dr. George E. Brooks. He is the person who introduced me to both African and world history, and for over a quarter of a century he has kept me engaged with fresh ideas and new challenges involving each field. He is Chaucer's Oxford Cleric: "still a student though, One who had taken logic long ago. . . . And he would gladly learn, and gladly teach."

NOTE ON SOURCES AND ABBREVIATIONS

In addition to standard published sources, I have used unpublished materials in several archives and libraries. These include the following:

Archives Nationales de France, Paris. These include records of French traders under "Colonies: Sénégal et Côte Occidentale d'Afrique" (prefix B4) and "Marine: Service General" (prefix C6).

Archives Nationales de Sénégal, Dakar. These include correspondence relating to the French post at Albreda (prefix 13G).

Bodleian Library, Oxford. The Rawlinson Manuscripts, which include Minutes of Council from James Fort in the eighteenth century (prefix C745-7).

The Gambia National Archives, Banjul. These documents are identified with the prefix CSO. They include British records from the nineteenth and twentieth centuries and a small number of documents relating to the post-independence period.

Public Record Office, Kew Gardens, England. These include records of the Treasury (African Companies, prefix T 70) from the seventeenth and eighteenth centuries and the Colonial Office (Gambia, General Correspondence, prefix CO 87, and Sierra Leone, General Correspondence, prefix CO 267) from the nineteenth and twentieth centuries. Some documents from the CO series are duplicated in The Gambia National Archives. I site the source I used.

The World
and a
Very Small Place
in Africa

INTRODUCTION

"Don't forget who taught us how to drive."
—Bakary Sidibe, to the author, in September 1974, after tiring
of the author's complaints about Gambian drivers

The Gambia River may not be the calmest and most easily navigated of the world's great waterways, but to seamen entering the river after a week or two of tossing in the choppy Atlantic, it may seem so. The Gambia flows into the ocean 115 miles below Cape Verde, the westernmost tip of the African continent. The river's mouth is surprisingly broad—twelve miles across at its entrance into the Atlantic—and funnel shaped as if designed to catch vessels coasting down around the cape from the north. Inside the mouth, the river is a sailor's delight: its main channel is deep, and its strong tidal flow helps vessels pass upriver. In days of sail most ships could ride the winds and tides 120 miles eastward to a port on the river called Niani-Maru. Smaller craft that could tack more easily between the narrowing banks were able to pass another eighty miles eastward to Barokunda Falls. These were not really falls so much as a series of laterite ledges on which craft drawing a little more than three feet of water scraped bottom. Fair-sized canoes could pass Barokunda and travel another 140 miles southeasterly toward the edge of the Futa Jalon highlands. Thus, from as early as West Africans put vessels on the water, the Gambia served as a highway into the interior.

On the north bank of the Gambia, at its mouth, lies a territory known locally as Niumi. For five hundred years it was a separate political unit—a state, or kingdom, in Western terms—one of many such small units that spread across West Africa's savannas over the centuries before European rule. Niumi was never large—it is difficult to say how large because African rulers were far more concerned with control of people than of land, and they seldom delineated political boundaries with much care, especially in lightly populated parts of their realm. Still, historical records and notions of local residents tend to agree that Niumi never comprised more than about 400 square miles, and even that figure is deceptively large because most of

4

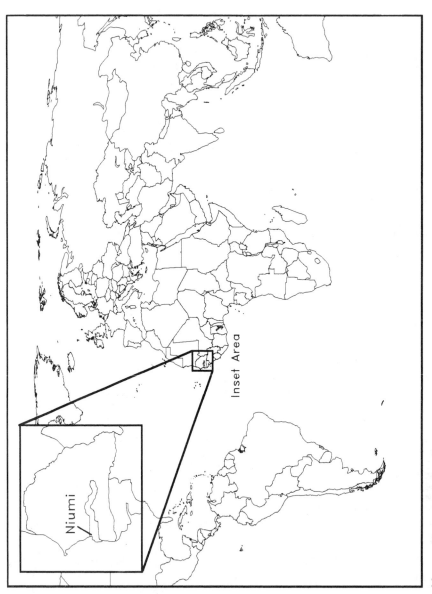

Map 1. **Niumi and the World**

its population before recent times lived within a few miles of the Gambia. Thus, Niumi was more a long strip of land along the riverbank under a single political authority than a compact, squared-off territory. And at the height of its control, even including uninhabited forests as well as the populated riverside, it was only about one-third the size of such small entities as the Duchy of Luxembourg or the state of Rhode Island.

I first saw Niumi in 1974 as I was coming into The Gambia by air. The plane made the short hop down from Dakar, Senegal, along the Atlantic Coast, and it passed seaward of Niumi as it approached Gambia's airport, across the river. The farther south we flew, the brighter and whiter grew the coastal stretch. In the vicinity of the Saloum River, north of the Senegal-Gambia border, great flats of land near the ocean were treeless and barren— a white moonscape, though absent of any elevation. It was here that the tide spilled across huge segments of the flatlands and then evaporated naturally, leaving a crust of salt that people gathered in baskets and exchanged toward West Africa's salt-starved inlands. For a thousand years, probably much longer, Niumi's residents had participated in, marshaled, and sometimes controlled the passage of salt up the Gambia River. It was a key to Niumi's power and wealth, and it would play an important role in much of the state's early history.

I could not spot the handful of buildings that served as the customs post on the border, but I knew from the coastline, having pored over maps of the area for a year or more, about where Senegal stopped and The Gambia began. It was late August, the height of the rainy season, and everything was green. What immediately became evident was how Niumi was a combination of two landscapes: watery coast and rolling, wooded grasslands. The northwestern part of the territory was a stretch of low, sandy, wooded islands separated from a mangrove-lined coast and crisscrossed by a maze of waterways. Only a small number of the area's inhabitants ever learned their way around these tidal creeks and backwaters. The mangroves hugged Niumi's riverbank in a sweeping arch from the Gambia's mouth down past Barra Point around a big eastward bend, and they clogged the bank on up river for a hundred miles or more. Oysters clung to the mangrove roots and, when exposed at low tide, made fair picking. A few little creeks and streams cut through the band of mangrove green and flowed a mile or two into the interior.

Inland from the coast and riverbank, savanna made up all the rest. I was surprised at how much this reminded me of my eastern Indiana home: grasslands and tall trees, with little elevation, rolling on for what seemed like forever. It was thick and verdant, waving in the August breeze. By the next April, six months into the dry season when the wind they call the *harmattan* blows hot off the Sahara, it would be crisp and dusty, everything tinted orange by the wind-blown soil.

From above, it all looked charming. Villages seemed to pop out behind the jet's wing, a mixture of thatch and metal roofs underneath canopies of majestic silk-cotton trees and broad, squat baobabs. I thought I recognized Essau, Berending, Bakendiki—old villages I had read about. I did not see many people—it was during the hottest part of the afternoon and the plane was still at several thousand feet—but I thought I spotted a few men in their fields of peanuts, a few children scattering birds from stands of millet. I saw the narrow scar of tarmac running down the fifteen miles from the Senegalese border to the ferry dock at Niumi's Barra Point. At Essau, near Barra, it intersected with a red-gravel road that struck off toward the far end of The Gambia, 200 miles dead east. A ferry full of people, cows, and a few cars was churning over toward Barra from the river's south side, where The Gambia's capital, Banjul, is situated. Covered pickups and station wagons— the "bush taxis" that convey people about West Africa's less-populated areas—were lined up near the terminal. It was all a pretty picture.

I would make the same trip by car just a few days later. A problem with arrangements for my long stay forced me to fly back to Dakar, and to save money returning to The Gambia, I joined a crowd of nine people in one of those station wagons riding down the tarmac road to the ferry. Close up, Niumi was not so charming. It was hot and humid almost beyond belief. Just north of the Senegal-Gambia border we passed a couple of men working in fields of peanuts. They were squatting, it looked like weeding, chopping up clouds of dust with broad, flat, short-handled instruments. One of them stood as our vehicle approached. He wore a long shirt that I thought was a faded imitation of camouflage until I got closer and saw the reddish-brown and black and olive blotches were soil and plant stains mixed and blended with perspiration. He did not wave—just looked at us with a face lacking expression, as sweat rolled down from underneath the bottom of his stocking cap. We came upon a bicyclist, an older man wearing glasses and a short-brimmed hat, who, when he heard us approaching, got off the bike, picked it up, and walked a good five yards off the road. It was something I would see repeatedly. Cyclists had a history of bad experiences with automobiles.

We stopped longer than we wanted at the border station between Senegal and The Gambia, a handful of yellowish buildings with tin roofs built close to the road. Not far away was one of those massive silk-cotton trees I had spotted from the air. The Gambian border guards, nice-looking, officious young men in khaki shorts and knee socks, made us open our luggage. Arguments ensued. One woman passenger did not want to retrieve a large, blue-plastic-wrapped package that the driver had tied snugly to the wagon's top. The guards were adamant. For a while she spoke loudly and waved her long arms. Other passengers spoke on her behalf. Then there was quieter talk. In the end she passed them a couple of small bills. Gambian officials accepted Senegalese currency. But the guards saved their most careful scrutiny for the driver's papers. They just were not in order, it seemed. Driver, passengers, and guards formed a tight huddle of loud discussion. I took the opportunity to look around.

Just down the road, vendors had set up shop. They knew that people did not cross the border speedily. Skinny young men were selling skinny loaves of bread, adolescents were offering sandwiches made with a spicy meat-and-oil mixture kept warm in enameled tubs, women were passively peddling green oranges, and two men, tall and dark with narrow, angular faces, were smoking animal carcasses—these looked like goats—over a slow-burning fire. They offered to cut off a strip of meat from one. I declined. There were flies everywhere. I walked another thirty yards to a low, roofed platform where old men were sitting. One of them had a milky-blue film over his eyes and was not seeing anything. The rest looked wan and listless. It was the "hungry season"—the months immediately preceding the harvest, when grain stores were low and few had cash, normally acquired by selling peanuts, to buy rice. It was also the time of year when mosquitoes bred in the standing water and then passed malaria among human hosts. Two women walked by slowly, balancing calabash bowls of greens on their heads. Each wore long, wrapped shirts of colorful, tie-dyed fabric and rubber, flip-flop shoes. One wore a yellowish T-shirt showing a faded Bob Marley. Both had infants attached to their backs by cloth wraps. One child's red-tinged hair was the telltale sign of *kwashiorkor,* a disease resulting from protein deficiency. Like almost all the children I encountered, these two had runny noses. Neither was asleep; their eyes silently followed me as their mothers walked past.

Once we got to Barra, I had some time to kill. The noonish ferry had just left the pier—it was a hundred yards out, had completed its pivot to face the south bank, and now was revving its old diesel engines to high speed for the five-mile crossing. It would not return for three hours. An engine breakdown in its twin had occasioned the long hiatus in the schedule. The Gambia Ports Authority did not have the part needed to repair the engine and was not sure it could turn one up. The other passengers were not surprised and did not seem to mind, however. They were content to sit and wait in the canopied pavilion. I wandered over to the Barra market, a small, open-air gathering of people, tables, stools, and stalls where one could procure everything from fresh fish to woven baskets. I was not astute enough to consider the significance of all the imported things for sale there—dry-cell batteries from France, rubber shoes from Spain, T-shirts from American colleges, pablum-like breakfast cereal in metal cans from Great Britain, and the ubiquitous Nescafé—but I did note a few oddities: Huge bags of rice from Vietnam and Arkansas (in this rice-producing region); plastic bottles of peanut oil from France (in this country where peanut farming was the major economic enterprise); identical bars of soap in every stall, imported from England and selling for exactly the same price. As I stood sweating in the heat and humidity, 5,000 miles from my home, where there was no hungry season and no malarial languor, where (most) drivers did not aim at cyclists, where we extracted oils from the crops we grew, where we had parts to fix our cars, and where manufacturers of a dozen different brands of soap competed vigorously for my dollar, I recognized that something in that little place was awry.

What was wrong in Niumi, I eventually came to understand better, was the same thing that was wrong in a good part of the world. I remained in The Gambia for nine months, interviewing oral traditionists so that I could, with additional archival work, reconstruct the precolonial history of Niumi for my doctoral thesis at Indiana University. It was an interesting piece; no one ever said it was seminal. About halfway through my stay in The Gambia, in late January 1975, George Brooks, my dissertation adviser, sent me a welcome letter of encouragement and included a copy of Immanuel Wallerstein's new book, *The Modern World-System*. "By all accounts," Brooks wrote in typical understatement, "this book is very important." I was already acquainted with William H. McNeill's interpretive work on world history, *The Rise of the West,* and had taught a couple of world history courses, part time, at Auburn University at Montgomery, Alabama, so I was at least partially comfortable with the "global perspective." Now, I found plenty of time to read about the modern world system—all the more because I had to make frequent trips on the Barra ferry, which was forever under repair. I struggled with Wallerstein's ideas of how events associated with the growth of European capitalism after the sixteenth century brought together increasing numbers of people of the world—brought them together not under a grand political authority but in a series of economic relationships he called the "modern world system." These economic relationships were more important than political ones, Wallerstein argued: how people fit into the world system, as participants from the stronger and wealthier "core" nations or as part of the weaker and poorer "periphery," determined important aspects of their lives. I suppose that reading was the beginning of my awareness of the influence of global events on local history. It is a perspective I have tried to maintain by following—sometimes at considerable distance—the evolution of arguments about world systems.

In 1976 I accepted a position in history with the liberal arts College at Cortland of the State University of New York; in 1978, for my sins, I thought at the time, I began teaching world history; and I have taught African and world history ever since. It has been the teaching and reading in both of these expanding fields, over quite a long time, combined with my experience of living in The Gambia and studying its history, that has given me a sense of what has long been the key to problems in Niumi and much of the rest of the world. More directly, I think that I have come to understand how dealings with large economic complexes and, eventually, incorporation into an ever-growing world market, or world economy, or world political economy, or, indeed, world system, have affected the way people lived for a long time in Niumi—this very small place in Africa. What follows is that story.

PART I

BACKGROUND

BEFORE A.D. 1450

In the late summer of 1446, nearly half a century before Christopher Columbus crossed the Atlantic, a Portuguese knight and adventurer named Nuno Tristão sailed an armed caravel down Africa's west coast and into the mouth of the Gambia River.[1] He had reason to expect a hostile reception. For several years prior to this, sailors like Tristão had been capturing Africans along the Atlantic coast north of the Gambia and spiriting them back to Portugal. According to Gomes Eanes de Azurara, a contemporary Portuguese court chronicler, "the disposition and conversion of these prisoners occupied a good portion of [Prince Henry's] time."

Just inside the river's mouth Tristão launched two boats, with twelve armed men (including Tristão) in one and ten in the other. They began to ride the tide upriver, intent on locating more "prisoners." Soon, however, they altered their route and, writes Azurara, "made for some habitations that they espied on the right hand." Their concentration on these habitations must have been intense, for they did not immediately notice the approach of twelve boats launched from the north bank, "in the which," Azurara records, "there would be as many as seventy or eighty Guineas, all Negroes, with bows in their hands." Then men in one of the boats beached their craft, got out, and began to rain arrows on the Portuguese. The others came near and, in Azurara's words, "discharged that accursed ammunition of theirs all full of poison upon the bodies of our countrymen." They chased the two Portuguese boats back to the caravel, outside the river's mouth, where the seamen tied up to the larger vessel, the crew cut their anchor cables amid the hail of arrows, and the invaders limped away. Of the twenty-eight who had entered the river on the caravel, only seven remained alive two days later because, Azurara notes, "that poison was so artfully composed that a slight wound, if it only let blood, brought men to their last end." Over several days, the survivors rolled twenty-one bodies off the caravel and into the Atlantic Ocean off Africa's west coast.

Because there was not a trained navigator among the remaining crew, the caravel's return to Portugal was indirect and long. Luck apparently played a role, though Azurara credits "heavenly aid." After two months out of sight

11

Box 1. A Sale of Slaves in Portugal

Azurara was a strong court supporter, who took the side of his countrymen in disputes with Africans, but he was mindful of the pain associated with the commerce of slaves. Of some of the earliest Africans
auctioned in Lisbon to work in the canefields of southern Portugal, he
writes:

> On the 8th of August 1444, early in the morning on account of the heat, the
> sailors landed the captives. When they were all mustered in the field outside
> the town, they presented a remarkable spectacle. . . . But what heart so hard
> as not to be touched with compassion at the sight of them! Some with
> downcast heads and faces bathed in tears as they looked at each other;
> others moaning sorrowfully, and fixing their eyes on heaven, uttered plaintive
> cries as if appealing for help to the Father of Nature. Others struck their faces
> with their hands, and threw themselves flat upon the ground. Others uttered
> a wailing chant, after the fashion of the country, and although their words
> were unintelligible, they spoke plainly enough the excess of their sorrow. But
> their anguish was at its height when the moment of distribution came, when
> of necessity children were separated from their parents, wives from their
> husbands, and brothers from brothers. Each was compelled to go wherever
> fate might send him. It was impossible to effect this separation without ex-
> treme pain.

---

of land, keeping the vessel sailing "directly to the north, declining a little to
the east," the crew sighted a ship piloted by a Spanish pirate, who informed
them they were not far off Portugal's southern coast. They put in at Lagos
and informed their patron, Prince Henry, of the tragedy. Azurara writes that
the prince "had great displeasure at the loss of the men," and "like a lord
who felt their deaths had come to pass in his service, he afterward had an
especial care of their wives and children."

Nothing is known of the immediate actions of the African bowmen,
residents of a small political unit called Niumi, occupying the north bank of
the Gambia's estuary, following the successful defense of their territorial
waters. They must have returned up the creeks and backwaters of their
homeland and, like the Portuguese, reported their exploits to their ruler, a
person with the title of *mansa*. He was surely elated at the news. If true to
later form, he led a celebration enhanced by palm wine and called in praise-
singers—a *mansa*'s equivalent of court chroniclers—to extol the gallantry
of the bowmen.

In time, though, however pleased he must have been with the defensive
efforts, Niumi's *mansa* seems to have thought deeply about relations with
the sharp-nosed intruders. Perhaps he recognized that the Portuguese would

be as persistent as they were pugnacious, or gained respect for the fighting potential of crossbowmen and caravels. More likely, with information trickling down of Portuguese trading with Africans along the Senegal River, far to Niumi's north, providing access to horses, iron bars, and other valuable commodities, the *mansa* and his advisers recognized how their commercial interests intertwined. In any event, nine years later, in 1455, when the Venetian Alvise da Cadamosto, sailing for Portugal, brought three caravels into the Gambia River, friendly traders from Niumi advised him on products he could obtain there. A year later Niumi's *mansa* befriended Portuguese trader Diogo Gomes and apparently mediated a dispute other Portuguese merchants were having with coastal peoples north of Niumi.[2] What had begun as hostile relations turned friendly with prospects of trade. Or, as Azurara concludes his account, after mid-century, "deeds in those parts involved trade and mercantile dealings more than fortitude and exercise of arms."

What brought the two groups—residents of the small southwestern European kingdom of Portugal on the one hand and the small West African kingdom of Niumi on the other—into conflict that summer day in 1446, to be followed within a decade by friendlier commercial contact, was a process of history that began centuries earlier and involved peoples across the central expanse of the Old World. By the middle of the fifteenth century western Europe and West Africa were being drawn increasingly into a wider world or, more particularly, into a restructuring and expanding world economic system that forever after would alter the ways of life of people living in each place.

Notes

1. Tristão's episode in the Gambia is described in Gomes Eanes de Azurara, *The Chronicle of the Discovery and Conquest of Guinea,* ed. C.R. Beazley and E. Prestage, 2 vols. (London: Hakluyt Society, 1896–99), 2: 252–57.

2. Alvise da Cadamosto, "The Voyages of Cadamosto," in *The Voyages of Cadamosto and Other Documents in Western Africa in the Second Half of the Fifteenth Century,* ed. G.R. Crone (London: Hakluyt Society, 1937), 97–100.

1

WORLD SYSTEMS

A BACKGROUND FOR NIUMI'S HISTORY TO A.D. 1450

Of all the general phenomena that have affected the way groups of people have lived—anywhere, at any time, through nearly all of the human past—two are of particular importance for students of world history. One is the relationship of groups of people with others who had ways of thinking and acting that were different from theirs. The other has to do with the way groups of people related to large-scale economic organizations—integrated trading complexes or commercial systems. Because many persons who appeared from afar, where people had new and different ideas and ways, were long-distance traders, the two phenomena often were related.

The first is important simply because people have changed most thoroughly, in relatively short periods of time, by borrowing ideas or adopting technologies from others. Anthropologists call this process *diffusion;* examples of it abound. The Plains Indians of North America altered their lifestyle considerably once they adopted the horse, brought across the Atlantic by the Spanish in the sixteenth century, and adopted a culture related to its use. Western Europeans changed over a longer time through the Middle Ages, but they certainly used others' ideas and technologies to their advantage when, after 1500, they employed such Chinese inventions as gunpowder, printing, and the compass to help assert themselves economically, and eventually politically, on the rest of the world.[1] Today, contact and borrowing have led to such thorough change among groups of people around the world, as ideas have spread with ease across the global communication network, that we encounter others who have distinctly different ways with less and less frequency. We are moving ever faster toward a global culture where many of the people of the world do things alike. But such was not the case just a few hundred years ago, and sometimes people changed dramatically, over a relatively short period, because of having come into contact with others whose ways were different from their own.

The second phenomenon still holds strongly in its effect on human lives, however. How any group fits into a regional, intercontinental, or global network of commercial relations is an important determinant in the ways individuals within the group live. Today, people residing in countries that are centers of world finance and production—Japan, the United States, or one of the nations of western Europe, for instance—live differently from those in countries that have little capital and industry and rely primarily on production of cash crops or raw materials for export. For an example of the latter one can pick most countries of the so-called Third World. Many now consider the major reason for the differences in the lives of people in the "developed" and "underdeveloped" worlds—differences in everything from income and productivity to caloric intake and life expectancy—to be how the groups have related to the world economic system of the past four or five centuries.

World Systems

Immanuel Wallerstein was the first to bring clear emphasis to the importance of world systems. In *The Modern World-System* (1974, 1980, 1988),[2] Wallerstein established a model for explaining how the world has come to be as it is today. This model rests on the rise of capitalism in Europe in the fifteenth and sixteenth centuries and the establishment of a Western-dominated capitalist economy involving peoples of all parts of the world in unequal relationships. According to Wallerstein, this "modern world-system" has remained in place, without major structural change, ever since. Several others have stretched Wallerstein's model to fit earlier times and smaller "worlds."[3] For this book, an informed acquaintance with basic elements of world-systems theory is useful for understanding the central argument—that events of a global scale affected the lives of people in a very small place in Africa for a very long time, and they still do.

World Systems Based on Economic Relationships: The Standard Model

Through much of the human past, groups of people have interacted with others some distance away through trade.[4] What they traded, primarily, were goods each produced that the other did not, or did not produce so well, or produced equally well but at much greater cost. The meeting places for exchange usually were towns or cities. Eventually, some of the trade goods were carried on to other sites, sometimes in other cultures, where they, in turn, were exchanged for products from elsewhere. Over time, those interacting in such economic arrangements came to exchange ideas and ways of doing things, as well.

In some places these relationships became regular, systematic patterns of economic and cultural interchange—a form of intercultural interaction that lasted for long periods. Historians and others have come to call these broad and lasting patterns of exchange "economic complexes," "economic systems," "world economies," or, from Wallerstein's lead, "world systems." It is important to recognize that they were called *world* systems not necessarily because they involved people over the entire world—indeed, only the world system in place since the sixteenth century has done so—but because they involved people living in separate political units beyond the recognized boundaries of states, beyond empires, or even beyond what we have tended to call civilizations.

Why is it important to recognize the existence of world systems in the past? Simply because the way societies in different areas were involved in a world system determined much about how individuals in that society lived. In most world systems, relationships among the various involved groups were not equal. Some areas of competing cities or states slowly grew into more central, or "core," positions in the network by becoming particularly efficient producers, efficient users of resources, and effective accumulators of wealth. The core areas tended to grow strong politically and militarily too. Other areas tended to remain in less central, or "peripheral," positions by becoming more suppliers of unprocessed resources to, and acquirers of processed goods from, the core or cores.[5] Indeed, one of the glaring ironies of such economic relationships is that groups on the periphery often found themselves trading for processed goods made from their own raw resources. But in addition, peripheral areas remained weak politically and economically. Such wealth that people in the peripheral areas possessed tended to flow toward the core areas of the network. These dissimilarities in production, labor, power, and wealth meant that persons living in core and peripheral areas of a world system lived quite differently—those in the core generally better in a sense of material goods, security, and general welfare, and those in the periphery generally worse.

Such political-economic relationships often became long-standing because the groups involved, especially on the periphery, became more or less trapped into them—not so much by deceit, stealth, or raw power as by circumstances. It was to the core areas' advantage to maintain their strong, central economic positions, so they tended to take what measures they could to do so. This might involve using their military to keep trade routes open or sending managers or advisers to the peripheral areas to make more efficient the production of primary products. And the circumstances themselves, with wealth and resources flowing to the core, enabled the core areas to act in such manner. On the periphery, the slow growth of production for the core areas became institutionalized. People who once put their efforts toward tasks vital to their own group's survival—food production, for instance, or tool or clothing production—found themselves working to produce raw resources for the core and then obtaining food, tools, or clothing via trade with the core. The dependency for vital products made it difficult to quit. Abrupt alteration of the relationship was likely to lead to economic, social, and political problems—everything from hunger and starvation to social upheaval and political turmoil. For their well-being and even their survival, many on the periphery grew dependent on the relationship with the core.

As with most political or economic theories, one can take such generalizations to an unwarranted extreme. All people in the same locale did not necessarily have similar living conditions, world systems notwithstanding, and there was uneven incorporation of people across the expanse of any world system.[6] Still, most of those living within the loosely defined boundaries of a world system had their ways of life affected, for better or for worse, by the relationships involved with the patterns of exchange. So understanding relationships in a world system is critical for understanding how and why people lived as they did in a particular place and time.

World Systems Based on Cultural Relationships: The Islamic Variant

Because world-systems theory is fairly new and its principles a long way from being set in stone, interesting variants of the theory have appeared. Some include elements of the cultural diffusion model. One that is particularly relevant to this study comes from historians of Islam, who are in the best position to recognize the overemphasis on Western civilization in historical study and who smart over the past dismissal of Islamic history as something "Oriental" and thus less important in global matters. Some of these historians believe that after the thirteenth century Muslims created their own kind of world system. According to Richard M. Eaton, the Muslim world system did not link people through commercial relationships but through "shared understandings of how to see the world and structure one's relationship to it." Based on Muhammad's words in the Qur'an and subsequent interpretations on how to build a religious community, Muslims from West Africa to Southeast Asia were drawn together in their efforts to follow the law on earth and make it possible to gain access to paradise after life.[7]

Muhammad had in mind a religious state and society based on law wherein a person could readily achieve salvation through doing God's will. To clarify and set out the law, a group of clerics studied and wrote for two centuries after The Prophet's death, so that by the tenth century a largely-agreed-upon body of law, the *Shari'a*, was in existence. Further interpretation of the law fell to learned men, most of whom lived in Islam's great central cities: Baghdad, Damascus, Cairo. Their interpretations tended to be conservative and the religious practice they authorized, while conforming to their literate culture, had less appeal for Muslims outside the urban centers of the Middle East. Eventually, a number of scholars found ways to give Islam more appeal for other peoples through the growing popularity of religious practice that emphasized Islam's spiritual and mystical dimensions. Such practice came to be called *sufi.*

Incorporating the likes of saints, shrines, spirits, dreams, altered states of consciousness, emotional frenzy, and ecstatic worship, *sufi* held appeal for the less educated and could accommodate aspects of pre-Islamic religious practices of peoples around the Muslim world. Such worship made it easier for nonbelievers to enter the realm of Islam. *Sufi* leaders, called *shayks,* formed brotherhoods, which had their own litany and unique forms of worship. Some brotherhoods grew and spread widely with the leader's popularity. One, the Qadiriyya, named after its founder, 'Abd al-Qādir, a twelfth-century Baghdad scholar, expanded about the Middle East and through North and West Africa; others had large numbers of adherents too. In time these brotherhoods became the primary vehicles for spreading Islam beyond the large empires closer to the heart of the Muslim world.

The way *shayks* and their followers spread their ideas was through travel and personal contact. These religious leaders came from a peripatetic tradition. Muhammad, himself a widely traveled merchant, had told the faithful they must "journey in the land, then behold how He originated creation." Muslim scholars ever after took him at his word, and their traveling, whether to trade or teach or learn or perform religious pilgrimage, brought a continuity to the realm of Islam across the land. Eaton shows that in the fourteenth century, Ibn Battuta, the Moroccan who crossed seventy-odd thousand miles of Africa, the Middle East, central Asia, Southeast Asia, and China, "moved through a single cultural universe in which he was utterly at home" and "intuitively understood that the Muslim world of his day constituted a truly global civilization." The Islamic community of today may be divided into competing nation-states, but that is a function of recent history and is, as Eaton argues, "fundamentally hostile to the Islamic vision of the *umma,* the community of believers, the 'abode of Islam.' "[8] Even more than today, West African Muslims of several centuries ago believed themselves a part of a vast community, an *intellectual* world system stretching across the desert they knew and into lands they could barely imagine, held together by scholars and saints and mystics and jurists and common folk all praying toward the same central shrine and living by the same law, parts of which they memorized in the same language. For this world system, economic unity was a factor, but not the major one. Perhaps it was spiritual unity as much as anything that tied together peoples of the Muslim realm across the Afro-Eurasian landmass.

Restructuring World Systems

A valuable exercise for understanding general patterns in world history is to chart the progression of world systems over time. Several persons have done so; one has identified thirteen world systems in existence before the rise of the "modern Central Civilization" in 1500 B.C.;[9] others count fewer. Naturally, such examinations can never be as precise as historians would like, because world systems are not established formally or legally and given names. Also, world systems do not "rise" and "fall" as we commonly think when considering the history of nations, empires, or civilizations. Instead, as historian Janet L. Abu-Lughod argues, world systems evolve and sometimes "restructure":

> They rise when integration increases and they decline when connections along older pathways decay.... [W]hen the vigor of a given dynamic of integration dissipates . . . , the old parts live on and become the materials out of which restructuring develops, just as the earlier system inherited . . . a set of partially organized subsystems. By definition, such restructuring is said to occur when *players who were formerly peripheral* began to occupy more powerful positions in the system and when *geographic zones formerly marginal to intense interactions* become foci and even control centers of such interchanges.[10]

In recent decades we have witnessed what some consider a gradual restructuring of the modern world system: countries that once were core areas of capital, industry, and wealth—Great Britain and France, for instance—have become less important in the world economy, while countries once on the periphery around the Pacific Rim increasingly are becoming efficient producers of goods. World capital is flowing toward these emerging countries, their governments have the means to assert themselves more forcefully in internal matters and international affairs, and the ways of life of people living there are slowly changing.

But this is a digression to modern times. According to some theorists, then, for the past several thousand years world systems have been appearing, thriving, and restructuring. Whole generations of people in Europe, Africa, Asia, and the Americas lived better or worse lives depending on how they were involved, at what time, in one or another of these large-scale economic complexes. One such complex, the biggest to its time, is a point of beginning for this study.

The World System of the Old World Before A.D. 1450

Historians, sociologists, anthropologists, archaeologists, and others have identified the existence of world systems of varying size and scope far into the past. Ancient Rome was part of an economic system, for example, that extended from modern England and Spain in the west to Mesopotamia and Egypt in the east and included all lands bordering the Mediterranean. Mesopotamia was in indirect commercial contact with China, India, Southeast Asia, and Africa's east coast. Even West Africa was connected via irregular trans-Sahara traders. Across thousands of miles of dusty Asian steppes, monsoon-blown waters of Asian oceans and seas, or balmy stretches of the Mediterranean, people passed goods and ideas back and forth in regular, perhaps even systematic, fashion. Rome's decline after the fourth century A.D. cut western regions from the system, but east and south of continental Europe a world system continued to operate.

The growth of this world system for a period after the mid-seventh century is related to the expansion of the Muslim world. Islam is a monotheistic religion, influenced heavily by Judaism, that evolved in the Middle East for several centuries before the time of Muhammad.[11] Over the century following Muhammad's death in A.D. 632, Muslim Arabs poured out of their homelands and conquered most of the Middle East, North Africa, and the Iberian Peninsula. Early in the eighth century Muslim armies followed across the trade routes of central Asia and swept down into northern India, where they fought to establish themselves as purveyors of the fineries of the East. By the ninth century, Arab and Persian sailors were coming into direct contact with East Africa, India, Southeast Asia, and even China. The result was dramatic. The Muslim world, stretching from northwest Africa to India, was tied into a vast commercial complex that included the Pacific Rim. East Asian goods flowed westward in unprecedented amounts; East African goods moved north and eastward. A Persian geographer, al-Muqadassi, listed items one could obtain just prior to A.D. 1000 in Oman at the eastern tip of the Arabian Peninsula: the list included drugs, perfumes, saffron, teakwood, ivory, pearls, onyx, rubies, ebony, sugar, aloes, iron, lead, canes, earthenware, sandalwood, glass, and pepper. Nearly every one came to Arabia through the thriving Indian Ocean–East Asian–East African trade.[12]

To finance this commercial expansion and efforts at collateral political consolidation, Muslims needed bullion. They found it south of the Sahara Desert, in the gold deposits of Africa's western savannas, and in gaining access to this gold in the eighth and ninth centuries, Muslim merchants established firmly the previously tenuous links that tied West Africa into the growing world system.[13] A trickle of trans-Sahara trade, with indirect

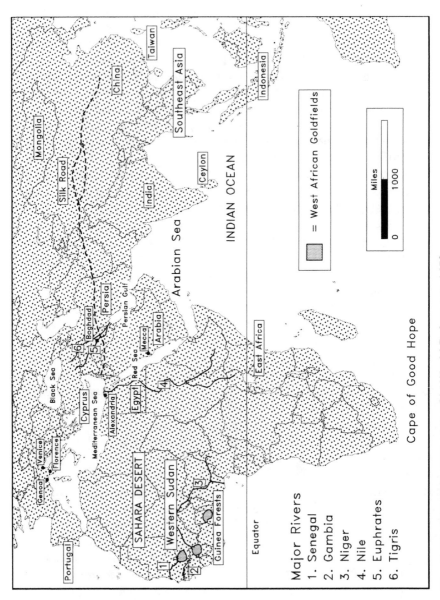

Map 2. The World System of the Old World Before A.D. 1450

Major Rivers
1. Senegal
2. Gambia
3. Niger
4. Nile
5. Euphrates
6. Tigris

= West African Goldfields

Miles
0   1000

Portugal

Genoa Venice
Florence

Black Sea

Cyprus

Mediterranean Sea

Alexandria

Egypt Red Sea

SAHARA DESERT

Western Sudan

Guinea Forests

Equator

East Africa

Cape of Good Hope

Boghdad Persia

Persian Gulf

Mecca

Arabia

Arabian Sea

INDIAN OCEAN

Mongolia

Silk Road

China

Taiwan

India

Ceylon

Southeast Asia

Indonesia

commercial connections between the populated savannas of West Africa and the plains of North Africa, probably predated the Roman Empire, but such trade grew in the fourth century A.D. with the introduction of camels among North Africa's Berber population. Camels quickly replaced horses and pack oxen to become veritable ships of the desert, voyaging from oasis to oasis under the guidance of Berber masters, carrying slabs of salt from mines on the desert's north side to the continually salt-starved inhabitants of the savannas along with dates, figs, woven cloth, and copper articles. They returned northward with gold, which West Africa had in greater supply than anywhere else in reach of the world system of the time, and also kola nuts, a popular stimulant from the Guinea forests, and ivory. Slaves usually accompanied the northward treks for sale in North Africa or the eastern Mediterranean. West Africa thus supplied a good part of the bullion that oiled the pre-Islamic commerce between the Mediterranean and China. The Islamic stimulus to the trade across Eurasia increased the importance of the West Africa link and led to cultural transferrals back and forth across the desert accompanying the products of trade. This connection to the large economic system had important political and economic effects for the West Africans who were involved.

Interested parties could argue long and hard over which area or areas were cores of this world system. One could build a strong case for the Middle East–India corridor, where prior to A.D. 1000 Muslims controlled much of the international exchange that took place. Another could weigh China's growing land and sea connections with the world to its west and south after the end of the first millennium, in company with Southeast Asia's increasing involvement with the carrying trade of the East Indies, to argue that a restructuring was under way by the eleventh century and that eastern regions were more central to the system for several centuries thereafter.[14]

One thing seems more certain, however: before A.D. 1000, Europe was not a core in any economic network. When thinking of the vast Eurasian world system of the time, some of the isolated reaches of northern and western Europe were barely peripheral. Through the several centuries when residents of these regions were tied to a narrow existence on the feudal manor, a network of economic interaction existed from the southern and eastern rims of the Mediterranean, across the Sahara, down the East African coast, and over the expanse of central and eastern Asia that brought a material and cultural fullness to the lives of urban dwellers and some others. Northern and western Europeans were far removed from the commercial or cultural centers of this vast and thriving system.

But over the next several centuries, that situation would change. The world system that incorporated central parts of the Old World continued to grow after A.D. 1000. Across much of the central Eurasian landmass and extending to West and East Africa, production of agricultural and manufactured goods increased, short-distance trade continued to bustle, and long-distance trade grew, involving more merchants from different parts of the Old World. Growing in importance with the central Asian land trade was that of the vast Indian Ocean complex, which connected East Africa, the Red Sea and Persian Gulf, India, Malaysia, and China in one vast commercial network of production and exchange. The steady monsoon winds that reversed direction semiannually facilitated travel by sail across the system. Well known are the great voyages under the direction of Chinese mariner Cheng Ho that reached coastal East Africa early in the fourteenth century. But Arab, Persian, Indian, and Indonesian vessels operated across various parts of the network as well, and a peaceful coexistence enabled waterborne trade to pass back and forth in this grand operation.[15]

Abu-Lughod believes that this early Old World commercial system, with China, India, and central parts of the Muslim Middle East as core areas, reached its peak around A.D. 1300 and then began to restructure. "Indeed," she writes, "the century between A.D. 1250 and 1350 clearly seemed to constitute a crucial turning point in world history, a moment when the balance between East and West could have tipped in either direction. In terms of space, the Middle East heartland that linked the eastern Mediterranean with the Indian Ocean constituted a geographic fulcrum on which East and West were then roughly balanced."[16]

As we know, the balance eventually would tip toward the West. Slowly, the world system restructured after the middle of the fourteenth century, leading to the centrality of western Europe, by the sixteenth century, in a system that was expanding to include the continents of the New World as well as more parts of the Old.

Western Europe in a Restructuring World System

It is not possible to point to a specific date when western Europe began to move out of its provincial narrowness and become a more active participant in the world economy. The long, slow process probably began in the ninth century and became much more noticeable some time in the eleventh. By the fourteenth century, western Europe was very different indeed: it was participating fully, and nearly equally, in the economic complex that spread goods and ideas across central parts of the Old World.[17]

Rising Western Europe

Here and there, even before A.D. 1000, venturesome European seamen began to sail farther from their ports, to come into contact with others from some distance away, and to exchange products to their advantage. European trade in the Baltic and North Seas connected the Low Countries and northern Germany with the British Isles. To the south, growing numbers of Italian seamen were spreading across the eastern Mediterranean, meeting again with Byzantine and Muslim merchants, elbowing their way into the trade of the region. By the eleventh century, Venetian merchants were carrying a portion of Byzantium's seaborne trade.

The earliest Crusades, the drawn-out Christian attempt to recapture the Holy Lands from the Muslims that began at the end of the eleventh century, heightened European interest in the eastern Mediterranean and beyond.[18] The first part of the 1100s saw the appearance of a string of European Crusader kingdoms—small city-states along the eastern Mediterranean coast—where enterprising Italians began producing foodstuffs and other marketable commodities to exchange for items that were available, through indirect contact, from East Asia. Europeans were awed by the products: "spices" were the main item—several hundred different flavors and scents that Europeans soon craved to enhance their almost tasteless cereals and often rancid meats—but there were also silk and cotton cloth, porcelain, cutlery, precious stones, and a host of other luxury goods that European lords of the land and successful squires believed to be their due.

Yet, there was little future in relying on Crusaders' booty as a source for these commodities. Northern and western Europeans recognized that if they wanted the luxuries, they would have to produce something in demand for the eastern Mediterranean and Middle Eastern market. So, ever slowly, but noticeably by the end of the twelfth century, people in parts of western Europe were growing crops or mining metals or cutting trees or weaving woolen cloth that could be traded south and eastward to Italian merchants, to the Crusader states, or to anyone else who could provide access to the luxury products in demand.

The increasing trade stimulated Europeans to greater internal change. On the European manor new events and activities were evident: a growing peasant population, the clearing of more land, and the production of more agricultural goods than the manor's population could consume. Lords acquired surplus foodstuffs and exchanged them at crossroads, which grew into towns. By the 1100s towns sporting commercial fairs dotted some areas of the European landscape; by the 1200s the towns were centers of bustling market exchange and craft production; by the 1300s the craft production was becoming more like small-scale industrial activity, and urban merchants were regularly casting their eyes farther afield for commercial opportunities. As the Mongolian peace spread across central Asia in the fourteenth century, much of Europe was tied into the major commercial system of the Old World. Participation in the system was important in determining economic, social, and material aspects of their lives.[19]

Connecting the commercial and manufacturing centers of northwestern Europe with the markets of the eastern Mediterranean and beyond were the fleets of the great medieval Italian port cities, Genoa and Venice. These cities benefited greatly from the Crusades, carrying goods and supplies for the European armies, trading for their booty, and in time broadening their commercial activities into the Red and Black Seas. By the time Muslims had retaken the last European Crusader kingdom at the end of the thirteenth century, sailors from Italian ports were carrying a good part of the Mediterranean trade and venturing farther and farther beyond Constantinople in an effort to get closer to the goods from the eastern markets. Back in the Italian cities, new methods of consolidating capital, both public and private, were behind financing of shipbuilding and trade. Abu-Lughod describes Genoa and Venice as "*almost* capitalist by the thirteenth century," and notes that "in Marco Polo's Venice virtually every 'dandy' in the city had money invested in ships at sea."[20]

Fourteenth-Century Setback

Large parts of northern and western Europe were on the political and economic rise at the start of the fourteenth century. Perhaps Europeans would have ventured earlier into the Atlantic, on their way to direct contact with West Africa and East Asia, had it not been for a series of economic and demographic setbacks they experienced in the difficult 1300s. At the root of these was the Black Death, which between 1348 and the end of the century carried off one-third to one-half of Europe's population.

It is ironic that Europe's economic woes and, in fact, its disastrous encounters with the Black Death came about in large part *because* of its participation in the existing world system.[21] Prosperity throughout the system rested on the connections and efficient movement of goods across the entire network. When connections to an important part or parts broke down, the system declined. This seems to be what happened with the onset of the Black Death, the flea- and rat-transmitted bubonic plague that spread across the Eurasian landmass after 1330, killing without discrimination. From southwest China in the 1330s the Black Death spread with Mongol horsemen, whose mounts carried infected fleas, across the steppes of central Asia to the shores of the Black Sea. There, rats carried fleas aboard ships bound for the resurgent Italian ports in the mid-1340s, and the disease then spread up trade paths through central and western Europe by mid-century. Mongol unity in central Asia fell apart, and without the order that the Khan's army provided, goods ceased traveling smoothly across the Silk Road. The sea link to Southeast Asia and China continued to function—albeit with interruptions caused by individualized outbreaks of the Black Death—and Venetian merchants traded through Egypt and the Red Sea to India, but the spread of merchandise across the Indian Ocean from Southeast Asia fluctuated by decades. There was a brief resurgence of trade from China along the southern sea route, when the new Ming government took momentary interest in external trade, but following the dramatic voyages of Chinese fleets into and across the Indian Ocean to East Africa between 1403 and 1430, the Ming rulers decided that external contact was not for them.[22] Neither Arabs nor Indians were strong enough to fill the void that the Chinese left. So there was, writes Abu-Lughod, a "Fall of the East" in the early fifteenth century that preceded, and was important in, the "Rise of the West."[23]

The Lure to Expand

Yet, there were difficulties in continental Europe that were separate from those caused by the Black Death or the fall of the East.[24] Agricultural productivity declined soon after 1300, the result of climate change, land exhaustion, and technological stagnation. Europeans needed new sources of food, new fishing grounds, new stands of timber for shipbuilding and other construction. Some argue, too, that lords of the European manor had reached the limit of their ability to extract surplus production from their serfs and that European serfs, or European peasants generally, were therefore becoming disruptive. Related to these difficulties was the ever-growing European need for bullion to finance the eastern trade. Muslims continued to have monopolistic access to West Africa's gold. Some in Europe began to wonder if expansion away from the Continent, into new lands where agents of European lords could produce cheap foodstuffs, fuels, and new surpluses might solve these problems. Such expansion might indeed enable Europeans to outflank the Muslims and get direct access to the West African gold—and maybe even the luxuries from the East. To some economically depressed Europeans of the fifteenth century, expansion loomed as their main hope for economic and social salvation.

And there was another kind of salvation that brought Europeans by the 1400s to want to expand into new lands.[25] European Christians had been fighting against Muslims for over half a millennium. The last Crusader kingdom fell to Muslim advances in 1291, but that hardly signaled the end of Christians' desire to take on the infidel. Rumors of a Christian prince, Prester John, thought to possess a formidable force but to be surrounded and beleaguered by Muslims out in the lands beyond, fueled a general

European desire to find new fields whereupon to resume the battle. A Christian missionary zeal that had been growing since the thirteenth century added strength to the religious motive for expansion.

So as the fifteenth century dawned—as the worst devastation of the plague faded into the past and Europe's population and economy slowly began to recover, and as the eastern realms of the Old World's commercial system were sending trade goods westward at irregular times, in insufficient amounts, and at high prices—a number of kings and princes and lords and persons of means on the western side of Europe were wondering how they might get away from it all—literally—and find new lands to help bring about their economic, social, and spiritual recovery.

Portuguese Expansion into the Atlantic

Well positioned to lead this effort were the Portuguese.[26] There has long been a notion that Portugal was always poor and backward and that it was mainly the efforts of Dom Henrique—"Henry the Navigator" of many Western texts—a brother of Portugal's king, possessing funds from a wealthy religious order and a crusading and exploring spirit, who brought Portuguese and Italian seamen to make the discoveries that opened the Atlantic and soon the world to European commercial contact. But there is much more than Henry's activities behind the Portuguese maritime ventures of the fifteenth century. Portugal had finished winning back its lands from the Moors in 1249. Since then, Portuguese seamen had been ranging wide in their quest for trade—to Flanders and Ireland in the north, to the Canary Islands and the northwest African coast in the south. Supporting this quest after 1385 was a new dynasty of Portuguese rulers and a landed aristocracy ready and able to fight for glory, God, or loot. When it became clear by 1400 that Venice was in control of the trade of the eastern Mediterranean (and thus access to the products from the East) and able to prevent the participation of others, Genoese and Florentines looked west and brought their sailing know-how and mercantile instincts to cities of coastal Spain and Portugal. All the elements that made up the commercial community of such ports as Lisbon in the fifteenth century hoped they could find a way to outflank Muslims and Venetians, who held the keys to the doors of African gold and luxury goods of the East.

But such outflanking was out of the question so long as the maritime technology and navigational wisdom available to Mediterranean and northern European mariners limited their ability to sail down Africa's west coast and return home.[27] Winds and currents were the root of the problem. Strong northeasterly winds blow steadily down from Morocco to Cape

Verde, and the Canary current flows briskly in the same direction. Vessels could leave Portugal and sail down Africa's northwest coast with relative ease, but beyond a certain point not far into the voyage, returning home was nearly impossible. The square-rigged vessels could not sail close enough to the wind to allow them to make headway against the current. Sailors needed more maneuverable ships that were rigged differently, and they needed more knowledge of the Atlantic winds. Without both, they were on a European tether, forever removed from the prizes of the East—or the West and South.

Prince Henry did not single-handedly bring about a revolution in ship building and ocean navigation. Instead, he played a small, but not insignificant, role in bringing along the steady compilation of knowledge of construction, guidance, and map making that had been going on for several centuries. Italian sailors, who had been in contact with seafarers in Europe's northern seas for over a century and knew also of such Muslim maritime advances as the lateen sail, added to the effort to build more maneuverable ships that could haul bulkier cargo.[28] Equipped with the increasingly popular caravels, which sported triangular lateen sails along with the traditional square rigs to allow for easier maneuvering and closer sailing to the winds, Portuguese sailors began venturing farther down the western coast of Africa. To return against wind and current, they had to make long and laborious tacks that took advantage of slight changes in wind direction, on and off shore, between morning and evening. In this fashion they sailed to Madeira in 1420, past Cape Bojador in 1434 and Cape Blanco in 1441. Arguim Island, just south of Cape Blanco, quickly became a Portuguese base for fishing fleets and coastal traders, who were successful in acquiring enough gold and slaves to keep their attention. Then, in quick succession, Portuguese mariners passed the Senegal River in 1444 and Cape Verde a year later. Not long afterward, an unknown Portuguese captain discovered that he could leave the latitude of Cape Verde on a long northwesterly tack toward the Azores, and there pick up the strong trade winds blowing from the west that would bring him back toward continental Europe. It was a discovery as important as any for increasing contact among the world's humanity. From the middle of the fifteenth century, the south Atlantic and, essentially, all of the remaining oceans of the world were open to European shipping.

It was in this context that, in the summer of 1446, as part of a leap-frogging line of Portuguese adventurers advancing down Africa's west coast, Nuno Tristão sailed his caravel into the broad mouth of the Gambia River. So far as he knew, no European seaman had ever sailed that far southward and returned to tell of it. One can think of the long-range ideals of reaching the

Indies, finding beleaguered Christians, or tapping West Africa's gold, but goals of a more immediate nature drove men like Tristão.[29] As his predecessors to the north had done, Tristão was intent on capturing Africans and taking them back to Portugal. Some could provide information about the prospects for trade or the existence of belabored Christians, some could learn Portuguese and serve as interpreters on future voyages, and all could be put to work serving Portuguese lords or cutting cane on the expanding sugar plantations around the Mediterranean. Though he had no reason to be surprised by either fact, Tristão was probably not aware of the existence of the state of Niumi at the Gambia's mouth, nor of its relationship to the regional system of West Africa that connected, across the Sahara Desert, into the grand commercial complex of the Old World. That may be why, when he spied habitations on the river's south bank, he mistakenly believed he had easy picking.

West Africa in a Restructuring World System

The trans-Sahara trade, which had existed into the distant past in indirect form and had grown in volume and efficiency with the introduction of the camel in the fourth century A.D., received a new stimulus with the Muslim conquest of North Africa early in the eighth century. Muslim traders tied West Africa to the thriving economic complex that fanned out from the eastern Mediterranean. This alone brought a sharp rise in demand for sub-Saharan products. Then, as the world system grew in strength into medieval times, so did demand—especially for gold, the product needed for coinage and eventual shipment to India to pay for the spices and silks entering the Mediterranean trade, but also for slaves and lesser amounts of ivory and kola nuts. Export of gold from West Africa seems to have peaked at an annual average of considerably more than a ton in the thirteenth and four-teenth centuries.[30] It was the driving engine of the trade northward across the desert, just as salt occupied the same place for the caravans trekking south.

Islam's Movement into West Africa

Commercial centers like Sijilmasa grew on the Sahara's northern fringe, and in such places North Africa's Sanhaja Berbers, who controlled desert trading, began to pay the Arabs' Islamic religion more heed. By the tenth century nearly all Berbers were familiar with the religion's tenets, and many of the Sanhaja considered themselves part of the larger brotherhood of Islam. It was thus with Berber merchants at the head of camel caravans that

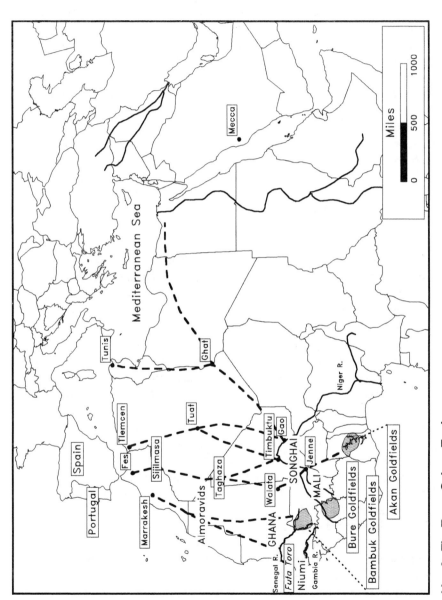

Map 3. The Trans-Sahara Trade

Islam crossed the Sahara to the more heavily populated regions of West Africa's sahel and savanna.

As is often the case, the long-distance traders brought more than commodities intended for exchange. Once Arabs had conquered eastward and opened the door to extensive contact with India in the eighth century, they brought to the Middle East a host of agricultural products the likes of which peoples in the western half of the Old World never had seen. These included several citrus fruits, eggplant, and watermelon, but they also included cotton. Production of the latter spread westward across North Africa with considerable speed, and then the idea of cotton cultivation, cotton seeds, and techniques of spinning and weaving passed southward across the Sahara with Berber caravans. In the heat of tropical West Africa, cotton cloth became a prized commodity. Between the upper Senegal and upper Niger Rivers in particular, cotton production and weaving grew to be important segments of the regional economy by the tenth century.[31]

The Islam that crossed the Sahara was a far cry from the *sunni,* or orthodox, Islam settled on generally by the learned followers of Muhammad not long after his death. Berbers seldom paid heed to orthodoxy of any kind, and they tended to prefer heretical versions of the Islamic faith that allowed for more emotional religious practice and inclusion of more of the local, pre-Islamic rites. This should have boded well for conversion of the masses in West Africa, for across the grasslands below the Sahara people were involved deeply in spiritual forces and the supernatural.

Yet throughout that area, peasants clung tenaciously to their animist practices and the veneration of ancestors that tied them to their land. The earliest West African converts to Islam and the ones who acted most effectively to spread the religion across the lands of their travels below the Sahara were itinerant traders, called *wangara* or *jula.* Detached from the peasant villages of their ancestors and thus not tied to spirits of the soil or local deities as were sedentary farmers, these merchants, like their Berber contacts before them, recognized the value that the sense of Islamic community provided them with fellow traders and among strangers in foreign lands. As they obtained trade goods from Berber caravans at portlike cities along the southern edge of the desert and then spread the goods with donkey and human caravans, they created a commercial complex of some sophistication that stretched from the western Atlantic coast below the Sahara, eastward across the expanse of what Arabs called *Bilād al-Sūdān*— the land of the blacks.

For a time these West African Muslims must have considered themselves on the distant periphery of the larger Islamic political and cultural realm. The militant Almoravid movement that swept many nonbelievers and loose practitioners before its armies in the eleventh and twelfth centuries was largely a Berber initiative with a focus on Morocco and Spain. Moreover, no matter what was going on among nominal Muslims as distant as sub-Saharan Africa in the west and the Indian sub-continent in the east, the political and cultural center of the Islamic world remained in Baghdad, where Arab culture held sway and Abbasid *caliphs* (successors of The Prophet) attempted to guide the vast Islamic state. But the once-great caliphate lost power and influence through the twelfth and thirteenth centuries, and the Mongol sack of Baghdad in 1258 effectively ended the political centralization of the worldwide Muslim community. What happened with Muslim civilization thereafter was not the steady decline that has long been pictured by Western scholars, however. With political fragmentation came a rapid cultural florescence and a slower but more steady spread of spiritual unity among Muslims about the Old World. Those instrumental in this steadily growing and unifying Islamic identity were scholars and mystics, who, according to Eaton, "elaborated an immense corpus of rituals, dogmas, legal structures, social forms, mystical traditions, modes of piety, aesthetic sensitivities, styles of scholarship, and schools of philosophy that collectively defined and stabilized the very core and substance of Islamic civilization."[32]

In West Africa, the process of Islam's spreading, gaining cohesiveness, and thereby tying sub-Saharan West Africa into the greater Islamic world was long and fitful. It is indeed one of the fundamental themes of the history of West Africa north of the Guinea forests. Here and there, where trade routes crossed or exchange was particularly brisk, the itinerant Muslim traders sometimes settled separate villages. In such villages they supervised trade in the dry season of the year and set up practices of Islamic scholarship, teaching, mysticism, and healing through the months of the rains. Some members or branches of large families might come to specialize in commerce, while others concentrated on divination, charm making, and healing. In this area Muslims had advantages over traditional African practitioners of magic and the supernatural, for the Muslims were inheritors of Indian, Iranian, and Greek systems of astronomy and mathematics. Their astute combination of science, numerology, and aesthetic mysticism gave many Muslims deserved reputations as the best at their work.[33]

And there were practical advantages associated with the combination of trade and scholarship. Both traders and teachers could acquire slaves, who could work their farms and provide for their families and passing caravans. Young Muslim scholars did their share of agricultural work for their teachers too. Such enclave, Islamic-commercial villages spread steadily throughout West Africa's savannas. They would be the nodes from which Islam, in later centuries, would spread or be assimilated by Africans from a variety of cultures and traditions.

State Building in West Africa

The planting of an Islamic seed that would sprout and grow for a millennium was just one effect of the desert trade. As the commerce expanded through the latter centuries of the first millennium A.D., and as the number and intensity of pastoralist raids on settled communities along the sahel and adjacent savannas increased, people south of the desert recognized a need to organize themselves in larger and stronger political units. Groups of agricultural people speaking one of the Mande languages and living in the heart of the savanna trading country between the upper Senegal and upper Niger Rivers, whose basic unit of social and political organization and identity long had been the village of a few hundred to a few thousand inhabitants with its hinterland, began to combine their resources to protect themselves from raids and to enable them to control and tax the passing commerce.[34] The slow, gradual transition to political organization beyond the village level had been occurring as a reaction to necessity for a long time—back to the time of the introduction of the camel or even earlier, it seems. By the eighth century, an Arab geographer in Baghdad was writing about the territory of Ghana below the Sahara as "the land of gold," and by the tenth or eleventh century it is apparent that many Mande-speaking peoples were organized in state structures of varying size and complexity. The smallest and simplest consisted of handfuls of villages with the leading lineage of one providing the head of state; the largest was indeed Ghana, which held authority through much of the eleventh century and possibly longer over people occupying several thousand square miles of desert, sahel, and savanna.

After A.D. 1100, several things occurred that would change the focus of power in the western savannas. The principal occurrence was the gradual onset of a long period of decreasing rainfall, which eventually made the existing sahel uninhabitable and forced herders and farmers to move south toward better-watered lands.[35] Also, by the thirteenth century the Bambuk goldfields between the upper Senegal and Faleme Rivers, long the major source of gold for the trans-Sahara trade, seem to have become less productive, to be replaced by those of the Buré area, south and a little east, on the upper Niger. By the same time, probably aided by the dry period that reduced ground cover and forced tsetse flies southward, speakers of Mandinka, the mother tongue of the Mande languages, living along the upper Niger and its tributaries, found it possible to breed horses in number. Mandinka horsemen perfected tactics of cavalry warfare and the lightning-swift raid. Under the leadership of the great folk hero Sunjata, in the 1220s, Mandinka horsemen overcame the successors of Ghana and established the Mali empire, greater still in the wealth and prestige of its rulers and the extent of its political and economic control.[36]

The Mali Empire

Regardless of its size—village, small state, or grand empire—at the center of a Mandinka political unit was a ruling lineage, or lineages, that were wealthy, powerful, and prestigious far beyond all others. The ruler of a Mandinka state was a *mansa*, head of the lineage in power. It was the role of a state's *mansa* to settle disputes between lineages or villages, coordinate planting and harvesting, oversee relations with traders and other strangers, intercede with the ancestors or spirits of the land for the good of the living community, and organize forces for the state's protection from its enemies and deal with such matters related to warfare as booty and captives.

Expenses of running such a state were considerable. To perform all his functions efficiently, a *mansa* needed a large court establishment, which consisted mainly of a body of men who saw to it that state policies were executed and that the state was policed and defended. Taken away from normal tasks of food production, these specialized individuals had to be fed. Armies also needed weapons, supernatural protections that adorned each soldier and his mount and weapons, and horses, which required care, fodder, and tack. And there was more. As representatives of the state, the *mansa*, his court, and members of the royal lineage expected to enjoy a style of living much higher than the rest of the population. This came mainly through access to luxury goods—various fineries of clothing and jewelry, alcohol, fine saddlery, tasty foods—almost all of which were not produced locally but had to be obtained from outside.[37]

The *mansa* had basic ways to meet these expenses. One was to take a portion of the produce of the nonroyal lineages in the state to provide for the royal court and state soldiers. As any taxing of a state's populace, this had obvious limits, so ruling families often established their own farms, worked at times by a draft of labor from the state's population, but more frequently by slaves, to provide food and fodder. Royal slaves also produced trade goods, especially woven cloth. Such slaves were usually captives from state warfare or organized raids. When such activity was frequent and successful, the *mansa* increased his wealth by selling or trading some of the captives.

Taxing trade was the other important element in financing the state. Rulers levied tolls on trading caravans and taxed commercial transactions in markets. Thus, wise rulers understood that they could greatly increase their revenues by stimulating trade in lands under their control or by gaining control of areas where trade flourished. Indeed, this last seems to be just what Mandinka lineages did from villages on the upper Niger in the early thirteenth century: they conquered and gained control of some of the most commercially important areas of West Africa, with active trade routes leading to and from the Sahara and passing horizontally across the Western Sudan. They then set up rulers in these areas who would be loyal, assessed payments of tribute on the people under their rule, and taxed the brisk trade to the extent it would bear. This large conquest state was the Mali Empire.

Over time, rulers of Mali extended their control of commerce south of the desert's edge across much of the Western Sudan, from Hausaland in the east, to the forests in the south, and to the Atlantic border of the savannas in the west. At the Gambia's mouth, Niumi existed at the western edge of this regional trading complex. There was an increase in trade over this vast region through the thirteenth and fourteenth centuries, as Mande-speaking merchants fanned out from their homelands between the Senegal and Niger Rivers to connect salt producers along the Senegambian Atlantic, kola-nut producers of the southern forests, and cotton-cloth and slave producers from all across the Western Sudan into a large and sophisticated commercial network. All of it tied into the trans-Sahara trade, through cities near the desert edge, and thus connected West Africa to the major world system that spread out across central parts of the Old World.

Mali extended its political control greatly to incorporate many parts of the Sudanic trading complex. Its ruling lineages may have considered Niumi the empire's westernmost extension, though not enough evidence exists to determine this with precision. Some rulers of Gambian states acknowledged Mali's authority but were far enough away from the empire's center that such control had to be indirect, sporadic, and not too taxing. The primary relationships were probably economic and cultural.

Mali's Decline

For a variety of reasons that included declining productivity of the Buré goldfields, Mali's power began to wane in the fifteenth century. Another Sudanic empire, Songhai, with its center on the port cities of Timbuktu and Gao on the big buckle of the Niger River, eclipsed Mali by about the time the Portuguese were sailing down the West African coast. Mali did not disappear entirely, however; it pulled in its imperial tentacles and held on as the political, cultural, and spiritual center for Mande-speaking peoples throughout West Africa. As Mali's political control declined, a smaller, but still powerful, empire emerged among Mandinka-speaking peoples to the west of the old Mali heartland on the upper Niger. Called Kaabu and centered on several Mandinka states south of the Gambia, this empire assumed some of Mali's authority toward the Atlantic and remained politically strong for some time. But after the fifteenth century Mali was a shadow of its former imperial self, and most of the far-flung states it had once controlled, at least indirectly, while still thinking of the upper Niger region as the center of their cultural world, owed Mali little more than nominal allegiance.

Political decline did not mean a falling off of trade, however. The trans-Sahara trade continued as Songhai monitored and marshaled its southern connections; the trade of the Western Sudan extended farther south toward goldfields deeper into the Guinea forests. And out on the western edge of West Africa's commercial complex, the very small state of Niumi continued to function as it had for some time. Mali's fall and Songhai's and Kaabu's rise were less important to the ways of life of its people than its connections to the larger world. Its leaders controlled the exchange of much-needed salt toward the interior and received products and cultural influences from as far away as Timbuktu, Muslim North Africa, and a part of the world beyond.

Notes

1. Lynda N. Shaffer, "Southernization," *Journal of World History* 5 (1994): 1–21.

2. Immanuel Wallerstein, *The Modern World-System: Capitalist Agriculture and the Origins of the European World-Economy in the Sixteenth Century* (New York: Academic Press, 1974); *The Modern World-System II: Mercantilism and the Consolidation of the European World-Economy* (New York: Academic Press, 1980); and *The Modern World-System III: The Second Era of Great Expansion of the Capitalist World-Economy* (San Diego: Academic Press, 1988).

3. For examples of those who extend the world-system model farther into the past, see Andre Gunder Frank and Barry K. Gillis, eds., *The World System: Five Hundred Years or Five Thousand?* (New York: Routledge, 1993); and Sharon R. Steadman, "Isolation vs. Interaction: Prehistoric Cilicia and Its Role in the Near Eastern World System," Ph.D. dissertation, University of California at Berkeley, 1994.

4. Good summaries of world-systems theory are found in Thomas Richard Shannon, *An Introduction to the World-System Perspective* (Boulder, Colo.: Westview Press, 1989); and Charles Ragin and Daniel Chirot, "The World System of Immanuel Wallerstein: Sociology and Politics as History," in *Vision and Method in Historical Sociology,* ed. Theda Skocpol (Cambridge: Cambridge University Press, 1984), 276–312.

5. In addition to economic zones labeled "core" and "periphery," Wallerstein's model has an intermediate zone, the "semi-periphery," which includes nations in transition from core to periphery, or vice versa, and consequently shares characteristics with each group. For the sake of simplicity, I have omitted discussion of the semi-periphery in this brief treatment.

6. Janet Lippman Abu-Lughod, *The World System in the Thirteenth Century: Dead-End or Precursor?* (Washington, D.C.: American Historical Association, 1993), 4–5.

7. Richard M. Eaton, *Islamic History as Global History* (Washington, D.C.: American Historical Association, 1990), 43; John O. Voll, "Islam as a Special World System," *Journal of World History* 5 (1994): 213–26. Discussion in this section is based almost entirely on these two sources.

8. Eaton, *Islamic History,* 44–45.

9. David Wilkinson, "Core, Peripheries, and Civilization," in *Core/Periphery Relations in Precapitalist Worlds,* ed. C. Chase-Dunn and T. Hall (Boulder, Colo.: Westview Press, 1991), 113–66.

10. Janet L. Abu-Lughod, *Before European Hegemony: The World System A.D. 1250–1350* (New York: Oxford University Press, 1989), 367.

11. Eaton, *Islamic History,* is a good, brief discussion of the conflicting interpretations of recent Islamic history.

12. Abu-Lughod, *Before European Hegemony,* 203.

13. The standard, now dated, general treatment of the trans-Sahara Trade is E.W. Bovill, *The Golden Trade of the Moors,* 2nd ed. (London: Oxford University Press, 1968). Chapter 2 of Ralph Austen, *African Economic History* (Portsmouth, N.H.: Heinemann, 1987) is a good summary of the trade based on more recent findings.

14. William H. McNeill suggests a "Chinese primacy between A.D. 1000 and 1500" in *"The Rise of the West* after Twenty-Five Years," *Journal of World History* I (1990): 5–7. Abu-Lughod (*The World System,* 2–11) argues for eight circuits, or subsystems, integrated into the larger world system of the thirteenth century.

15. Abu-Lughod, *The World System,* 3; K.N. Chaudhuri, *Trade and Civilisation in the Indian Ocean: An Economic History from the Rise of Islam to 1750* (Cambridge: Cambridge University Press, 1985); Chaudhuri, *Asia Before Europe: Economy and Civilisation in the Indian Ocean from the Rise of Islam to 1750* (Cambridge: Cambridge University Press, 1990); Jung-Pang Lo, "The Emergence of China as a Sea Power during the Late Sung and Early Yuan Periods," *Far Eastern Quarterly* 14 (1955): 489–503.

16. Abu-Lughod, *Before European Hegemony,* ch. 11; Abu-Lughod, *The World System,* 2, 11–18.

17. For Europe's rise to prominence in this early world system, see Abu-Lughod, *Before European Hegemony,* pt. 1; and Fernand Braudel, *Civilization and Capitalism, 15th–18th Century,* vol. 3, *The Perspective of the World* (New York: Harper & Row, 1994), ch. 2.

18. A good discussion of the importance of the Crusades to European commercial and political growth is in William D. Phillips Jr. and Carla Rahn Phillips, *The Worlds of Christopher Columbus* (Cambridge: Cambridge University Press, 1992), 17ff.

19. Abu-Lughod, *Before European Hegemony,* 352–64.

20. Ibid., 108, 116, 118.

21. Discussion of the Black Death is based on William H. McNeill, *Plagues and Peoples* (Garden City, N.Y.: Anchor Books, 1976), 165ff.

22. Jung-Pang Lo, "The Decline of the Early Ming Navy," *Oriens Extrêmus* 5 (1958): 149–68.

23. Abu-Lughod, *Before European Hegemony,* 361.

24. Wallerstein, *The Modern World-System,* 37–45; Eric R. Wolff, *Europe and the People without History* (Berkeley: University of California Press, 1982), ch. 4.

25. For religious motives for European expansion, see Phillips and Phillips, *Christopher Columbus,* 38–43.

26. Braudel, *Perspective of the World,* 138–43, deals with "the unexpected rise of Portugal."

27. For the problems Europeans encountered trying to sail into the Atlantic and the

technological discoveries that enabled them to do so, see Philip D. Curtin, "The Slave Trade and the Atlantic Basin: Intercontinental Perspectives," in *Key Issues in the Afro-American Experience*, 2 vols., ed. Nathan I. Huggins, Martin Kilson, and Daniel M. Fox (New York: Harcourt Brace Jovanovich, 1971), 1: 77–80; John Thornton, *Africa and Africans in the Making of the Atlantic World, 1400–1680* (New York: Cambridge University Press, 1992), ch. 1; and Phillips and Phillips, *Christopher Columbus*, ch. 4.

28. Thornton, *Africa and Africans*, 22–23.

29. Ibid., 24–29.

30. Austen, *African Economic History*, 36, and Appendix A3.

31. Andrew Watson, *Agricultural Innovation in the Early Islamic World: The Diffusion of Crops and Farming Techniques, 700–1100* (Cambridge: Cambridge University Press, 1983), ch. 6.

32. Eaton, *Islamic History*, 27.

33. Ibid., 25–26; Thomas C. Hunter, "The Development of an Islamic Tradition of Learning among the Jahanke of West Africa," Ph.D. dissertation, University of Chicago, 1977.

34. For the formation of states in the Western Sudan, see Nehemia Levtzion, "The Sahara and the Sudan from the Arab Conquest of the Maghrib to the rise of the Almoravids," in *The Cambridge History of Africa*, vol. 2, *From c. 500 B.C. to c. A.D. 1500*, ed. J.D. Fage (Cambridge: Cambridge University Press, 1978), 637–84. Roland Oliver offers useful thoughts on the issue in *The African Experience: Major Themes in African History from Earliest Times to the Present* (London: Weidenfeld & Nicholson, 1991), 93–95.

35. George E. Brooks, *Landlords and Strangers: Ecology, Society, and Trade in Western Africa, 1000–1530* (Boulder, Colo.: Westview Press, 1993), 7.

36. Nehemia Levtzion, *Ancient Ghana and Mali* (London: Methuen, 1973), ch. 5.

37. Robin Law, "Slaves, Trade, and Taxes: The Material Basis of Political Power in Precolonial West Africa," *Research in Economic Anthropology* 1 (1978): 37–52.

2

NIUMI IN A RESTRUCTURING WORLD SYSTEM
BEFORE A.D. 1450

Strangers make the village prosper.

—Old Mandinka Proverb

People living in Niumi, on the north bank of West Africa's Gambia River, have been involved in the exchange of goods and ideas with people some distance away for as long as there is any record. From the eighth century A.D., if not earlier, West Africa was connected to the commercial complex of the central part of the Old World through the trans-Saharan trade, and Niumi was part of a commercial network of considerable scope and sophistication that was tied to that exchange. The increasing importance of West African gold and slaves to the Mediterranean and the expanding Old World trade in the thirteenth century affected West African history generally and Niumi in particular. By the fifteenth century it is likely that residents of the small, coastal-and-riverain kingdom were just as eager as Europeans to find access to greater and more direct participation in the expanding market of the world system.

The Physical Setting

The most striking physical feature of Niumi is not its mundane landscape but its glistening water. Atlantic breakers lap against the northern shores of the territory and the Gambia River's broad estuary, sometimes with good-sized waves of its own, flows past the rest. Only here and there along Niumi's shore or riverbank, where man has slashed and cut and carved away and dug and built, can one see the distinct point where land meets water. The rest is covered with the spiderlike roots and woven branches of mangroves, a green wall at high tide and a maze of gnarled, skeletal obstructions at low. Upsetting the mangrove line along the Atlantic especially is a series of creeks, estuaries, lagoons, sandbars, and tidal islands, all connected by water, that Niumi's residents used effectively. The various barriers protected the waterways from the rougher Atlantic and facilitated fishing, gathering of mollusks, and rendering of salt by solar evaporation.

40

The sheltered watercourses also made possible the large-scale movement of goods by boat, an activity Niumi's residents had been involved in for as long as there is any historical or archaeological record.[1] No matter who ruled Niumi—1,000 years ago or the day before yesterday—a good proportion of its residents found their livelihood from the products of the river and sea or the trade that the waters facilitated.

Yet, Niumi's other physical feature played an equally important role in its history. This was its flat or barely rolling, wooded terrain. Niumi was located at a point where West Africa's savannas stretched out to the continent's edge. British colonial officers occupying posts in similar savanna regions sometimes referred to the landscape as *M.M.B.A.*—"miles and miles of bloody Africa"—a reference to how across vast stretches holding few visible signs of human activity the gently rolling brush, the grasses and trees, seemed to run on forever, meeting the wide sky at the distant horizon and passing beyond. The expanse of grass and scrub, tree and thorn, anthill and stalking animal, and more grass and scrub seemed to boggle the British mind, so foreign was it to the confines of hedgerows and stone walls in the England they knew. This was what Mandinka bards called the "bright country," the agriculturally productive lands that have always held a good part of West Africa's population.[2] These savannas lie between twelve and sixteen degrees north latitude—deep into the tropics, where it is hot and humid for a little less than half the year, roughly June through October, and hot and dry for the rest.

The north bank of the Gambia River lies on a boundary that, according to more technical geographers, separates pure savanna from savanna-woodland.[3] This means simply that in the rolling savanna country north of the line there are progressively fewer trees until one encounters the sahel, or marginally habitable desert edge, in the vicinity of the Senegal River, and in the rolling savanna country south of the line there are progressively more trees until one begins to encounter the galleried vegetation of true tropical rainforest after about 100 miles. This is not to suggest that Niumi lacked trees. Before the twentieth century, when steadily increasing peanut cultivation prompted more people to come to Niumi and clear more land, there were forests across the whole central core of the state. In fact, Niumi's Mandinka inhabitants knew a good half of the 400-square-mile area as "the bad-devil place," a region where *jinns* or evil spirits ruined the lives of anyone attempting to settle there. Some still do not care to venture across Niumi's middle stretches, though in the twentieth century a good number of Wolof have built and sustained villages there. Colonial Commissioner Emilius Hopkinson found Niumi's midsection much more wooded than its coastal regions and thus less healthy. He reasoned it was the diseases to man and animals of

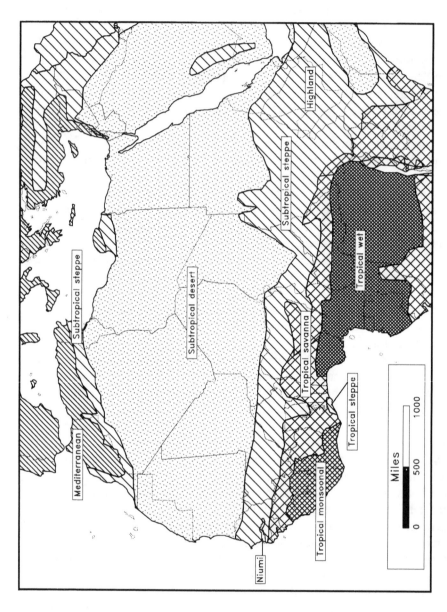

Map 4. Niumi's Physical Setting

Mediterranean

Subtropical steppe

Subtropical desert

Subtropical steppe

Highland

Tropical savanna

Tropical wet

Tropical steppe

Tropical monsoonal

Niumi

Miles

0   500   1000

the forests that brought the Mandinka to think of the land as being inhabited by bad devils.[4] These forests held occasional elephants and lions, more baboons and warthogs, and an abundance of smaller wild game. Just as important for Niumi's commerce with Europeans, they were homes to bees that provided honey and wax. But in terms of habitable area, this meant that until recent times Niumi was more a strip of land along the Gambia River and the adjacent Atlantic, under the single political authority of several ruling lineages, rather than a carefully delineated, confined state as most of the early Gambian histories, full of maps with tidy boundaries, would have us believe.

Creating the north-south differences in vegetation is the amount of rain that falls—less as one moves north from the Gambia and more as one travels south. Niumi lies in an east-west band that receives, on average, about forty inches of rain each year, or as much as some of the best farm-lands of the American Midwest. However, all of Niumi's rain falls within about five months, from June through October. This is the crop-growing season, when men and women have to produce what their families will consume through the seven- or eight-month dry season that follows. It is not an easy task. The soils of the region lack fertility; they are similar to the reddish clays of the American South, impregnated with iron oxide, and they are alternately leached by the heavy rains and cooked by the sun until a thin, heavy crust is all that remains to nurture plants. The lower Gambia region had another agricultural cross to bear—high salinity of soils that make farming that much more difficult. Niumi's residents had to practice shifting cultivation, rotating crops frequently and allowing long periods of fallowing between plantings if they were to coax crops out of the soil and nurse them along toward harvest. The food crops Niumi's farmers grew in these soils, for many hundreds of years before they had contact with Europeans, were the savanna grains—several varieties of early- and late-ripening millet and sorghum, which before the last century provided the majority of calories in their diet. Up some of the small streams that entered the Gambia, where there was slightly less salt in swampy areas, people grew wet rice, and they broadcast rice onto lands above the swamps for dry-rice cultivation. Women have assumed all the work in growing rice. Niumi's farmers also grew cotton, which had been introduced into West Africa across the Sahara back into the first millennium A.D. Women spun the cotton into thread; men wove it into cloth on narrow looms. Once the Portuguese had substantial contact with West Africans, they introduced a number of crops from Asia and the New World that gradually altered agriculture and nutrition across the region.[5]

In addition to marking the geographer's artificial division between savanna and savanna-woodland, the forty-inch rainfall line sets the approximate northern limit of the thick brush that supports the tsetse fly, the vector for *trypanosomiasis* ("sleeping sickness"), a disease that is fatal to most large animals.[6] Because of its heavy vegetation, Niumi was one of the worst areas along the river for the disease. Until recent years, when Niumi's population had grown and people cleared more land for human habitation, neither cattle nor horses lived well or long—they had to be kept away from areas of heavy undergrowth—and it was nearly impossible to breed them there. This had important implications for agriculture, for in other parts of West Africa where cattle thrived, residents used dung to return fertility to exhausted soil. In Niumi this was hardly possible. It meant that crop production was less successful there than other areas not far away; it probably meant that for a long time people in Niumi relied more on trade, exchanging products they could obtain from the sea for foodstuffs that others could grow in greater abundance. Also, people in Niumi who were intent on making use of such large animals as horses knew they would have to have a steady supply from outside the state, particularly from areas to the north that were free of the tsetse fly.

Other diseases that were endemic to the region shortened people's lives and had considerable effect on Niumi's history.[7] Malaria was probably the most important. West Africans inherited immunities to the disease from their parents, but these were mostly weak and thus not significant. Transmitted between hosts by the anopheles mosquito, malaria infected humans as infants and, if they survived the experience, infected them again though with progressively less serious results throughout their lives. With high fevers, headaches, and chills that could last for weeks, the disease was particularly debilitating. Because the mosquito population bred in puddles, pools, and swampy areas created during the months of heavy rains, malaria was a seasonal disease. It was unfortunate that it was the season of farming when success required hard work. Yellow fever was another disease that Niumi's residents lived with. Also mosquito-borne, it came in epidemic waves, and it, too, was debilitating. Surviving yellow fever left one with a longer period of immunity before contracting the disease again.

West Africans gained an ironic benefit from malaria and yellow fever: coming from an environment entirely free of such diseases, Europeans had no immunities to either one. Thus, in West Africa's tropics they acquired the diseases easily and, when they did, frequently died. Annual death rates of Europeans living in West Africa before the middle of the nineteenth century, when quinine came into regular use to prevent malaria, varied between 250 and 500 per 1,000 per year. That was enough to keep the European presence small and weak.

Of course, Niumi's residents lived with more tropical diseases—dysentery, yaws, snail fevers, and more. All of them combined to give the region an unhealthy cast and a high rate of mortality, especially among infants and children. As late as 1960, life expectancy at birth in The Gambia was only thirty-two years, and more than one of three children died before age five.[8] These figures were worse several centuries ago. The adult population had to produce about twice as many offspring as they would end up with as adults in the future, and many youngsters had to be fed who would never become productive members of society. Also, most men and women carried with them microbes for these diseases, which flared up now and again. The situation brought about lethargy when it did not bring an early end to life.

The fact that the natural habitat for humans changed relatively quickly, from north to south, and that what people could produce in each habitat was different, meant that exchange of products from one region to another was a regular aspect of people's lives. With the desert edge a few hundred miles to its north and the rainforest a few hundred miles to its south, and with the ocean and its abundant supply of seafood on its border and a river connecting it to the seasonally dry interior, Niumi was ideally situated to be an active participant in regional commerce. Long before any Europeans sailed into the Gambia River with products of their own to exchange, residents of Niumi were trading with persons from long distances away to get items they wanted or needed but did not produce.

The Cultural Setting

Today's population of just over a million in the tiny Republic of The Gambia is a thorough ethnic mixture.[9] A person traveling up and down the length of the country on either side of the river may encounter people speaking six different languages as their primary mode of communication. Yet official ethnic classifications and linguistic differences mask the fact that today, and for a long time in the past, many aspects of people's ways of life in the region—and in a larger portion still of West Africa—were similar. These similarities made it easy for persons from different linguistic or ethnic backgrounds to live together, mix, intermarry, and generally to move about within and through whatever boundaries a sense of ethnicity imposed.[10]

Chief among the similarities was the role of kinship in individual and collective identity. As for nearly all West Africans at most times in the past, kinship provided individuals their sense of who they were and provided families the formal connections to others that tied together local groups and enabled the formation of larger political, social, and cultural groupings. The

Box 2. The Problem of Evidence for Precolonial African History

Writing or speaking about the way Africans lived more than 500 years ago requires a disclaimer related to the certainty of what we know. Stated simply, there is not much good evidence for studying African cultures so far back in the past, and thus one cannot be as certain as one would like of many statements one wishes to make about them. Anthropologists have done historians of Africa great service with their cultural studies, but they often have lent confusion to historical study by their reference to societies in the cultural present, treating them as if they never had different ways of doing things until fairly recent times (normally, when the anthropologist came into contact with the culture). In such studies there is an implied sense that only the complex modern world of the past century brought change to the traditional ways. Of course, this is not historical; it is not a way of looking at cultures through time. As all people in all cultures, African societies changed over time. The difficulty is that for most of those societies there is not sufficient evidence of the way things used to be.

For historians, though, it is important to know the way things were. A number of historians of recent years have argued, for example, that the Atlantic slave trade altered many aspects of society and polity along coastal West Africa. But in most cases they do so without good or complete evidence of the way people lived, and lived together, before the Atlantic trade began. It is a frustration for all concerned. The best one can do, it seems, is to use such evidence as is available for the area under study, draw analogies from comparable societies under similar circumstances, and make inferences from regional cultural patterns of the time to reconstruct, in general terms, the relevant cultural setting. Such an effort is what appears in this book.

extended family, two or three generations of male relatives with their wife or wives and children, was society's building block.[11] An extended family lived together in a compound—a section of a village that was fenced off from others in which there were separate dwellings; several compounds of extended families formed a village; village members had rights to use surrounding land, but not to *own* land, and they cooperated in projects that would benefit them all. Groupings of villages often joined together under formal agreements to form statelike structures, with one or several large lineages providing the rulers. Niumi was such a grouping.

Kinship was important in chronically underpopulated Africa because it was through the family that offspring were produced to ensure group survival. Thus marriage was a critical social function. Marriage alliances linked separate lineages and, through mutual obligations of support and assistance, merged many of their interests, including procreation and survival. Bride wealth, a payment from the male's family to the female's to compensate the latter for the loss of a productive worker and reproducer, cemented the interfamily relationships. This payment often was substantial; frequently it was in such a form of wealth recognized widely throughout West Africa as pieces of woven cotton cloth or decorative personal items. It could include much else, however, from the popular stimulant kola nuts and storable foodstuffs to gold and slaves. As a way to maximize fertility, multiple marriage was nearly universal: if a man, through the resources of his family or the assistance of his age mates, could amass sufficient bride wealth, he could marry two, three, four, or a dozen or more different women at the same time. In the centuries before the coming of Islamic law, which theoretically limits a man's wives to four, wealthy men—especially rulers, who generally had access to the greatest wealth and used marriage ties for reasons of state, cementing relationships with allies—might have a substantial household of wives and their children. Of course, the greater the wealth in the society, the greater the number of wives men tended to have and the broader and stronger tended to be the kinship ties across village and state lines.

There probably was a time in Niumi when most lineages could intermarry. Before Serer and Mande influences grew strong in the region, people living there may not have recognized status groupings. According to a handful of studies of the population, they were more egalitarian than most other West Africans. Age, knowledge, and talent were the factors that differentiated among individuals.[12]

But influences of groups that came to dominate Senegambian society after A.D. 1000—the Mandinka, Serer, and Wolof in particular—gradually put an end to whatever egalitarianism existed in the earlier population and brought limits on relationships of marriage. For a long time into its past, Niumi's population had different levels of rank and regard—groupings of people, with boundaries often more rigid than those of ethnicity. (A "free-born" Mandinka might marry a freeborn Serer, for instance, but no freeborn Mandinka would marry a person belonging to the group of skilled artisans or slaves, regardless of the person's language or ethnic identity.) Students of African cultures often call such divisions social *classes;* it is not clear that West Africans thought of them as such. George Brooks argues that it was the Mande-speaking peoples who imposed their basic tripartite social structure on other groups in much of West Africa when they infiltrated and sometimes conquered others several centuries ago.[13] It is clear that a stratified social structure has existed among a number of West African peoples for a long time.

Persons occupying the highest level of Niumi's social structure were those whom Western social scientists often term simply "freeborn," and sometimes identify as "farmers and nobility."[14] These were not African concepts, however; they conformed to European notions of what the highest classes ought to be. Actually, a member of the so-called freeborn group was not necessarily a farmer or a nobleman, nor was the person always independent, since certain individuals or even extended families of the freeborn group lived as clients among nonrelated families or among other ethnic groups, depending on their hosts for food and shelter, at least until they harvested a crop or fulfilled some other economic function. The freeborn group might better be defined by what it was not: it did not include persons who were members of skilled occupational groupings or slaves. Rulers as well as common farmers, traveling merchants as well as Muslim clerics were "freeborn." At some point in the past—in the sixteenth century in Niumi, it seems—ruling lineages set themselves apart from the rest of society to the extent that they formed an elite surclass, making the rest of the freeborn families clearly in a second rank. Universally, birth and personal accomplishment combined to establish an individual's position among the freeborn population. One could be born into a lineage that provided rulers of a state, but if the individual did not prove himself successful at those things expected of male members of the ruling lineage—riding, performing brave deeds, gaining a large and influential nuclear family with numerous offspring, garnering wealth, dressing opulently, owning slaves—he would never become a ruler and indeed might not have much status at all. Conversely, a person born into a nonroyal freeborn family could elevate his status through hard work, economic success, increasing the size of his family, and being generally wise in word and deed. The most respected freeborn persons of nonroyal lineages were persons with whom all others had to reckon, but they could never become rulers of a state.

A second general social category in Niumi consisted of lineages whose members performed skilled activities.[15] Blacksmiths, potters, leather workers, and bards were the major ones. Because they were endogamous, lived separately, and were often spoken of with contempt by members of the freeborn grouping, students of West African cultures sometimes refer to these lineages as *castes*. It is not an entirely appropriate term. The blacksmith was a necessary adjunct to farmers and warriors, for he alone knew how to fashion cultivating tools, spearheads and arrowheads, and swords. He also served as a diviner, pre-Islamic religious specialist, and manufacturer of protective charms. And blacksmiths were the traditional leaders of secret societies that did everything from ensuring social order to perpetuating Mande culture.[16] Women in blacksmith lineages were society's potters, and they, too, had special relationships with the earth wherein resided the powerful spirits of the potter's materials. The leather worker used special ingredients to tan hides and then turn them into saddles and bridles, sandals, and pouches, and he covered with leather the charms and amulets, made by Muslim diviners or traditional spiritualists, that nearly everyone in society wore on the body or attached to weapons, tools, saddles, or garments. The bard (popularly called a *griot*) was necessary because he kept the histories of clans, families, and individuals; served as diplomat, adviser, and confidant of common patrons and rulers; and entertained all elements of society. Bards also had a teaching role, for it was they who passed along real and fabricated genealogies and knowledge of the past that helped provide personal, family, and state identity, and political legitimacy, over large areas.

Members of these occupational groupings filled an odd niche in society—one, frankly, that we still do not completely understand. It was typical for a farmer, warrior, or trader to hold a skilled artisan in outward contempt, but to recognize his usefulness to society and maintain an inward respect for the person and his skills. Because artisans had access to special knowledge and skills, feelings toward them could combine fear and awe of their mastery of the occult and access to spiritual and worldly powers with resentment, for artisans kept to themselves and guarded selfishly the knowledge of their skill that was essential to their economic well-being. Lineages of artisans often were wealthier than typical freeborn lineages too. Blacksmiths and leather workers were revered for their craft secrets and expertise: both worked with trees and minerals from the earth, the dwelling places of spirits. Their dealings involved spiritual rituals that others were incapable of performing and just as glad to leave to the artisans. Perhaps because they were entertainers, who are set apart in many societies, but just as likely because they often had intimate ties with persons at the heart of political power, bards were regarded as social separates. They often were constrained to live on the edge of villages, physically detached from the residences of others. Bards were normally associated with a specific lineage for patronage, but blacksmiths and leather workers were more independent. They moved about to find the materials they needed for their work—ore, wood, hides, certain fruits and berries— and settled when it was to their advantage, sometimes allying themselves to a freeborn lineage through a system of varying-term credit whereby the artisans would perform services on promise of sustenance and protection through the following year or longer. Such relationships, continually renewed, appeared permanently binding to foreign observers, and in a sense they were, though in theory either party could break them when it had fulfilled its part of the bargain.

Slaves, who made up the third social grouping, are the most difficult to describe and, with artisans, the most misunderstood by outside observers of precolonial African society.[17] Before the twentieth century there were many slaves in states like Niumi. Estimates made from the late eighteenth century into the colonial period suggest that from two-thirds to three-fourths of some societies in West Africa consisted of slaves, and there is no good proof that this proportion had increased significantly from earlier times.[18] Today there is no doubt: most precolonial African societies, even before they had contact with Europeans, had large slave populations and participated in a trade of slaves. Why they did so and what slavery in precolonial West African societies was like are questions that have perplexed outside observers for a long time.

The nature of African slavery varied considerably and differed from forms of the institution more familiar to Europeans. This has prompted students of the subject, like the blind men and the elephant, to stress only the aspects of its nature that they encountered. Some prefer to emphasize that African slavery was a property relationship;[19] others stress how, in a society where kinship defined the individual's place, slaves were those without kin.[20] It is clear that, for the continent as a whole, slavery encompassed a range of relationships of dependency.

For much of West Africa, John Thornton has provided a clear and logical discussion of slavery in a recent study of the early years of Atlantic commerce.[21] "Slavery was widespread in Atlantic Africa," Thornton argues, "because slaves were the only form of private, revenue-producing property recognized in African law."[22] Almost nowhere in precolonial Africa did the law recognize private landholding; land was owned communally, by the state in some settings and by the village or the large clan in others, and parceled out to lineages for their use according to need. That need was based on the number of laborers the lineage had to work the land. So to increase production, lineages had to invest in more laborers. This they could do, in a sense, by paying the bride price for sons to marry, benefiting from the woman's productive efforts, and then waiting for the offspring of the marriage to mature, but this latter was investment that might never pay off, and not for over a decade at best. They could, however, invest in a slave, who could be put to work almost immediately and bring rapid return on the investment. Women slaves could also bear children, who eventually would add to the size of the labor force. Thus, slavery was, according to Thornton, "possibly the most important avenue for private, reproducing wealth available to Africans."[23]

Who owned or sought to acquire slaves? All those who had wealth and an interest in increasing it. Agriculturalists obtained slaves to augment crop production. Rulers owned slaves to do their routine work, grow their crops, tend their horses, weave cloth, mine ores, and more. When societies became more militaristic and required larger armies for protection or offensive raiding, rulers obtained slaves and made them soldiers of the state. Traders used slaves to provide foodstuffs for them and their families as they indulged in nonagricultural pursuits and to serve as porters on commercial forays. Muslim clerics had slaves who produced food while they and their male offspring conducted religious training or did any of a variety of supernatural work for their clientele.

Given the varied circumstances in which slaves might live, it is easy to understand that the lot of West African slaves varied considerably from one circumstance to another. One role that varied less than others, however, was that of women. The majority of slaves in West Africa during precolonial times were women, and typically they brought a higher price than men. This was for the obvious reason that women produced useful offspring, but also because females tended in many ways to be the main producers in the society. Women also had the advantages of being more easily assimilated into a society than men and less likely to escape.[24] Besides sex differences, slaves associated with a lineage often did the same variety of tasks as other family members, though sometimes they specialized in a single craft, such as weaving. Over several generations, and increasingly with marriage and childbirth, slaves could become recognized members of the household, no longer liable for sale and movement. Slaves of royal lineages might serve in offices of state, as soldiers or administrators, and become particularly important in such matters. The difference was that slaves and their descendants were always outsiders, making them liable for exploitation by the insiders, the original family members. Although slaves' fortunes rose with the wealth and position of the family, they never entirely lost their personal status as being persons other than kin.

As in most places where slavery existed, West African societies obtained slaves by more or less violent means. Warfare, including raids, banditry, and kidnapping, was the most common method. Even wars not fought to gain slaves had that effect when successful, for prisoners of war were normally enslaved and sold or put to work to help defray the costs of the wars. If ransom was impossible, there were other considerations. Young boys could train as future soldiers; girls and women could become concubines; slaves of either sex could be given as gifts to religious persons or shrines. But generally captives were not especially valuable near their place of capture. They were close to home and likely to escape. Wise captors

moved prisoners rapidly and sold them away quickly if there were no pressing needs for their labor. Even if the need for labor was strong, it was often
better to sell off local captives and buy slaves from some distance away. For
these reasons, African armies often had a following of merchants eager to
buy prisoners at low prices and then march them off to more distant markets
where their value would be greater.[25]

Less violent methods of enslaving involved condemnation through judi-
cial or religious proceedings for civil crimes or supposed religious wrong-
doing. As the slave trade in West Africa grew heavy, slavery probably
became a more common punishment for an increasing number of offenses
to society.[26] And, finally, there is evidence of individuals voluntarily enslaving themselves, almost always because they could not feed or otherwise
care for themselves or their families.[27] In the worst of times, people chose
dependence over starvation.

The stratified societies described here had elements besides kinship in their
culture that lent them cohesion. One was the age grade. Groupings of adolescents went through several-month-long periods of training for adulthood and
then were initiated together into the society. Such "bush schools" took place
every few years. Those initiated at the same time formed a grouping of
individuals of the same approximate age with particularly close ties. Members
of age groups had obligations that ranged from serving as a labor brigade on
communal projects to looking after elderly villagers. They lent assistance to
one another at various stages in life, helping poorer members accumulate bride
wealth, for instance, or joining to build dwellings for spouses.[28]

Secret societies, sometimes called power associations, also cut across lines
of class and kin and helped bring and keep social order. Brooks makes the
strongest case to date for the existence and importance of secret societies
among Mande speakers.[29] Blacksmiths were the principal keepers of Mande
cultural tradition, Brooks argues, and where they settled across the Mande-
speaking world they established local chapters of such associations. Masked in
public to hide their worldly identity, leaders of secret societies provided for
social order, arbitrated disputes between lineage members, saw to it that trade
routes were protected and free of banditry, and generally, writes Brooks, "influenced other—possibly all—matters of consequence in communities under their
purview."[30] Secret societies probably played a role in the spreading of Mande
culture and the assimilation of peoples to a hegemonic culture by inducting
children of host societies and teaching them Mande ways. Also, over time they
adopted and then perpetuated local beliefs and practices.

One final institution that was common throughout much of West Africa
made possible the free movement of travelers and traders in foreign societies with minimal regard for protection, food, and lodging and provided a

way for foreigners to assimilate into a new society. This was an age-old custom of reciprocity that anthropologists call the landlord-stranger relationship.[31] Traditionally, persons living in West Africa provide food and shelter without question or fanfare for visitors. For those staying for a few days, a farming season, several years, or permanently, the relationship with a family, village, or larger group is institutionalized. A person coming to a West African village without the ability to subsist or succeed alone obtains a host, or landlord, who agrees to provide food and lodging. The landlord also provides proper introductions and generally serves as the stranger's connection with local society, taking the stranger's side in disputes, guaranteeing debts, or serving as guardian for the stranger's children. In these societies where kinship ties are necessary for having a place, kin of the landlord become kin of the stranger, and the responsibilities of kinfolk and landlord become similar.

For their part, strangers must get along in the village on the landlord's terms, following local customs carefully and providing services for the landlord—perhaps working in the landlord's fields several days a week or, if appropriate, trading on the landlord's account. If the stranger is successful, the landlord can expect gifts in a quantity related to the stranger's prosperity. Because one of the landlord's assumed responsibilities is to assist the stranger in amassing bride wealth and finding a suitable marriage partner, it often happens that the stranger who remains for a long period marries into the family of the landlord and thus becomes a part of the family and community. Wealthier strangers might marry into other, more prosperous or prestigious families—maybe even into families of rulers. In such ways, one-time outsiders integrate themselves into local communities.

The landlord-stranger relationship played a particularly important role in such a society as Niumi's, where for a variety of reasons alien peoples were forever coming to farm, fish, trade, proselytize, or otherwise attempt to prosper. Indeed, Niumi's history, early or late, is in large part the story of individuals or groups coming to live from some distance away and bringing with them material goods, cultural values, or religious practices that altered the circumstances of life for people in the region. Before the nineteenth century, when Europeans used force to bring about change in Niumi, it was the landlord-stranger relationship for accommodating strangers that made possible this cultural melding.

Niumi's Early Residents, Their Commercial Milieu, and the Niumi State

It is not possible to determine a great deal in detail about the earliest inhabitants of the coastal regions in and around the lower Gambia. Such evidence that exists for the period before Europeans sailed down Africa's west coast and began leaving a written record of what they encountered is from archaeology (with only a few sites investigated), linguistics, or oral traditions and is considerably limited in what it can tell us. We know that the region long had natural advantages that lured migrants, in good times and bad, so Niumi's population was a mixture of people from different ethnic backgrounds. This was typical of a wide area of West Africa. When Alvise da Cadamosto spent fifteen days at a commercial entrepot some sixty miles up the Gambia in 1456, he found "each day fresh people of various tongues down at the ship" and generally people "constantly journeying from place to place up and down the river in their canoes."[32]

An interesting recent study of Senegambian place names suggests that the earliest inhabitants might be identified most closely with one of several related groups—Bainunk, Kasanga, Beafada—who once populated a much larger area than they do today between the more arid lands to the north of the lower Gambia and the more humid lands to the south.[33] To these were added Serer, who moved southward during the first millennium A.D. from the Senegal River valley, and Mande-speaking peoples, who arrived later still from the east.[34]

There were, it seems, certain residential and occupational tendencies that characterized people's lives in Niumi. Nearly everyone who lived there before the mid-nineteenth century resided near the water, either ocean or river. The interior that today holds a sizable population of farmers was overgrown with forests and did not have many permanent residents at all. Cadamosto found the lands along the Gambia "covered with numerous and very large trees which are everywhere throughout the country"—so much so that they stifled the breeze and made travel on the river much less comfortable than on the Atlantic. He reported on an elephant hunt in Niumi's forests wherein men "advanced scrambling and jumping from tree to tree," shooting the elephant with arrows and throwing poisoned spears.[35]

Those inhabiting the sixty or seventy miles of islands and seacoast stretching north from the Gambia's mouth were long identified simply as *Niuminka,* which means simply "the people of Niumi." They were a mixture of the earliest residents, the Bainunk and others, with Serer and Mandinka. The language and customs of Serer seemed generally to predominate to the north. After the sixteenth century, more Mandinka customs entered into their ways. The sea was their livelihood; they were excellent boatmen in dugout canoes of varying sizes, some large enough to hold scores of men, and they fished, gathered mollusks, and extracted salt from the Atlantic's waters. They grew some of the savanna grains too, and they traded what they obtained from the sea up the coastal rivers, into West Africa's interior, for cotton cloth, gold, agricultural products, and more.[36]

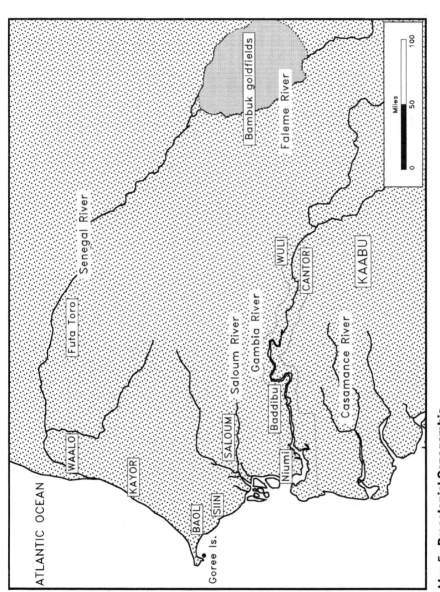

Map 5. **Precolonial Senegambia**

ATLANTIC OCEAN

Goree Is.

BAOL

SIIN

KAYOR

WAALO

Futa Toro

Senegal River

SALOUM

Saloum River

Gambia River

Baddibu

Niumi

WULI

CANTOR

KAABU

Casamance River

Bambuk goldfields

Faleme River

Miles

0   50   100

Box 3. **Ethnicity**

Ethnicity as we think of it—a clear identity with, and strong loyalties to, an ethnic group—almost certainly did not exist in precolonial West Africa. Europeans, who developed national loyalties and intense feelings about ethnic and national identity in recent centuries, brought their notions of ethnicity, nationhood, and national loyalty to Africa in the late-nineteenth and early-twentieth centuries and applied them to Africans. Europeans assumed that Africans had the same identity with a "tribe" as Europeans had with an ethnic grouping—English, Irish, French, Italian, German. For the benefit of order, colonial authorities attempted to label each African man, woman, and child as a member of one or another ethnic group. There was no room for multiethnicity. It did not matter if a person in colonial Gambia had a personal, primary identity as "Mandinka," "Jola," or "Serahuli": early in the twentieth century he or she became such on the books—formally and officially. Gambia's British administrators could state the exact percentage of the colony's "native inhabitants" who were Mandinka or Jola or Serahuli. Then, the development of African nationalisms, which came into existence in the anti-Western, anticolonial culture of the first half of the twentieth century, heightened many of these prescribed ethnic divisions, especially when colonial political parties came to be based largely on ethnic designations, and rendered Africans, indeed, downright "tribal."

But Africans did not always think of themselves as members of tribes or ethnic groups. Before the nineteenth century, ethnicity in Senegambia was much more fluid than we tend to think of it—a permeable membrane through which passed marriage partners, members of secret societies or occupational groupings, magico-religious figures (Muslims and non-Muslims), and just about everybody else. People frequently reached adulthood speaking several languages and existing comfortably among persons who did things differently from the way they did them. Thus, there is little doubt—and oral traditions bear this out—that Niumi's early population was a conglomeration of peoples who had various individual and group identities and who lived together without many of the troubles that today we identify as "ethnic conflict."

Along the river banks south of the Niuminka settlements was a small number of villages that were primarily commercial in nature. These were outposts, or nodes, of what Philip D. Curtin identifies as a trade diaspora, the initial element of what would grow to become a dominating presence of Mande-speaking peoples along the banks of the middle and lower Gambia by the seventeenth century.[37] What was behind the existence of these Mande commercial enclaves in an alien Niuminka polity were the patterns of trade that existed in and around the lower Gambia. It was a commercial milieu that had long been among West Africa's most active, but, like most of the rest of the region, it became considerably more active in the thirteenth and fourteenth centuries with the growth of a Western Sudanic trading complex, tied into the trans-Sahara trade, and the rise of the Mali Empire.

The Gambia had long been an artery for trade between the Atlantic and the interior.[38] The commodity that made the river trade brisk was salt—the same commodity that had always been of fundamental importance to the desert trade, that had brought Berbers across the Sahara with slabs of it tied to camels, that had prompted West Africans to exchange gold for it. For the Niuminka, salt did not move in hundred-pound slabs, but in peck-sized baskets. Extracting the salt from seawater was never easy. The activity required flooding large basins with tidal waters, closing off dikes, then waiting for the tropical sun to evaporate the water and scraping up the residual salt from the basin floor. Yet, it was an ideal activity for the dry season of the year, when crops were in and there was less work of other kinds to do. Because of greater humidity and cloud cover, areas not far south of the Gambia could not produce salt so efficiently as those along the Atlantic coast north of the river.[39] So it was, in the coastal lands not far north of the Gambia's estuary, that residents extracted the creamy reddish-looking mineral, put it in baskets made from woven palm fronds, loaded the baskets into large canoes, and conveyed the salt upriver. Beyond the Gambia's headwaters and off across several thousand miles of West Africa's savannas, there was almost no salt except that which was imported from the mines north of the Sahara. Thus the river was a salt highway eastward and southeastward to areas of considerable demand. The traders took with them dried seafood and kola nuts (obtained from areas some distance to the south) for the eastward trade or savanna grains—millets and sorghums—that peoples in the rice-producing regions to the south of the Gambia could not grow so efficiently.[40]

Wherever along the river the coastal canoe men met traveling merchants from distant places, they exchanged their products. For a long time the state of Cantora, on the Gambia's south bank at the head of navigation, was a regional center for such exchange.[41] From Mande-speaking merchants in Cantora the coastal traders obtained cotton cloth, especially, but also iron, copperware, or gold; from Banyun merchants in the river's southerly tributaries—especially Vintang Creek, which entered the Gambia from the southeast some fifty miles upriver from the mouth—they received kola nuts, malaguetta pepper, or rice. Over land, from the north, came a trickle of horses, more cloth, and leather goods. And captives from one or another episode of local or regional warfare were an important part of this trade. These slaves carried goods as they marched and were sold along with them to end up working in the fields of a state's ruling lineages, working to produce crops for a nonroyal lineage, or marching across the Sahara for sale in the slave markets of the Mediterranean.

Over the years of such heavy commercial activity, a trade diaspora came into being along the Gambia's banks. Individual or small groups of Mande traders, perhaps Soninke speakers originally, from the region between the middle Senegal and upper Niger Rivers, traveled to trade in alien territory toward the Gambia's mouth and remained in one or another village along the river. In time, more of such traders, perhaps relatives of the original, followed and settled in the same villages. As rapidly as possible they would learn the languages, cultural nuances, and commercial ways of the people among whom they were living. Such villages thus became nodes of a trading network that stretched its arms some distance from the original homes of the traders. The settled merchants served as cross-cultural brokers, facilitating trade between the local population and traveling merchants from the Mande-speaking areas of the western savannas.

By the fourteenth or fifteenth century, there were a dozen or more of such commercial enclaves of a Mande trade diaspora that stretched from Mali's political and economic center on the upper Niger to the Gambia's mouth and tied people and polities along the river to the trading complex that stretched across the savannas toward Lake Chad and connected into the trans-Saharan trade. *Julakunda,* the "place of the traders," these villages were called, and they caught the attention of the earliest Europeans to visit the Gambia because they were the points of exchange of products of all types, for all comers.[42]

But the villages were not only commercial centers: they were known also as *morakunda,* the "settlement of the Muslims," and indeed they were the places where Soninke, Fulbe, and Mandinka merchants who spread southward from the Senegal and westward from the Niger had established themselves as practitioners of Islam. Trade could take up a good part of residents' activities in the dry season of the year, when roads and paths were passable; then *moriya,* the magico-religious works of Muslim holy men constituted their work through the rains, when slaves could be growing crops to sustain them all. If for some Africans and Europeans the villages were primarily the locus of trade, for many Africans from a surrounding region they were the places where ascetic and wealthy Muslims divined, made charms, and worked to cure people of their maladies.

This mixture of more numerous, coastwise settlements of Niuminka and a small number of at least mixed-Mandinka commercial and Islamic villages along the Gambia's banks was organized into a state that, into the sixteenth century, was ruled by a lineage of the more numerous Niuminka.[43] The lack of evidence makes it difficult to determine much in specifics about the state, and one forever must be wary of applying modern Western notions of states as carefully bounded territories under one government. Early rulers of West African states seem to have been concerned more with control and protection of people than of land. In the fourteenth and fifteenth centuries, the Niumi state may have had more in common with the Wolof or Serer polities to the north than it would several centuries later, when Mandinka political influences were stronger. It had a hereditary ruler—the title *mansa* that Cadamosto and Gomes use for Niumi's ruler in the 1450s shows either a borrowing from the Mandinka that indicates, again, how mixed were customs, practices, and language, or more simply that the Portuguese relied on an interpreter who spoke one of the Mande languages. One suspects that Niumi's ruler had officials in the commercial villages to oversee and tax trading activities there.

The state of Niumi was apparently independent at the time of the Portuguese arrival.[44] On the south bank of the Gambia, some distance upriver, several states owed at least nominal allegiance to a Mandinka *farim,* or governor, located, writes Cadamosto, "inland towards the south-south-east, . . . at nine or ten days journey," and this governor "was subject to the Emperor of Melli, the great Emperor of the Blacks."[45] The earliest Portuguese did not report Niumi as being subject to imperial Mali or any particular overlord. This may have been true because it was farther away from the center of Mandinka authority, on the upper Niger, or because its ruling lineage was more powerful and bellicose than those of the upriver states. Or maybe the Portuguese simply failed to make note of some hierarchical political situation involving Niumi.

Of course, there existed important differences in the first half of the fifteenth century between little Niumi and mighty Mali. A major one was the nature of their military forces. The key to Mali's power was cavalry. Horses had been important to West African rulers for centuries, but often more for the prestige they conferred than for their tactical use in battle. But by the thirteenth century, perhaps aided by a long dry period in West Africa that reduced ground cover (and thus the shade-loving and disease-bearing tsetse flies) along the upper Niger, Mandinka elites found it possible to sustain large herds, Mandinka horsemen perfected raiding tactics, and Malian horse warriors gained command of the battlefield. The men of Mali's royal lineages were horsemen, who rode and raided and defended on horseback.

This was not the case in early Niumi, where any lifestyle based on horses remained a problem. The lower Gambia had enough seasonal rain to keep low brush growing, so tsetse flies spread the deadly trypanosomiasis among large animals. And unlike Mali, Niumi did not have a steady source of horses through trade. So while Niumi's royal lineages may have clung to the trappings of horsemanship, keeping a few mounts about for use on ceremonial occasions, they were not able to marshal a cavalry force sufficient to raid others for slaves or to protect themselves from alien raiders. Instead, they had a different medium to command—the coast and river— and a different means of conveyance: the dugout canoe. If Mali remained master of the western savannas' overland trade routes into the fifteenth century with its formidable cavalry, Niumi kept strict control of the ocean and riverain trade routes in and around the lower Gambia with its fleet of large canoes, each capable of holding two or three score of warriors wielding bows that fired arrows tipped with deadly poison. One can suppose that Niumi's rulers used the wealth they garnered from the aquatic trade to acquire slaves, whom they employed in household production, perhaps the rendering of salt, and the manning of the canoes that were so important to the state's power.

When Nuno Tristão entered the Gambia River and tried to acquire slaves by force, he experienced the power of Niumi's riverain forces and the efficacy of their weapons. The lessons the Portuguese learned from Tristão's experience were ones that Europeans trading in West Africa were loath to forget over the next three and one-half centuries: surrounding them were complex societies that were active participants in a sophisticated regional commerce that was growing in response to a restructuring world system. In virtually every situation, power was in the hands of the Africans; the vulnerability of the alien Europeans, who were outmanned and eternally dependent on local peoples for water, food, shelter, and cultural and commercial mediation, was palpable. Survival and success depended not on force of arms but on finding a mutuality of interests and then fostering those interests to the benefit of African states and foreign traders alike.[46] This is precisely what the Portuguese did in dealing with Niumi and others, once they understood the circumstances of cross-cultural trade along Africa's west coast, toward the end of the fifteenth century.

Notes

1. Olga Linares de Sapir, "Shell-Middens of Lower Casamance and Diola Protohistory," *West Africa Journal of Archaeology* 1 (1971): 41.

2. George E. Brooks, *Landlords and Strangers: Ecology, Society, and Trade in Western Africa, 1000–1530* (Boulder, Colo.: Westview Press, 1993), 12.

3. A good, concise discussion of the region's physical geography is in ibid., ch. 1.

4. Annual Report, North Bank Province, June 1921, CSO 1/163.

5. J.R. Harlan, J.J.J. de Wet, and A.B.L. Stemler, eds., *Origins of African Plant Domestication* (The Hague: Mouton, 1976).

6. Philip D. Curtin, *Economic Change in Precolonial Africa: Senegambia in the Era of the Slave Trade* (Madison: University of Wisconsin Press, 1975), 218–19.

7. Philip D. Curtin discusses "Killing Diseases of the Tropical World" in *Death by Migration: Europe's Encounter with the Tropical World in the Nineteenth Century* (Cambridge: Cambridge University Press, 1995), ch. 5.

8. *Human Development Report 1991* (New York: Oxford University Press for the UNDP, 1991), 123, 127; *World Tables 1995* (Baltimore: Johns Hopkins University Press, 1995), 295.

9. Except where otherwise noted, information on Gambian society is from Brooks, *Landlords and Strangers,* 33–47; Curtin, *Economic Change,* 29–37; or Donald R. Wright, "Niumi: The History of a Western Mandinka State through the Eighteenth Century," Ph.D. dissertation, Indiana University, 1976, 16–27.

10. For a good discussion of West African ethnicity and the role colonial officials played in defining African ethnic groups, see David C. Conrad and Barbara E. Frank, "*Nyamakalaya*: Contradiction and Ambiguity in Mande Society," in *Status and Identity in West Africa: Nyamakalaw of Mande,* ed. David C. Conrad and Barbara E. Frank (Bloomington: Indiana University Press, 1995), 7–10.

11. This describes a patrilocal society, as most Senegambian societies are today. Evidence from oral tradition suggests that society in Niumi may have been matrilocal, and perhaps matrilineal, a long time ago, but this is impossible to determine.

12. F. Lafont, "Le Gandoul et les Niominkas," *Bulletin du Comité des études historiques et scientifique de l'Afrique occidentale française* 21 (1938): 414; Paul Pélissier, *Les paysans du Sénégal: Les civilisations agraires du Cayor à la Casamance* (Paris: Imprimerie Fabrèque, 1966), 411.

13. Brooks, *Landlords and Strangers,* 4, 45–46.

14. Curtin, *Economic Change,* 29–37.

15. Conrad and Frank, *"Nyamakalaya,"* 10–16; Tal Tamari, "The Development of Caste Systems in West Africa," *Journal of African History* 32 (1991): 221–50.

16. Brooks, *Landlords and Strangers,* 73–77.

17. Good sources for precolonial African slavery are Paul E. Lovejoy, *Transformations in Slavery: A History of Slavery in Africa* (Cambridge: Cambridge University Press, 1983); Claude Meillassoux, *The Anthropology of Slavery: The Womb of Iron and Gold,* tr. Alide Dasnois (Chicago: University of Chicago Press, 1986); Suzanne Miers and Igor Kopytoff, eds., *Slavery in Africa: Historical and Anthropological Perspectives* (Madison: University of Wisconsin Press, 1977); and Arthur Tuden and Leonard Plotnicov, *Social Stratification in Africa* (New York: Free Press, 1970).

18. Martin A. Klein summarizes some of these data in "The Demography of Slavery in the Western Sudan in the Late Nineteenth Century," in *African Population and Capitalism: Historical Perspectives,* ed. Joel Gregory and Dennis Cordell (Boulder, Colo.: Westview Press, 1987), 50–62.

19. Tuden and Plotnicov, *Social Stratification,* 12.

20. Miers and Kopytoff, *Slavery in Africa,* Introduction.

21. John Thornton, *Africa and Africans in the Making of the Atlantic World, 1400–1680* (New York: Cambridge University Press, 1992), ch. 3.

22. Ibid., 74.

23. Ibid., 86.

24. Martin A. Klein, "Women in Slavery in the Western Sudan," in *Women and*

Slavery in Africa, ed. Claire C. Robertson and Martin A. Klein (Madison: University of Wisconsin Press, 1983), 67–92.

25. Curtin, *Economic Change,* 154–55.

26. Walter Rodney, *A History of the Upper Guinea Coast, 1545–1800* (Oxford: Oxford University Press, 1970), 258ff.

27. During a drought at the end of the eighteenth century, Scottish physician and explorer Mungo Park noticed women who had turned over their children to local rulers in exchange for provisions to keep themselves alive. He related, "There are many instances of freemen voluntarily surrendering up their liberty to save their lives. During a great scarcity, which lasted for three years, in the countries of the Gambia, great numbers of people became slaves in this manner." *Travels in the Interior of Africa* (London: Cassell, 1887), 57, 108.

28. Carol Spindel discusses the importance of age groupings in the past and shows how they are considerably less important today in a part-Mande village in northern Ivory Coast in *In the Shadow of the Sacred Grove* (New York: Vintage Books, 1989), 93, 124–27.

29. Brooks, *Landlords and Strangers,* 44–46, 73–77.

30. Ibid., 74.

31. Ibid., 38–39; V.R. Dorjahn and Christopher Fyfe, "Landlord and Stranger: Change in Tenancy Relations in Sierra Leone," *Journal of African History* 3 (1962): 391–97.

32. Alvise da Cadamosto, "The Voyages of Cadamosto," in *The Voyages of Cadamosto and Other Documents in Western Africa in the Second Half of the Fifteenth Century,* ed. G.R. Crone (London: Hakluyt Society, 1937), 69.

33. Stephan Bühnen, "Place Names as an Historical Source: An Introduction with Examples from Southern Senegambia and Germany," *History in Africa; A Journal of Method* 19 (1992): 1–57. This argument is supported generally by Jean Giraud, *L'or du Bambouk: une dynamique de civilisation ouest-africaine: du royaume de Gabou à la Casamance* (Geneva: Georg Editeur, 1992).

34. Curtin, *Economic Change,* 19–22; Pélissier, *Paysans,* 192–96; Wright, "Niumi," 9–12.

35. Cadamosto, "Voyages," 70–71.

36. Felipe Tejada, "The Ñiominka," unpublished paper, Indiana University, c. 1980, 2–4.

37. Philip D. Curtin, *Cross-Cultural Trade in World History* (Cambridge: Cambridge University Press, 1984), 1–2, 17–18, 26–28, 38–39; Curtin, *Economic Change,* ch. 2; Abner Cohen, "Cultural Strategies in the Organization of Trading Diasporas," in *The Development of Indigenous Trade and Markets in West Africa* (Oxford: Oxford University Press, 1971), 267ff.

38. Giraud, *L'or du Bambouk,* passim.

39. Leon Pales, *Les sels alimentaires: sels minéraux, problème des sels alimentaires en AOF* (Dakar: Direction Général de la Santé Publique, 1950), 13–14, 39, 93–96.

40. George Brooks calls attention to the importance of the kola nut trade in "Kola Nuts and State-Building: Upper Guinea Coast and Senegambia, 15th–17th Centuries," Boston University African Studies Center Working Papers, No. 38, Boston, 1980. The trading of kola is a principal theme of Brooks, *Landlords and Strangers.*

41. Giraud, *L'or du Bambouk,* passim.

42. Diogo Gomes argued over religion with a Muslim from one such establishment in Niumi and visited an emporium in Cantor, a state noted as being a commercial hub far up the Gambia. Gomes, "The Voyages of Diogo Gomes," in Crone, ed., *Voyages,* 92–95.

43. Evidence that the state's rulers were not Mandinka and, indeed, were Atlantic-oriented Niuminka is from oral traditions and Diogo Gomes, who, when in the Gambia River in 1457, sent the ruler of Niumi "many presents by his own men in his own canoes, which were going for salt to his own country." Such salt, which "was plentiful there, and of a red colour," was in the coastal territory occupied by the Niuminka. Gomes, "Voyages," 97.

44. Here, again, one can get bogged down by European concepts of political independence. Virtually every state had relationships of reciprocity and dependence with others in its neighborhood, through marriage alliances and other mutual obligations. To say that the state of Niumi was "apparently independent" in the middle of the fifteenth century simply means that the Portuguese did not refer to its owing allegiance, including payment of tax or tribute, in any formal way, to another political authority.

45. Cadamosto, "Voyages," 67.

46. Ivana Elbl, "Cross-Cultural Trade and Diplomacy: Portuguese Relations with West Africa, 1441–1521," *Journal of World History* 3 (1992): 174–75.

PART II
THE PRECOLONIAL PERIOD, 1450–1800

For 400 years following the opening of the Atlantic to European shipping, a group of merchants, planters, shippers, and bankers constructed and maintained an economic system that affected people on all four continents bordering the ocean. The system's primary purpose was to produce commodities for the European market, but it involved obtaining and transporting laborers—mostly slaves—for the staple-producing plantations, supplying the laborers with their basic needs, and maintaining ancillary trade around the rim of the Atlantic basin.

People in Niumi had been involved in trade along West Africa's Atlantic coast long before the Portuguese arrived. They controlled a part of the regional exchange of salt, dried seafood, and kola nuts with their canoes and boatmen; they were on the edge of the desert-side trade that connected them, across the Sahara, to the economic system of central parts of the Old World. But the appearance of Portuguese sailors in the Gambia in the middle of the fifteenth century marked Niumi's entrance into the broader trade of the growing Atlantic complex, an international economic network Niumi would continue to be involved in for more than 350 years. In a variety of ways, over several centuries, participation in the Atlantic economy altered politics and society in the state. Various Europeans active in the Atlantic commerce brought to Niumi new means for political control, first providing access to horses and much later access to firearms; new markets for what people in Niumi could produce, including slaves; and new sources to tap for revenue. The trade also brought new persons to reside in Niumi—Africans, Europeans, and mixtures of the two. Some of the Africans would come to take advantage of the new means to political control, and their descendants would participate in ruling Niumi for the remainder of its existence as a sovereign state. Most of the Europeans would come to trade and then, to a degree Niumi's residents allowed, their offspring would assimilate into the society. Eventually, European private companies and governments established permanent commercial outposts on Niumi territory that would benefit Niumi's rulers. Over time, as Niumi was fully integrated into the Atlantic commercial network, it came to have an economy, polity, and society that were dependent on such a thorough connection to the Atlantic trade. When the plantation complex or Niumi's relationship to it changed significantly, the lives of everyone in the state faced change as well.

3

NIUMI BETWEEN TWO SYSTEMS

WAXING ATLANTIC TRADE, CONTINUING SUDANIC TRADE, 1450–1600

When you go to a new land and find the people all
hopping on one leg, you, too, must raise a leg.
—*griot* Unus Jata, in an interview in The Gambia,
September 1974

The period between 1450 and 1600 was one of partial reorientation for Niumi. Portuguese merchants came by sea and connected westernmost sub-Saharan Africa to a growing plantation complex centered on the Atlantic Ocean. Among other things for Niumi, this meant a significant heightening of the trading of slaves. Before Portuguese arrival, persons in Niumi may have sent slaves northward toward the Sahara, but the numbers were not large and the importance of the trade to Niumi's economic well-being was not significant. The state's main commercial activity was the trading of salt from the Atlantic toward the savanna hinterland of the upper Gambia, mainly for cloth, iron, and gold. But within a few decades of the appearance of Portuguese caravels in the Gambia River, Niumi, with other states along and near the Senegambian coast, became a supplier of commodities for the Atlantic economy: gold, hides, beeswax, foodstuffs, and slaves, and more importantly, it taxed the trade passing through the state and in and out of the river's mouth. Participation in the Atlantic commerce did not diminish the amount of trade taking place across the western savannas, however. If any-thing, it heightened that trade, and Niumi continued to exchange goods between the Atlantic, the upper Niger River, the southern edge of the Sa-hara, and the Guinea forests.

The growing trade led to gradual change for Niumi's residents. The heightening demand for slaves brought an increase in slave raiding and associated political and social instability. Over half a century or more, people across coastwise Senegambia had to find new political institutions and social structures that would enable them to live with a reasonable level of security. People in Niumi found it necessary to change a number of their basic institutions, from the nature of the state to the form and structure of villages. But the new trade brought something besides instability: it provided some residents of Niumi with access to new wealth and new products, and it brought new people with fresh ideas from different parts of the world. Each of these would play a role in a century and a half of political, economic, social, and cultural change in the state.

Western Europe and the Rise of the Plantation Complex

From the perspective of world history, a series of events that occurred over the century following 1450 stand at the beginning of the long process of the coming together of peoples of the world. The steady Portuguese exploration of Africa's west coast, Bartolomeu Dias's 1488 rounding of the Cape of Good Hope, Vasco da Gama's voyage to India in 1497–99, and subsequent Portuguese efforts to rest control of the Indian Ocean spice trade from Muslim merchants are widely known events of "European expansion." By early in the sixteenth century Portugal had gained control of key points of access to the Indian Ocean, defeated a strong Arab fleet, and established trading posts in East Africa, India, Indonesia, and China. Each year Portuguese fleets sailed out to "The Indies" and back, returning with spices, mainly, but also Indian cottons, East Asian silks, and a host of foods and plants that were entirely new to them. Iberian and northern European cities became more important suppliers for the European market, at the expense of trade through eastern Mediterranean and southern European ports.

In the other direction, the Genoese sailor Christopher Columbus enlisted Spanish rulers to back his 1492 voyage to the west to reach the same Indies, but he underestimated the earth's size and located what to Europeans was a new world in the Americas. With considerable speed, Spanish *conquistadors* rested control of central and southern regions of the Americas from the resident Indians, gaining access to an enormous expanse of land that held vast quantities of silver and gold and on which grew scores of plants entirely foreign to Europeans. The Spanish did not hesitate to begin exploiting the mines of Mexico and South America's highlands. Using Indian labor primarily, Spain brought from the earth and transported home nearly 20,000 tons of silver and over 200 tons of gold between 1503 and 1660. It was bullion that would grease the wheels of capitalism and international trade throughout western Europe.

But spices, cottons, silver, and gold were not all that flowed from one region to another in greater abundance after 1450 and affected the lives of people around the world. With slightly less speed, perhaps, but inexorably nevertheless, the Portuguese, Spanish, and eventually northern and western

69

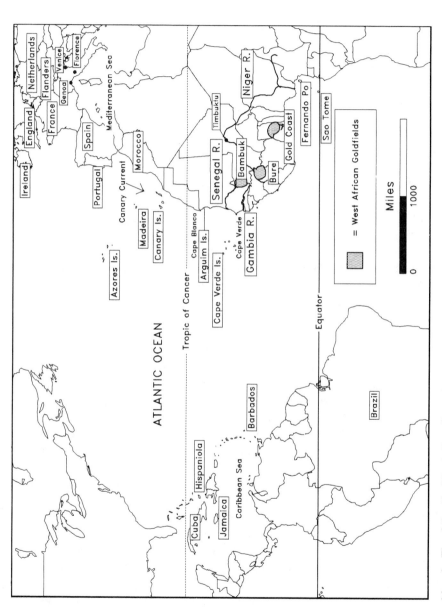

Map 6. **The Atlantic Plantation Complex**

Europeans began spreading new plants and animals (and sometimes more simply new strains of the same plants), to parts of the world where they were unknown. Over time, wheat and most common barnyard animals for the Americas; maize and potatoes for Europe; maize and sweet potatoes for East Asia; maize, cassava, and peanuts for Africa—to name a few—would alter the caloric and nutritional basis of populations and enable regions to sustain larger numbers of people with less labor. Such changes, often overlooked, would underlie much of the history that transpired, Old World and New, over the last half a millennium.[1]

For a century and more after 1450, as most of these events were taking place, a number of Portuguese and Portuguese-African (Luso-African) sailors and entrepreneurs focused attention on West Africa, where they found riches of their own to exploit. What interested the Portuguese most in Africa south of the Sahara was gold. For several centuries, word of rich West African potentates had circulated around the Mediterranean, causing ambitious south Europeans to dream of reaching the lands below the Sahara. Rumors gave way to fact once Malian ruler *Mansa* Musa took a hundred camels laden with gold on a pilgrimage to Mecca in 1324–25 and reduced the value of gold in Cairo with lavish spending and giving.[2] When crusading Portuguese knights wrested Ceuta in Morocco from the Moors in 1415 and learned greater details about the gold-bearing lands of West Africa, their dreams became more vivid. Gold was a commodity in great demand in the Mediterranean of the late Middle Ages, where polities of all sizes had been minting gold coins for several centuries. Portugal did so for a while, but was forced to stop in 1383 for want of bullion.[3] On a 1442 voyage past Cape Blanco, Portuguese merchant seamen traded for gold with Tuaregs along the Atlantic Coast. Then, as he ascended the Gambia River in 1456, Alvise da Cadamosto bartered with an African ruler for gold—not a lot of it, he reported, but "they traded it cheaply, taking in exchange articles of little value in our eyes."[4]

The Gambia turned out to be one of two important points of Portuguese access to West African gold—the other, after 1470, being El Mina on the Gold Coast. The river flowed directly toward the Bambuk and Buré goldfields. Oceangoing vessels could sail to within 100 miles or a little more of Bambuk and 250 of Buré. Besides that, African merchants had been bringing gold down to ports along the Gambia, to exchange for salt primarily, for a long time. Diogo Gomes was duly impressed at Cantor, 250 miles up the Gambia, where he saw African merchants "come loaded with gold" and learned of a "lord of all the mines" toward the east, who "had before the door of his palace a mass of gold just as it was taken from the earth, so large that twenty men could scarcely move it, and [to which] the king always fastened his horse."[5] Fairly quickly, Portuguese and Cape Verdean traders ascended the Gambia and began exchanging their "articles of little value" for gold, and the result in Portugal was almost instantaneous: in 1457 the Lisbon mint began issuing the *cruzado,* which Charles R. Boxer labels "a coin of almost pristine purity, which underwent no debasement until 1536." According to Curtin's estimates, by the beginning of the sixteenth century the Portuguese were obtaining an annual average of about seventy-five pounds of gold from Senegambia.[6] A good portion of that they acquired in trade from along the banks of the Gambia River.

If the amount of gold obtainable in West Africa was not as great as the Portuguese wished, the metal's availability captured their interest and brought them to recognize what Curtin calls "a fortuitous and unexpected by-product of the gold trade":[7] the availability of slaves. What the Portuguese could do with slaves initially was take them home to serve Europe's royalty and tend to the knights and squires who served as marginally productive members of European courts. Within decades of obtaining the first slaves from West Africa, however, new markets for them appeared. These were tied to an expanding economic complex of slave-worked plantation agriculture that was spreading into the Atlantic in the wake of Portuguese explorations. It was an enterprise that would have enormous and lasting consequences not just for West Africans but for persons residing today on all four continents bordering the Atlantic.

The origins of this grand, modern, intercontinental economic system, the Atlantic plantation complex, go back, once more, to the formative time of the Crusades.[8] As European Crusaders marched across Muslim lands bordering the eastern Mediterranean, they encountered a variety of products they never before had seen—or tasted. One they found particularly appealing was cane sugar, a product of central Asian origin that Muslims had been growing for an Asian market—it did wonders to mint tea—for many years. When they could, Italian merchants bought sugar from Muslim producers and imported it into southern Europe, where even the wealthiest of people had only honey to add sweetness to their foods. Once Christian entrepreneurs acquired land as part of the crusading effort, they began altering feudal customs regarding land tenure and labor use so they could concentrate productive efforts on growing cane for the export market.

Curtin explains the properties of sugarcane that lend it to plantation agriculture and an export market. It requires considerable labor for its cultivation and harvest, and it is so heavy and bulky that it must be concentrated, through pressing and boiling, into crystalline sugar and molasses before it can be moved any distance. Once concentrated, though, it has a high value relative to its bulk—qualities ideal for long-distance export. With such heavy labor demands for growing and processing, and with such concentrated value in a product that was a dietary luxury rather than a nutritional staple, widespread plantation growth of sugar for export was not long in coming.

Indeed, by the start of the twelfth century a sugar-growing plantation complex was in existence on Christian holdings in the Levant and on the eastern Mediterranean islands of Cyprus and Crete. Capital and management for the plantations came from southern Europe, as did shipping. Labor was mostly servile, but in a different sense than on the feudal manor. At certain times of the year, workers on sugar plantations were required to work extraordinarily long hours under the most difficult circumstances. Feudal laws and customs did not contain obligations for such work on the part of serfs. Fortunately for the plantation owners, the old Roman legal status of *servitus*, or chattel slave, still existed around the Mediterranean, as did an active slave trade. So owners of the prototype plantations began buying laborers. Many of the early slaves on these plantations were captives from the struggles between Christians and Muslims that were taking place on either end of the Mediterranean. With the opening of the Black Sea to European traffic at the start of the thirteenth century, more of the plantation slaves came from the sea's northern shores. Many were speakers of Slavic languages, from whence comes the word *slave* (*esclave, esclavo*) in several European languages. By the fifteenth century traders even were selling small numbers of black Africans in the Mediterranean slave trade, after a crossing of the Sahara. But on the sugar plantations, race or color were not of primary importance. Highest values were placed on strength and longevity.

Europe's growing population and its development of a commercial infrastructure of towns, roads, banks, and regular markets meant increasing demand for sugar and better methods of supply, so the Mediterranean plantation complex expanded. Sicily and Tunisia in the central Mediterranean became sugar producers; then southern Spain, southern Portugal, and northern Morocco. The fifteenth-century opening of the Atlantic to European shipping enabled the spread of sugar plantations to several ocean islands, where the warmer and wetter conditions were better still for growing cane. On Madeira after 1455 and São Tomé near the Equator in the 1470s, plantation managers took over and quickly made the islands the major sources for sugar for the European market. Spain wrested the Canaries from Portugal after 1480 and established plantations there, too. For these new and rapidly growing, labor-intensive agricultural enterprises in the Atlantic, and for some of the older ones around the Mediterranean, the Portuguese obtained slaves from Africa's west coast, below the Sahara, in exchange for commodities in local demand—horses, iron, cloth, metalware, and more.

Columbus took sugarcane with him on his second voyage to North America in 1493 and made at least a halfhearted attempt at growing the crop in the Caribbean, but this and more concerted Spanish efforts at cane production through the sixteenth century were not as successful as later. A major problem was that the laborers for these plantations, local Arawak Indians, could not live long enough to be productive, for they had no immunities to the Old World diseases—smallpox, measles, chicken pox, whooping cough, and several more—that came to the New World with the Europeans.[9] Once Spaniards located silver and gold deposits in Central and South America, mining held their attention, and they used local Indians and some imported African slaves for this enterprise. But purely African slave-based plantation agriculture was still some years away in the Spanish New World empire of 1600.

It was the Portuguese, with access to African slaves, who successfully moved plantation-based sugar production to the New World after the middle of the sixteenth century. Africans had much the same inherited immunities to Old World diseases as Europeans, and most adult Africans had some degree of immunity to malaria and yellow fever, largely because they had survived the tropical diseases in childhood. They could live longer in the New World tropical environment of the sixteenth century than anyone else, and this factor, more than others, made them pay off for Portuguese planters. Between 1550 and 1600 African slaves poured into Brazil, and by the latter date, Brazil had replaced the Atlantic islands as the major source for Europe's sugar. Slaves also were being taken to some of the Caribbean islands, Hispaniola especially, where planters continued their efforts to grow the crop.

Thus, whether for the West African, Atlantic island, western European plantation complex of 1500 or the West African, Brazilian, western European plantation complex of a century later, most patterns and institutions were the same. Capital, know-how, management, and shipping all came from Europe, where the market lay. The laborers on the plantations were enslaved, and nearly all of them came from the interior of Africa's west coast.

Early Atlantic Trade and Political Change in Niumi

Senegambia was the first region of sub-Saharan Africa to become a major exporter of slaves into the Atlantic economy. The Atlantic trade picked up rapidly following Portuguese arrival; when Gomes made a second voyage to Senegambia in 1460, he found two Portuguese vessels anchored and trading peacefully not far north of Niumi. Though records for the trade and

its timing are spotty, it is clear that by the start of the sixteenth century
Africans living along Senegambia's Atlantic coast and its major rivers were
fully involved in supplying captives, gold, hides, beeswax, and foodstuffs in
exchange for horses, cloth, metals, beads, and more.[10]

This increase in trade happened to be taking place at a time when
Senegambia's long-stable political situation was slowly beginning to
change. What role the Portuguese and their demand for some products and
supply of others played in altering Senegambian politics remains open to
debate, but several historians believe that the increased access foreign traders provided persons living along the Gambia River and southward to valuable commodities, horses in particular, helped bring about the long regional
upheaval of the late fifteenth and sixteenth centuries. Such commodities
clearly were important in the social and political change that occurred in
Niumi.[11]

As we know, when the first Portuguese arrived in the Gambia River in
the middle of the fifteenth century, they found Niumi existing on the river's
north bank, a political unit populated largely by Niuminka, some closer
culturally to their Serer kin in the northern coastal regions and others under
more Mandinka influence toward the Gambia's mouth. The state was ruled
by a prominent lineage of the same group. Prosperous families living in the
state owned slaves, who worked to increase production of foodstuffs. Existing at several locations within the state were separate commercial and religious enclaves, villages inhabited by Muslim, Mande-speaking traders and
holy men who had settled in the lower Gambia some time earlier as part of a
Mande trade diaspora, drawn mainly by the commerce in salt, dried fish, and
kola nuts, for cloth, iron, and gold between the Atlantic Coast and West
Africa's interior. Niumi's rulers derived revenue from tolls charged for the
coastal and riverain trade and from taxes on the state residents. They may
have owned a small number of horses and displayed or ridden them for the
prestige the animals provided for their position as heads of state, but early
Niumi in those years was not good territory for horse owning or for military
pursuits involving cavalry. The backbone of Niumi's military force, as
Tristão and his crew found out, was a fleet of war canoes, manned by
poison-arrow-firing archers. This force allowed Niumi's rulers to command
access to the waters of the lower Gambia and gave them control of the
coastal and riverain trade of the region.

Some distance to the north and east of the lower Gambia, the political
and military situation was different.[12] A vast Jolof Empire, populated by
Wolof-speaking peoples, had controlled much of the inland region between
the Senegal and Gambia Rivers since the thirteenth century. Along the
Atlantic coast from the Senegal River to south of Cape Verde, smaller

tributary states of Wolof speakers held sway. The Mali Empire, larger still, had been the dominant force through the vast interior lands east of the navigable Gambia for about the same length of time. Mali, too, had subsidiary and tributary states that at times of the empire's greatest power stretched to the banks of the Gambia.

The key to the military strength of Jolof and Mali alike was horse cavalry.[13] Elite Wolof and Mandinka forces used horses primarily for mobility—they specialized in the lightning-quick raid, galloping in on poorly defended villages and rounding up captives, whom they exchanged for slaves from elsewhere to work in royal fields or traded toward the Sahara for more horses and luxury items. The threat of raids from Jolof or Mali horsemen usually was enough to make people on the empires' peripheries render tribute payments. Access to a continuing supply of horses was necessary for the cavalry states because of the epidemiologically harsh savanna environment. Trypanosomiasis was the major scourge of large animals, but other tropical diseases added to the fact that horses did not live long in Africa's more wooded grasslands. In addition, it was difficult to breed horses very far to the south of the sahel, and it was all but impossible to do so in the latitudes of the Gambia River and southward. So Jolof and Mali maintained a brisk trade toward the desert. Mali had access to gold and kola nuts, in addition to slaves, that it could exchange for the horses (and salt, figs, dates, and more), but Jolof, long cut off from nearby goldfields by the more powerful Mali, traded mostly captives. Indicative of the importance of horses for the savanna empires was their price: Cadamosto reported that desert traders in the 1450s were getting from ten to fifteen slaves per horse, and the Portuguese received similar prices when they began importing horses into Senegambia soon after.[14]

In the second half of the fifteenth century, Senegambia and probably a good portion of the western savannas experienced a cavalry revolution.[15] The Jolof Empire quickly built its cavalry force to more than 8,000 horses, and other states tried to keep up. What brought this about was the combination of widespread adoption of the Arab stirrup, which made the beast much more effective as a tool of warfare; increasing numbers of horses imported from the desert edge; and the new supply of horses from the Portuguese. Use of the Arab stirrup, instead of riding bareback, enabled warriors to use their legs and upper bodies to thrust spears. It thus allowed for the combination of the mobility of the horse with the killing capability of the spear and made it possible for states with cavalries to acquire better means still to conquer and dominate agricultural communities. This caused demand for horses to rise, so Berber merchants all the way to North Africa responded with more mounts. At the same time, Portuguese traders interested in supplying what West Africans wanted began importing horses into Senegambia, originally from North Africa but eventually from herds developed on their newly acquired Cape Verde Islands.[16]

The Portuguese horse trade to the western savannas never eclipsed that from across the Sahara and the desert frontier, but it increased the supply of horses in areas where they could not be bred and thus played a role in altering the power relationships of some of the states in western Africa. After 1500 there were enough horses in Senegambia and a sufficient supply for replacements that states could afford to risk more of their mounts in bigger battles. Small political units that were peripheral to the largest cavalry states rushed to find ways to increase the size of their horse-borne forces—usually by acquiring slaves to exchange for horses—to avoid total dominance, or to come up with tribute payments that overlord states demanded in horses or slaves. By the sixteenth century, across Africa's westernmost savannas the rush to mount was on, and key to obtaining horses was obtaining slaves.

All of this occurred at a time when the Mali Empire, plagued by ineffective leadership, declining productivity from the Buré goldfields, and the growing strength of a new rival, Songhai to its northeast, was in a state of decline. Taking advantage of Mali's weakness, a new group of Fulbe cavalry warriors gained control of the Senegal River valley in the first years of the sixteenth century and effectively cut Jolof off from its desert-side supply of horses. Jolof had other problems at the time—internal warfare related to competition among brothers of the ruling lineage and the emergence within the empire of slave-based centers of power under nonroyal nobles—which the cutoff of its horse supply may have exacerbated. In any event, Jolof power declined rapidly as its coastal tributaries—Walo, Kajor, and Baol—with horses from the Portuguese and the westernmost sahel achieved independence. Other tributary and peripheral regions of Mali began to hive off as well.

Around the beginning of the sixteenth century a series of political realignments occurred among Mandinka-speakers living between the south bank of the Gambia and the Futa Jalon highlands.[17] Most noteworthy, with access to horses from Portuguese traders in the Gambia, Casamance, and Geba Rivers, a number of Mandinka lineages broke from Mali and joined their separate, small political units to form a larger state called Kaabu. In form and substance, Kaabu took much from its Malian heritage. The elite lineages of Kaabu, who called themselves *nyancho,* championed a Mandinka ethos that spurred young men to find areas of their own where they could command cavalry forces, dominate others, and rule. There were too many *nyancho* princes to achieve this in the dozen or so substates of

Kaabu, so young, proud, ambitious, elite Mandinka warriors did what their types had tended to do far into the past: they cast about for states where their lineages could take or share political control. Prime targets were those where there was sufficient production and trade to maintain the elite life-style and expensive cavalry. Important, too, was access to horses. Sitting at the end of a major artery for trade into the interior, with agricultural and salt production of its own, with enclaves of Mande and Portuguese merchants already paying for the right to participate in the commerce of the region, and with Portuguese ships bringing horses, iron, cloth, and other useful martial and luxury commodities with growing regularity, the region around the lower Gambia was a prime target for Mandinka conquest and settlement.

Evidence for what happened in Niumi during this formative period comes almost solely from oral data—stories collected in and around Niumi as told by family elders and *griots*.[18] The tales probably telescope into a short period events that occurred over a longer time because traditionists do not have sufficient ways of describing *processes* of change, but as most African traditions, they contain a core of truth, and these fit into the pattern of events that was taking place throughout the region.

In the last decade of the fifteenth century, a group of *nyancho* lineages from Kaabu moved north of the Gambia and took over an area on the southern edge of the weakening Jolof Empire.[19] From a central settlement near the mouth of the Saloum River, these lineages soon mixed with the existing Wolof and Serer population and established the state of Saloum. With access to horses from the desert-side trade to the north and from the Portuguese in the Saloum River, the rulers of the new Saloum state were able quickly to assemble a strong cavalry. To obtain commodities to ex-change for horses, Saloum warriors rode into neighboring lands to take captives. One of those lands immediately to the south was Niumi. Jolof bands might have done this earlier, on rare occasions, but Niumi's tradi-tions suggest that the incursions from Saloum became more frequent and damaging to the society and economy of Niumi once the Saloum state was in place.

The existing rulers of Niumi could not, by themselves, assemble suffi-cient force to deter Saloum's cavalry warriors. Niumi's military strength had long been in boatmen and canoes, which lent no assistance against cavalry raids. So it was in desperation that, some time during the first half of the sixteenth century, Niumi welcomed to the state several good-sized Mandinka *nyancho* lineages from two of the states of Kaabu: lineages named Manneh and Sonko. Then, from Portuguese merchants Niumi en-hanced its cavalry force with new mounts and, with the combined strength of the three clans, fought to hold off the raids of Saloum's warriors.

The result of these events was the gradual strengthening of the Niumi polity. What had been a largely Niuminka state with an orientation to the ocean and river, with Mande commercial and Muslim enclaves, slowly became a Mande-style state with a cavalry force of middling size adding to its military backbone. The cavalry force never was as large as the body of horsemen from many other savanna states. Niumi's dense interior forests and its more southerly setting meant that disease factors prevented horses from breeding easily there and shortened their lifespan considerably. Still, the state's increased strength through its newfound ability to maintain a cavalry force permitted Niumi to establish a relationship with Saloum more to its favor that would last for over two centuries. It was not at all times a peaceful relationship, but one characterized by raiding and reprisals, arrangements to limit raiding so as to prevent serious disruption of trade and farming, and sometimes tribute payments. Niumi's cavalry served less as a defensive force and more as an offensive threat that brought about deterrence. If strong enough to launch a damaging raid of reprisal into Saloum, a relatively peaceful and prosperous standoff would result. But when Saloum felt strong enough to raid within Niumi's borders and then to meet Niumi's reprisals with equal force, Saloum demanded tribute from Niumi—a kind of protection payment. And while marshaling human and material resources to build a cavalry force to maintain security from rivals across the land, Niumi's rulers kept a focus on their bread and butter: control of traffic on the lower Gambia with a body of armed boatmen that allowed them to levy customary taxes on trade passing between the Atlantic and upper reaches of the river.

The Mandinka lineages that provided the state's new military strength took up residence in Niumi and gradually mixed and intermarried with important lineages already present. They were not the state's founding families and thus could not rule the state on that important account, but they intended to achieve the elite status of the state's rulers for their efforts, so something had to be worked out. With three lineage groups wanting control, it is not surprising that it was not settled peacefully. Niumi traditionists speak of conflict among the competing royal lineages that broke out into warfare so intense, they say, that the shallow valley running north from Barra Point toward Jinak Creek "ran red with blood." Before civil war completely destroyed the state, however, wise counselors intervened. An old woman from a clan of blacksmiths residing in a remote Niumi village supposedly told one of the royal warriors, "Have peace. If you kill everyone you will have to work for yourself. The head that rests in the shade is supported by those heads that are under the sun. If you kill the rest of them off, no head will sit in the shade."[20] What came out of the tumult was a way of sharing political leadership and the elite lifestyle that accompanied it with a rotating system of succession.

Rotating succession was not unique to Niumi.[21] A number of states of the Western Sudan circulated political authority among prominent lineages. Why this was the case is evident: the cavalry warfare that dominated fighting in the grasslands required considerable investment in horses, training for horsemanship, and slaves to care for the horses, produce subsistence crops for the royal lineages whose members did not farm, and add soldiers when necessary and possible to the state's forces. Lineages did not make such investment without a payoff: they demanded a share of elite status and political control. Succession to high office was the lineage's opportunity to reap the material and emotional rewards of its investment in that state's military pursuits. Patterns of successional rotation among lineages usually reflected their relative investment.

In Niumi, no single lineage dominated the state after its political consolidation in the sixteenth century. The Sonko clan seems to have been the most populous, meaning it would have made a greater contribution to Niumi's cavalry force and owned more slaves, but traditional evidence is overwhelming that the Sonko alone were not strong enough to deter foreign forces or to provide a level of control sufficient to enable the state to benefit fully from the river trade.[22] The Manneh clan, whose members to this day guard most religiously their reputation as descendants of *nyancho* and the fiercest of horsemen, provided important numbers to Niumi's cavalry, and the Jammeh clan, besides being the territory's "owners" by right of precedence, controlled Niumi's formidable fleet of canoes that made possible participation in the salt and fish trade and the monitoring of river traffic. Each contributed enough to the communal welfare that, by Mandinka political custom, it could expect to participate in ruling the state.

The pattern of circulating succession that came out of Niumi's sixteenth-century restructuring—two Jammeh, two Manneh, and three Sonko lineages rotating political authority—was honored religiously thereafter. Succession disputes that took place over the years occurred *within* lineages, usually among brothers; royal lineages did not challenge others out of turn. It was a practical matter: the weight of force of the six other families, who would suffer if another broke the sequence and ruled out of turn, kept the system functioning as established.

Those who had the worst experience from the changing political structure were probably slaves. Before the political consolidation and the coming of the Mandinka royal lineages to share in political authority, Niumi's rulers, like other free lineages in the state, used slaves primarily for household production—to grow crops to help the lineage to subsist—and for reproduction—to produce offspring to add to the number of laborers supporting the lineage. Such persons would eventually be incorporated into the lineage as household slaves and as such be treated better and less likely to be sold. But with the change in the nature of warfare and political control came a corresponding change in the nature of slavery in the state. Royal lineages and others acquired slaves to serve particular functions for the state or the family. Those producing subsistence crops so that members of the lineage could engage in other activities—cavalry pursuits, trade, artisanal work, Islamic clericalism—tended to be kept separate from the lineage and were less likely to be assimilated. Many male slaves simply became soldiers, canoe men, or other functionaries for the state, never to be assimilated. Women were more likely to be assimilated, especially if they were concubines of freeborn men, but even the offspring of women slaves tended to remain separate, forever holding the badge of slave identity.

Trade Diasporas and New Identities

The increasing trade of Senegambia in general, and the Gambia River in particular, brought changes to the region beyond the political. Among other things, it brought a new set of commercial specialists to travel to and settle in enclaves along the Gambia's banks. These merchants developed personal and group identities—colonial officials probably would have identified them as separate "tribes"—with their distinct professions and their own languages, religions, and social customs. However much they differed from Niumi's indigenous population, they were welcome for their value to the state and its ruling lineages and their ability to bring material improvements to the lives of persons already residing in Niumi. It was customary to allow such groups to form villages on Niumi's soil, where they could live under their own laws and customs insofar as they did not conflict seriously with those of the state's majority. The two main groups were the Muslim traders on the one hand and Christian Portuguese and Luso-Africans on the other.

Muslim Traders

One group of new settlers in Niumi were persons who identified themselves with the Torodbe, a religious grouping mostly of former slaves among the Fulbe, who took on characteristics approximating those of a large clan. Once residents of the Futa Toro region of the middle valley of the Senegal River, these Muslim clerical lineages spread southward and eastward into various of the savanna lands, taking with them their own forms of worship and religious mysticism. The earliest Torodbe lineages came to Niumi around the beginning of the sixteenth century. The timing of their arrival and placement of their villages along the Gambian riverside suggest they came with commerce in mind.

A second, related group was that of Mandinka long-distance traders, called collectively *jula* by Mandinka speakers, who ventured down to the Gambia's mouth in larger numbers than ever before to participate in the waxing commercial exchange there. Nearly all of these merchants were Muslims and a good many were clerics, for they came out of the tradition of long-distance trade of West Africa's interior, where Islam and commerce walked together. Islamic clericalism provided the merchants an identity separate from those among whom they settled, and their religious beliefs and specialty in trade brought them to have a sense of solidarity with other merchant clerics across the region.[23]

The forerunners of these traders were Soninke-speaking merchants long associated with the Sudanic trade of cotton textiles. Because they dealt with Islamic Berber traders from the Sahara and because they were itinerant folk, detached from agricultural communities whose members were tied to animist spirits of the soil and trees, they were among the earliest West Africans to accept Islam. Learning Muhammad's word made some of them literate, and the literacy helped them with their commercial dealings, made them valuable to rulers eager to keep careful state accounts, and gave them another calling in the manufacture of protective charms out of written script.[24] With the long dry period that set in gradually after about A.D. 1100, forcing cotton cultivation and weaving along with habitation generally southward, these trading lineages moved south and west to new lands along the upper Niger and Senegal Rivers. From there they spread gradually across an ever-growing savanna region, purveying trade goods and establishing merchant-clerical communities. They could set up schools and teach the Qur'an when the rainy season kept them from venturing out in long-distance trade.

Some *jula* families had descended the Gambia River from its head of navigation prior to the fifteenth century, lured by the salt trade. The earliest Portuguese met "Mauri" men—Muslim Mandinka—interested in selling them cotton cloth and pepper; Niumi's *mansa* had a Muslim among his entourage when he came to the riverside to speak with Gomes in 1457.[25] The arrival of European traders in the Gambia and the heightening of trade that followed seems to have lured more *jula*. Over the course of the sixteenth century they positioned themselves where they could most effectively participate in the trade that was blossoming along the Atlantic coast and between the lower Gambia and the savannas to the eastward. By the end of that century they were tied through their trading interests and a sense of cultural solidarity with a group identified as *Jahanka,* the "people of

Jaha," a village on the Bafing River east of the Gambia, who were known as much for their specialized Islamic clericalism as for their commercial acumen and who dominated the overland trade between the upper Gambia and the upper Niger. Perhaps influenced by the Jahanka's avoidance of involvement in the political or religious affairs of their hosts, Muslim *jula* lineages in Niumi were not driven to proselytize. From their enclaves in one or two villages near Niumi's waterside, they traded—probably a great deal more than one recognizes in European records; did "Muslim works," which included divination, making protective charms, and practicing medicine for others; and conducted schools of Islamic learning. From this time on, albeit quietly, Niumi would be one of several centers of Islamic clericalism and magico-religious practice, as well as trade, along the Gambia River. And there would be prestigious and wealthy settlements of Muslims on Niumi territory some centuries later, when disaffection with the state's rulers became general and Islamic revivalist sentiments would be spreading throughout the region.[26]

Christian Portuguese and Luso-Africans

New Mandinka rulers and merchant clerics were not the only groups the economic situation lured into Niumi for settlement. Along the state's southern riverbank, in the neighborhood of the *jula* settlements where riverine trade seemed focused, other new and very different faces appeared. These were Portuguese or, rather quickly, the offspring of unions between Portuguese men with African women, who quickly became the cultural brokers between traders from the African and European societies.[27]

This was not the way Prince Henry or the kings of Portugal envisioned the African trade taking place. They intended to have their subjects explore and exploit Africa's western coast directly from ports in Portugal, and this happened as long as the prince managed Atlantic activities. But in 1455 Portuguese mariners sighted the Cape Verde archipelago, a dozen small, uninhabited islands lying 350 miles northwest of Cape Verde, and it was soon evident that the volcanic islands could serve as an advance base for Portuguese trading with the nearby coast. Henry died in 1460, just as European mariners were reaching the coast of Sierra Leone; two years later, Henry's cousin arranged for the first shipload of colonists to settle one of the Cape Verde Islands; and to stimulate further settlement of the archipelago in 1466, Portugal's King Afonso V granted Cape Verde colonists the right to trade along Africa's western coast. Within a matter of a few years the land lying along that coast between the Senegal River and Sierra Leone became, in Portuguese eyes, the "Guinea of Cape Verde"—the northern part was "Senegambia" and the southern, below the Casamance, the "Southern Rivers." For the next century and a half Portuguese and Cape Verdeans would operate out of a handful of the islands' ports to tie into the brisk African trade of the coast and vast hinterland of the Guinea of Cape Verde.

That commerce showed real potential. From the earliest voyages the Portuguese had learned of the great demand throughout Senegambia for horses. With the buildup of Jolof herds in the middle of the fifteenth century, followed by the growth of competitive cavalries among smaller states, Portuguese traders had their hands full trying to meet the demand, especially since one caravel could carry no more than ten horses on a single voyage.[28] In the beginning they brought animals from home or purchased them along the coasts of Morocco and Mauritania, but after about 1480 Cape Verde colonists began breeding horses on several of the islands, and soon the Cape Verdes became the major supplier for the Portuguese horse trade. Profits rolled in from the start. The earliest traders reported getting from nine to fourteen slaves per horse and making profits of between 500 and 700 percent per voyage.[29]

Of course, slaves were not the only commodities the Portuguese wanted, any more than horses the only items in demand in Senegambia. In a visit with traders in Niumi in 1455 Portuguese learned of the availability of gold and malaguetta peppers up the Gambia River, and within a decade others recognized the profits available competing with African merchants in transporting kola nuts from Sierra Leone coastal regions northward. Africans had a variety of needs and wants themselves. Besides horses, caravels soon began bringing raw cotton and woven cotton cloth—much of it after the 1470s woven on the Cape Verde Islands, using African techniques and slaves to do the weaving —as well as iron (some from elsewhere in Africa), copperware, and tobacco to exchange along Senegambia's coast and riverbanks.[30]

The earliest of this new group of foreign traders in Senegambia were from Portugal (with a few Genoese and one or two other south Europeans), but that was not the case for long. Portuguese men settled the Cape Verde archipelago. To grow their crops, tend horses, weave, and do most of the other work on the islands, these settlers imported slaves from Africa's west coast. The slave population of the islands soon outnumbered the free, eventually by a ratio of six or seven to one. Other coastal Africans immigrated to the Cape Verdes, some of them members of ruling elites. Once the inevitable unions between Portuguese men and African women occurred, a sizable population of mixed parentage came into being on the Cape Verdes. These Luso-Africans had the advantage of familiarity with Portuguese and African cultures and languages; they would be the ones, largely, who would conduct the growing trade of the Guinea of Cape Verde of the late fifteenth and sixteenth centuries.[31]

The first generation of Portuguese and Cape Verdeans in the Gambia River were content to trade from their ships. After only a short period of initial wariness, African merchants ventured to the caravels or longboats with their trade goods. In Niumi, once Gomes had worked out satisfactory arrangements with the ruler in the mid-1450s, shipboard trading proceeded smoothly for two decades. Then, Spaniards got involved and muddied the waters. Having gotten wind of the brisk trade and respectable profits that Portuguese merchants were taking, a Spanish captain led several caravels down the coast and into the Gambia in 1475. Not immediately recognizing the Spanish as different from the Portuguese and assuming the vessels' arrival meant more friendly discourse, with gifts for dignitaries and prospects for profit, Niumi's *mansa* led his retinue on board one of the Spanish ships. As the Portuguese had tried thirty years earlier, the Spaniard had his crew detain the ruler and his people; then he sent a force on land and rounded up another 140 men and women to take back to Cartegena in southern Spain. King Ferdinand of Aragon eventually heard of the incident and ordered the *mansa*'s return, but the others were sold into Spanish slavery. Not surprisingly, it was a while before Niumi's riverside villages were again receptive to Iberian visitors.[32]

But the lure of horses, inexpensive cloth, iron bars, and more eventually broke down suspicions, and the shipboard trade began again, as was happening all along West Africa's Atlantic coast. It was not long in Niumi and elsewhere before a disgruntled Portuguese merchant here or a venturesome Cape Verdean trader there turned his back on the islands and cast his lot on shore among the local population. Termed *lançados* (from the Portuguese verb *lançar,* to cast or throw [oneself]), these men and their descendants settled and became permanent members of West Africa's coastwise trading communities. Their numbers mounted rapidly—by early in the sixteenth century there were *lançado* groups in nearly every commercial village of coastal and riverine Senegambia—as they married local women, produced children, and added to their kinship groups with slaves and other dependents. They would serve as the linguistic brokers and cultural intermediaries for African-European commercial relations for several centuries.

When the first renegade Portuguese or Cape Verde Islanders came to live on Niumi soil, probably in the last decades of the fifteenth century, it was necessary for them to establish relationships with their African hosts that would enable them to fit into local society and exist in a way that would prove beneficial to themselves and Africans alike. The *lançados* were not entirely familiar with Niumi's language and culture, and it was their task, as rapidly as possible, to adopt certain customs and norms of local residents. What simplified this adoption and assimilation was the existence of the institutional landlord-stranger relationship. It allowed *lançados* entry into the society and monitored the synthesis of Portuguese (or Cape Verdean) and African ways of living.

The first *lançados* would have needed to make initial arrangements with the *mansa,* the state's ultimate landlord. It appears that Niumi's ruler, or perhaps it was more than one *mansa* over several decades, sanctioned *lançado* settlement in a line of villages along the then sparsely populated southern riverbank—Tubab Kolong (which means, in Mandinka, "white man's well"), Lamin, Juffure, San Domingo (no longer in existence), and Sika. The villages were founded by a combination of Africans and Portuguese (or Luso-Africans) for the specific purpose of becoming settlements for Niumi's growing population of "strangers," most of whom were advanced elements of one or another trade diaspora. Knowledgeable informants in Juffure say that their village was founded as a "stranger village" by members of an Islamic commercial and clerical lineage named Tall between 1495 and 1520. This lineage came to Niumi from Futa Toro on the Senegal River, possibly as horse traders. Descendants of the Talls admit, however, that their ancestors founded the village with the assistance of "some Portuguese," who already had settled their own village of San Domingo nearby.[33] Evidently, there was a symbiosis between enclave settlements of African, Portuguese, and Luso-African merchants.

These early *lançado*-African settlements quickly became the points of contact between Niumi's ruling families, its growing number of merchant lineages, and the trade with Europeans in the Gambia River. They symbolized the partial reorientation of the state's commercial focus from the seaside, where Niumi's boatmen controlled the salt trade, to the riverbank, where rulers would have to exert other kinds of control over a different sort of trade in the hands of merchants from new locations.

It is important to recognize, however, that the upper hand in these cross-cultural, commercial relationships remained in the hands of the Africans. Europeans who came to the Gambia River to trade did not have overwhelming power at their disposal. Some of the caravels mounted cannon, but the most effective fighting the Portuguese did was with the crossbow, and they always were badly outnumbered. Those settling on African soil had to rely on local rulers to ensure conditions for safe passage of trade goods and protection of merchants from outside forces. The Portuguese also came with more obvious, basic needs—water and food were the most important—and they required help with everything from navigating over shoals and shifting sandbars to communicating with African rulers and traders. So after the initial episodes like Tristão's, when they learned just how dependent they truly were, these early Europeans came to Niumi in an accommodating mode, ready to do what they must to work out a mutually beneficial trading relationship. Their lone trump cards were access to commodities that people in Niumi wanted and growing wealth from the lucrative trade that Niumi's ruling families desired to tax.[34]

Wherever Niumi's *mansa* might decide to settle a *lançado,* the person had to attach himself to a local landlord, a designated host who would oversee the person's dealings with others. The landlord would allocate a plot of land upon which the *lançado* would be allowed to construct a dwelling and would see to it that the individual had food—at least until the newcomer could make his own arrangements. Besides help with essentials, the landlord would represent and defend the stranger in disputes with others and in local councils. He would vouch for the *lançado* when commercial dealings might require trust or credit and generally do what he could to ensure the stranger's success in the foreign setting. Over time, if the *lançado* was indeed successful, the landlord might assist him in finding a spouse, one of his own daughters, perhaps, or another woman with good kinship connections. It was all an institutional way of integrating the stranger into Niumi's society.

Of course, Niumi's rulers did not allow strangers to settle, and designated landlords did not perform beneficial tasks for their strangers merely out of the goodness of their hearts or an ingrained sense of what ought to be regular hospitality. The newly arrived stranger was long on liabilities and short on assets, but as a *lançado* became successful, he had something valuable to offer and an informal obligation to see that his landlord and Niumi benefited from his success. This was done normally through the giving of gifts, with values commensurate to the stranger's success, and the payment of more regular fees and taxes to the family of the reigning *mansa.* No records exist for the size of such rents and fees until late in the seventeenth century, but by then Euro-African traders settled in Juffure on Niumi's riverbank paid the *mansa* an annual rent of fifty *écus* (the equivalent of 150 francs) and had to render a tax of one-tenth the value of all commodities traded.[35] Contemporary reports claim (in the fashion of complaint) that a *mansa* also could enter a Euro-African dwelling and take from the resident whatever he wanted, but Europeans who wrote of such incidents were probably biased in favor of the Euro-African intermediaries and may have been witnessing rulers coming to take their unpaid due.[36] In any event, reports of such activity on the part of rulers show the completely dependent status of Europeans and Euro-Africans on foreign soil.

Over the course of the sixteenth century the *lançado* population gained acceptance as part of Niumi's society. Much as the Muslim *jula* had done, the *lançados* developed their own individual identity, based not on their physical appearance, for soon they had none that was different from anyone else, but on several cultural characteristics they shared.[37] They referred to themselves as Portuguese because they retained outward elements of their Portuguese background: they constructed and lived in square dwellings with walls whitened with lime; wore European-style clothing; sported crucifixes and claimed to be Catholic, though many never had seen a cleric; kept Portuguese names; and considered themselves "white." Among other languages, *lançados* spoke Crioulo, a language with a Portuguese vocabulary and grammar and syntax largely from West African languages, which developed on the Cape Verde Islands and spread as a *lingua franca* for trade along Africa's western coast and up its rivers. Finally, as many did throughout West Africa, the *lançados* identified with their profession; one way or another, they were engaged in activities involving trade.

The most successful of these *lançados* were able to head sizable families and to gather about them slaves and retainers who could help in their commercial dealings. The retainers most noteworthy in European eyes were those they called *grumetes* (or *gromettas*), whom ship captains employed to serve as navigational guides, oarsmen, translators, and brokers. Successful Luso-African families in Niumi also might have hunters, praise-singers, blacksmiths, boat builders, fishermen, leather workers, African diviners, or Muslim holy men attached to their extended families. The longer they existed on Niumi soil, the more these extended families looked and acted like their hosts.

New Ways of Life

Over the several generations of heightened economic activity and political consolidation, everyday life in Niumi rolled on: men and women farmed; women pounded grain, gathered wood, cooked meals, and looked after childrearing; artisanal groups busied themselves with their skills; Muslim merchants went about their commercial or religious activities, the former with increased vigor; and slave men and women worked in fields, wove cloth, extracted salt, or, if royal slaves, served as boatmen or cared for horses. But few aspects of that life were the same in 1600 as they had been one hundred years earlier. Over the course of the sixteenth century, foreigners associated with the new commercial contacts brought a range of new material goods, new products, and alien ways of doing everything from propelling boats to building houses that altered the lives of the state's residents.

From the time of the consolidation and strengthening of the state around the middle of the 1600s, residents of Niumi must have been pleased that the powerful ruling lineages could marshal force enough to keep foreign raiders from their fields and villages. When effectively protected, most probably did not chafe at having to provide a portion of their produce to the royal families.

By the time the rulers had acquired such force, people in the state were residing in different kinds of villages. In the new setting, individual compounds were tucked behind palisades and entire villages were ringed by stockades. Valentim Fernandes, a German residing in Portugal who compiled information about the Gambia-Geba region in 1506, describes the compound of a "Mandi Mansa" in the lower Gambia—quite possibly Niumi's *mansa*—as consisting of several dwellings inside six rings of stockades with archers guarding the opening of the inner ring. André Alvares d'Almada, a Cape Verdean who made frequent trips up and down the Gambia, writes in 1594: "These blacks are very war-like. . . . [The Gambia] is a river which possesses a large trade in slaves. . . . Along the river and its creeks are certain military fortifications . . . made of very strong wooden stakes, their pointed ends embedded, and a rampart of earth behind . . . [each with] guard-towers, bastions, and parades." It seems reasonable to assume that the increased raiding for captives that appeared in response to heavy demand for slaves along the Atlantic coast and the fighting that accompanied the political reshuffling throughout the region—all affected by the new and increased supplies of horses—heightened insecurity in Niumi and brought its villagers to take these evident defensive measures. From the start of the sixteenth century until an effective *pax colonia* descended on the Gambia at the start of the twentieth century, residents of Niumi would only feel safe behind palisaded walls.[38]

Over time, the look of some of the dwellings inside the villages changed too—this because Portuguese and Luso-Africans brought with them their own architectural notions of form and function and blended them with materials, construction techniques, and styles they found in their new homes.[39] The sixteenth century saw the development of a housing style that European chroniclers referred to as *à la portugaise*. This was a square dwelling rather than a round one, constructed of stone in the early years but eventually of African-style mud bricks. The exterior walls were covered with chalk or white clay; roofs were of thatch; and inside was a vestibule for receiving guests and transacting business. Such houses appeared first in Luso-African quarters of commercial villages, but because their occupants had the elevated status of traders, a position often associated, rightly or wrongly, with material wealth, the houses themselves came to be symbols of high status. It was not long before Niumi's rulers, Muslim merchants, and persons of means from other callings constructed their houses "in the Portuguese style."

Boat building went through similar changes. Over the course of the seventeenth century, boat builders in Niumi picked up elements of European construction styles and propulsion techniques and blended them with the traditional dugout canoe to come up with an entirely new type of coastal and riverain trading vessel: the *pirogue*. This had a dugout as its basis, but had reinforced planking up the sides, husky wave breakers extending front and back, and sails. By 1600 the vessels were ubiquitous in the Gambia and up and down the Atlantic north and south of there. From then until the middle of the twentieth century, when motorized barges came to play a bigger role, the *pirogue,* in one form or another, was the primary vessel used to convey people and commodities about the region.[40]

Yet, the new products or adaptations that had the most far-reaching implications for life in Niumi had nothing to do with dwelling styles or means of travel on water. Bringing greater change to the lives of men and women resident in Niumi were things that were living: over the course of 150 years Portuguese and Luso-Africans introduced a host of new plants and animals—from Europe and from the more distant continents with which Europeans were recently in contact—that would alter the diets and affect the health and well-being of Niumi's residents.

Newcomers naturally wanted to eat and drink what they were accustomed to, so some of the earliest short-term visitors from Portugal or the Cape Verdes attempted to grow things that grew back home.[41] For one reason or another, many of their experiments ended in failure: European grains, grapes, peaches, olives, lettuce, cabbage, onions, garlic, and more failed early test plantings. But from their homes in southwestern Europe and contacts around the Mediterranean rim Portuguese sailors obtained and successfully introduced melons, figs, eggplants, and chick peas. They also brought pigs and a healthier strain of chickens, both of which reproduced adequately. Much more important still, after the European voyages to East Asia and to the New World at the end of the fifteenth century, Portuguese and Cape Verdeans introduced a number of other new fruits and vegetables: coconuts, bananas, plantains, and a much more productive strain of rice from East Asia; maize, cassava, chili peppers, peanuts, papayas, guavas, and tobacco from the Americas. It was fortunate that these plants happened to arrive in Niumi during a century and one-third of abundant rainfall, between 1500 and 1630.[42] The new crops grew well and the results were significant. Within a few generations the Asian rice had replaced indigenous African rice, making rice growers more important than before as providers for society. Local residents never took to maize as a staple of their diet—they seemed to prefer rice and millet—but they grew it eventually to sell to Europeans in the river and, over time, recognized its importance in ripening early and thus serving as a suitable food at the end of the growing season ("the hungry season"), until rice and millet were harvested. They did like the new chilis, however, and perhaps enjoyed better health from the vitamin C the fiery peppers provided. Relatively quickly, Gambian stews took the place they hold today among the spiciest foods eaten on the continent.

Farm work was made easier too, by the importation into Niumi of iron bars. Local blacksmiths had long been able to smelt iron and fashion tools appropriate for agricultural needs, but obtaining ore and producing charcoal were expensive operations that took time. Early European traders brought flat iron bars, the raw material for the blacksmiths to produce tools and weapons. Some came directly from Europe and some from local manufacture at other points along the West African coast, where traders had purchased and shipped them to areas of greater demand in the Gambia. Thus, before long the Niumi smiths could turn out many more hoes for cultivating and machetes for beginning and maintaining farm plots and kitchen gardens, and they could do it more cheaply than before. When combined with the new crops and the more productive varieties of old crops available to farmers, access to inexpensive iron must have contributed to a rise in food output in Niumi, an improvement of the diets of the state's residents, and an ability in the state to support a larger population. This combination of factors also made possible the production of sufficient surplus goods to provide for alien garrisons on European outposts in the seventeenth and eighteenth centuries and to stock slavers with grain as they left for the New World.[43]

The growing importation of iron bars had implications for Niumi's rulers and their offensive and defensive aspirations as well. As the sixteenth century progressed, Niumi's ruling elites could much more easily obtain the raw material for their blacksmiths to fashion weapons—spears, arrows, daggers, swords, and harpoons—so they could arm a greater military force, on land or water. This prompted them to seek more fighting personnel. The quickest way to do so was to purchase captives. They could obtain slaves in the traditional manner, by exchanging salt or dried fish for captives from the interior lands, or, with their expanding cavalry, they could capture slaves in the region and trade them to lands farther away in exchange for slaves from some distance. (Slaves were of limited value near their point of capture because they could easily escape and return home. Slave values increased with their distance from home.) In this fashion the internal capture and flow of slaves grew within a century or a little more of the beginning of West Africa's participation in the Atlantic economy.[44]

Thus, Europeans, mostly Portuguese, and Luso-Africans provided residents of Niumi access to a new economic endeavor, an Atlantic commercial complex. At the same time, Muslim African traders linked the shores of Niumi more thoroughly still to the trans-Sahara, sahel, and savanna network that had been in existence for centuries. Through steadily increasing participation in these economic systems between 1450 and 1600, people in Niumi gained new methods of control, new means to enhance and broaden old forms of social and political relationships, new sources of raw materials, new products, new residents in the state, and new ways of doing things. Some of them—rulers, artisans, merchants, many freeborn farmers—benefited from the novelties. Some others, perhaps many (though not all) slaves in particular, found life more difficult with new kinds of work and new punishments for not doing it. In all these ways, over that century and one-half, life in Niumi changed considerably. The Niumi of 1600 was different politically, socially, culturally, and religiously from the Niumi of 1450. For the next two centuries, however, change would come at a slower pace.

Notes

1. Alfred W. Crosby, *Germs, Seeds, & Animals: Studies in Ecological History* (Armonk, N.Y.: M.E. Sharpe, 1994), esp. chs. 1 and 9; A.J.R. Russell Wood, *World on the Move: The Portuguese in Africa, Asia, and America, 1415–1808* (New York: St. Martin's Press, 1992), ch. 5.

2. E.W. Bovill, *The Golden Trade of the Moors,* 2nd ed. (London: Oxford University Press, 1968), 87–88.

3. C.R. Boxer, *The Portuguese Seaborne Empire, 1415–1825* (New York: Knopf, 1975), 8.

4. Alvise da Cadamosto, "The Voyages of Cadamosto," in *The Voyages of Cadomosto and Other Documents in Western Africa in the Second Half of the Fifteenth Century,* ed. G.R. Crone (London: Hakluyt Society, 1937), 68.

5. Diogo Gomes, "The Voyages of Diogo Gomes," in Crone, ed., *Voyages,* 95.

6. Boxer, *Portuguese Seaborne Empire,* 18–19, 24; Philip D. Curtin, *Economic Change in Precolonial Africa: Senegambia in the Era of the Slave Trade* (Madison: University of Wisconsin Press, 1975), 198–206.

7. Philip D. Curtin, *The Rise and Fall of the Plantation Complex* (Cambridge: Cambridge University Press, 1989), 42–43.

8. Curtin has written the clearest treatments of the plantation complex: *The Tropical Atlantic in the Age of the Slave Trade* (Washington, D.C.: American Historical Association, 1991) is a short description; *The Rise and Fall of the Plantation Complex* is a more complete account. Discussion here is based on Curtin's work.

9. Crosby, *Germs, Seeds, & Animals,* 36–37 and ch. 3. Curtin ties disease factors to the centuries-long existence of the Atlantic slave trade in "Epidemiology and the Slave Trade," *Political Science Quarterly* 83 (1968): 190–216.

10. Curtin, *Economic Change,* 155–56; George E. Brooks, *Landlords and Strangers: Ecology, Society, and Trade in Western Africa, 1000–1530* (Boulder, Colo.: Westview Press, 1993), 130.

11. Suggesting that it was the Portuguese horse trade that set the stage for Senegambia's fifteenth-century political upheaval are Robin Law, *The Horse in West Africa: The Role of the Horse in the Societies of Pre-colonial West Africa* (Oxford: Oxford University Press, 1980), 52–53; and Jean Boulègue, *Le grand Jolof (xviiᵉ-xviᵉ siècle)* (Paris: Diffusion Karthala, 1987), 72–77. Ivana Elbl argues otherwise effectively in "The Horse in Fifteenth-Century Senegambia," *International Journal of African Historical Studies* 24 (1991): 85–110.

12. Excellent sources for the early history of West Africa in general, and Senegambia in particular, are Brooks, *Landlords and Strangers;* Curtin, *Economic Change,* ch. 1; Boulègue, *Le grand Jolof;* James F. Searing, *West African Slavery and Atlantic Commerce: The Senegal River Valley, 1700–1860* (Cambridge: Cambridge University Press, 1993), ch. 1; and James L.A. Webb Jr., *Desert Frontier: Ecological and Economic Change along the Western Sahel, 1600–1850* (Madison: University of Wisconsin Press, 1995), chs. 1 and 2.

13. The importance of the horse in the precolonial history of West Africa's savanna states is detailed in Law, *The Horse.* Discussion more particular to Senegambia is in Webb, *Desert Frontier,* ch. 4; and Elbl, "The Horse."

14. Cadamosto, "Voyages," 49.

15. Webb, *Desert Frontier,* 70–72.

16. Gomes's account shows how quickly the Portuguese recognized the importance of the horse trade and got involved. In 1458, on his way home from his first Senegambian voyage, Gomes admonished the ruler of the island of Gorée, just off Cape Verde, telling him, "It would be better for him to make peace with [the Christians], and that both might exchange merchandise, so that he might have horses, &c., as Burbuck [Walo] and Badamel [Kayor], and other lords of the negroes had." In 1460 Gomes made a second voyage to West Africa. When he arrived at Joal, the major Atlantic port of the state of Siin, immediately north of Niumi, he found two caravels, one commanded by a Portuguese and the other by a Genoese, each "conveying horses thither." Gomes, "Voyages," 99–101.

17. Much of the information on Kaabu is from oral traditions. Summaries and interpretations are found in Brooks, *Landlords and Strangers,* 109–13; B.K. Sidibe, *A Brief History of Kaabu and Fuladu, 1300–1930: A Narrative Based on Some Oral Traditions of the Senegambia* (Banjul: Oral History and Antiquities Division, 1974); and Mamadou Mané, "Contribution à l'histoire du Kaabu, des origines au xix siècle," *Bulletin de l'Institut Fondamental d'Afrique Noire,* series B, 40 (1978): 87–159.

18. A representative sampling of these oral data is in Donald R. Wright, *Oral Traditions from The Gambia, vol. 1, Mandinka* Griots, and *vol. 2, Family Elders* (Athens: Ohio University Center for International Studies, 1979, 1980).

19. Some of my earlier ideas of these events are in Donald R. Wright, *The Early History of Niumi: Settlement and Foundation of a Mandinka State on the Gambia River* (Athens: Ohio University Center for International Studies, 1977), ch. 3.

20. Landing Nima Sonko, oral interview, Berending, Lower Niumi District, The Gambia, November 1, 1974.

21. The best discussion of rotating succession in West Africa remains Jack Goody, *Technology, Tradition, and the State in Africa* (London: Oxford University Press, 1971), chs. 2 and 3.

22. It is a problem discussing Mandinka kinship groupings using such English terms as *clan* and *lineage,* for such terms are imprecise. Here, a clan constitutes all individuals with the same surname, who share a sense of having descended from a common ancestor, often a mythical figure, who lived in the distant past. Lineages of the same clan can be spread across broad areas of the western savannas. Clan members do not necessarily

have personal acquaintance with one another. A lineage is a smaller grouping of peoples with the same surname, normally several extended families in the same village, who know one another and share common descent from an ancestor they can identify from not so long ago.

23. Curtin, *Economic Change*, 66.

24. Jack Goody, "The Impact of Islamic Writing on the Oral Cultures of West Africa," *Cahiers d'Etudes Africaines* 11 (1971): 455–66.

25. Brooks, *Landlords and Strangers*, 129; Gomes, "Voyages," 97.

26. European accounts and maps of the region that include discussion or listing of Muslim clerical towns (*morecunda*) usually include one or more in Niumi. For the Jahanka and their trading network from the upper Gambia, see Lamin O. Sanneh, *The Jahanke: The History of an Islamic Clerical People of the Senegambia* (London: Oxford University Press, 1979); and Curtin, *Economic Change*, 67, 75–83. Thomas C. Hunter, "The Development of an Islamic Tradition of Learning among the Jahanke of West Africa," Ph.D. dissertation, University of Chicago, 1977, contains some of the best information on the role Muslim holy men played in divination, charm-making, and the supernatural.

27. Much of the information on early Portuguese and *lançado* activities is from Brooks, *Landlords and Strangers*, chs. 7–9. Also useful are Jean Boulègue, *Les Luso-Africains en Sénégambie, xvie-xixe siècle* (Lisbon: Instituto de Investiga, cao Cientifica Tropical, 1989); and Peter Mark, "Constructing Identity: Sixteenth- and Seventeenth-Century Architecture in the Gambia-Geba Region and the Articulation of Luso-African Ethnicity," *History in Africa: A Journal of Method* 22 (1995): 307–27.

28. Elbl, "The Horse," 102.

29. Cadamosto, "Voyages," 49.

30. Brooks, *Landlords and Strangers*, 165.

31. Ibid., 189–92.

32. J.W. Blake, *Europeans in West Africa, 1450–1560*, 2 vols. (London: Hakluyt Society, 1942), 1: 213–17.

33. Bakary Tall, oral interview, Juffure, Upper Niumi District, The Gambia, December 15, 1974.

34. Ivana Elbl, "Portuguese Relations with West Africa, 1441–1521," *Journal of World History* 3 (1992): 177–81.

35. Records of such payments are in the Gambia Castle Charge Book, 1737, T 70/1452.

36. François Froger, *Relation d'un voyage ... aux côtes d'Afrique* (Amsterdam: Chez les Heritiers d'Antoine Shelte, 1702), 31; Jean-Baptiste Labat, *Nouvelle rélation de l'Afrique occidentale*, 5 vols. (Paris: Chez Guilaume Cavalier, 1728), 5: 312–14.

37. Mark argues for the development of a Luso-African "ethnic group" along the Upper Guinea Coast and discusses how in Senegambia there was a "fluid understanding of identity as a cultural, a linguistic, and a professional identification, one which can and often does change over time," in "Constructing Identity," 317.

38. Mark, "Constructing Identity," 310–11, 315; Valentim Fernandes, *Description de la côte occidentale d'Afrique (Sénégal au Cap de Monte, Archipels)*, ed. and tr. Theodore Monod et al. (Bissau: Centro de Estudos da Guiné Portuguesa, 1951), 37; André Alvares de Almada, *Tratado breve dos Rios de Guiné*, tr. P.E.H. Hair, 2 vols. (Liverpool: University of Liverpool, 1984), 1:43–44.

39. Mark, "Constructing Identity," 315–16.

40. According to Brooks, the word *pirogue* "derives from sixteenth-century European usage of *pirague*, a Galibi Indian word from Brazil." It clearly was brought to Senegambia by the Portuguese. *Landlords and Strangers*, 209. One can still see *pi-*

rogues in the Gambia's estuary and along the adjacent Atlantic coast, small ones launched in the morning offshore breeze and larger motorized adaptations conducting fishing operations in deeper water.

41. Much of the discussion on introductions of plants is based on Stanley B. Alpern, "The European Introduction of Crops into West Africa in Precolonial Times," *History in Africa: A Journal of Method* 19 (1992): 13–43. Although Alpern's focus is on the Atlantic coast between Liberia and Nigeria, he includes information on plant introductions along the Upper Guinea Coast.

42. Brooks, *Landlords and Strangers*, 7.

43. Alpern, "European Introduction," n.1; Stanley B. Alpern, "What Africans Got for Their Slaves: A Master List of European Trade Goods," *History in Africa: A Journal of Method* 22 (1995): 12–13.

44. Curtin, *Economic Change*, 154–56.

4

NIUMI AT THE HEIGHT OF THE ATLANTIC COMPLEX, SEVENTEENTH AND EIGHTEENTH CENTURIES

The great number of canoes and men employed in this commerce gives great influence and respect to the king. Indeed, he is the most powerful and terrible of all the kings of the Gambia; he has imposed considerable duties on the ships of all nations.
—J.B.L. Durand, *A Voyage to Senegal* [c. 1800][1]

A body of mythology surrounds and confounds our understanding of West African societies that participated in the Atlantic slave trade. One myth of long standing is that powerful and wily European captains sailed their ships along Africa's western coasts, sent longboats ashore, and grabbed unsuspecting African men and women to fill their slave cargoes and, eventually, to sell in the Americas as slave labor. The absurdity of this portrayal of Africans—as hapless folks utterly unable to stop the kidnapping and as passive ciphers in the cross-cultural commercial dealings—has not reduced its tenacity in the minds of generations of people.

A similar and equally inaccurate myth is what Curtin calls "the old stereotype of gewgaws for slaves": the misconception that Europeans traded mostly worthless goods to Africans for the heart of their most productive manpower, implying that "the Europeans hoodwinked a group of ignorant savages into parting with something of considerable value in return for nothing, or even for goods that were positively harmful."[2]

Unfortunately, historians of a generation ago did little to dispel such myths. It is in the nature of those who write history to bring the ideas of their own, culturally chauvinistic place and time to consideration of others, and the mid-twentieth century was the end of a long period of particularly strong racist notions among Western intellectuals. Many historians of the time were unable to recognize anything resembling order and rationality in precolonial African state and social structures. As late as 1963 a noted historian stated on British television that African history before the late-nineteenth-century takeover by Europeans amounted to little more than the "unrewarding gyrations of barbarous tribes in picturesque but irrelevant corners of the globe."[3] In such an intellectual climate, African societies that participated in the Atlantic economy were not likely to receive an accurate assessment. There was no reason for Niumi to be an exception. Although the state existed in the same locale for half a millennium and its residents dealt with Europeans from a position of strength through most of the period, John M. Gray in his 1940 *History of the Gambia* termed Niumi and the other Gambian states "petty districts" that "lacked the unity and stability which really qualifies a territory for the title of kingdom." Gray described these states' rulers as nothing more than "war lords, who rose and fell very often with astonishing rapidity."[4]

It almost seems unnecessary now to state that Niumi was considerably more than a petty district commanded by warlords. Through the seventeenth and eighteenth centuries, when the state's participation in the Atlantic trade was at its height (and increasing amounts of evidence become available for its assessment), Niumi was a stable state with a typical Mandinka political and social structure that, over the decades, its rulers modified to meet new requirements imposed by extensive participation in the Atlantic complex. Europeans trading in the Gambia recognized the state's strength and, through the most active period of Atlantic commerce, curried favor from Niumi's *mansa* and scores of the state's other prominent people. Africans never dictated terms of the trade—the global market and laws of supply and demand did that—but Niumi's rulers determined much about how the cross-cultural exchange took place and controlled European access to Gambian commerce sufficiently to ensure the state's profit into the early years of the nineteenth century. Just as Europeans, people in Niumi made rational decisions about trading one body of commodities for another. No European merchant in the river believed otherwise.

Furthermore, there is an element of irony in Niumi's history through the two centuries of its most active participation in the Atlantic trade. It is a natural assumption that slave trading was disruptive to local politics and society—that raiding, capturing, defending, and dealing with acquisitive foreigners were activities that led to a breakdown in established polity and society. This simply does not appear to have been the case through the seventeenth and eighteenth centuries in Niumi. People in the state experienced considerable change over the first century and more of participation in the waxing Atlantic trade, before 1600, and as its position in the huge economic complex declined after 1800, the state's viability came under serious threat and its society changed considerably. But the two centuries or more when Niumi was engaged most fully in the Atlantic-oriented commerce that brought European manufactures in exchange for captive laborers and other African products was a period of relative political and social stability in the state. It is almost surely accurate to state that people in Niumi's villages in 1800 lived more like their ancestors had lived in 1600 than like their children or grandchildren would exist half a century later, in 1850. That seems to be the case for most of the states along the Gambia River: by 1600 ways of dealing with foreign merchants and shippers had become institutionalized, and the institutions would not come under serious threat and require drastic alteration until several decades after the ending of slave trading toward the Atlantic. By then, much in the rest of the world was changing and people in Niumi would experience the full, and indeed seriously disruptive, effects in many aspects of their lives.

Niumi's Expanding World

Three different kinds of events had the greatest effect on the ways people lived in Niumi in the seventeenth and eighteenth centuries. One was natural: the steady drying of the climate, forcing a gradual alteration of lifestyles of those who relied on crop growing and animal breeding. The second was driven by human hands and involved further incorporation into a world economic system: it was the expansion of the Atlantic complex, fueled by a growing European craving for sugar, that heightened demand on New World plantations for laborers and raised demand in West Africa for commodities from Europe, Asia, the Americas, and other parts of Africa in exchange for them. The third was less dramatic than the others: it involved the increasing acceptance by peoples from all levels of Niumi's society of some of the ways of living, thinking, and acting of Muslim clerics and mystics living in enclave villages in their midst. None of these events was entirely disruptive. Niumi's rulers found ways to adapt the polity, economy, and society to meet the changing circumstances. But, taken together, the events made Niumi a different place to live in 1800 than it was a little over two centuries earlier.

The Ecological Base

Historians who have studied climate phases in West Africa do not agree on when long wet or dry periods occurred in different places.[5] Data are not sufficient for careful climatic reconstruction by years or decades, and rains have always fallen unevenly and unpredictably across West Africa's savannas. But James L.A. Webb Jr. calls attention to one climatic fact that seems unassailable: since about 1600, with only minor regional fluctuation and short-term variance, West Africa's sahel and savanna have experienced a "marked trend toward increasing aridity." When he compared older maps of the region with more recent ones, Webb noticed "bodies of water [that] evaporate from the cartographic record," and from historical data on rainfall in Senegal he concludes that the same amount of annual precipitation judged "below average" in the mid-eighteenth century was considered "above average" for a typical year in the mid-twentieth century.[6] There is not much doubt that over the past several centuries West Africa, including the land of Niumi, has dried out.

One can only estimate the effects this gradual alteration of rain-based ecological underpinnings had on the lives of people in Niumi. One of the effects for farming communities is obvious: reduced rainfall means more difficult circumstances for the production of food crops generally and, more often than before, periods when there is not enough grown locally to eat. As annual rainfall declined, the season of rain shortened and such rains that fell came more frequently in storms. This meant that erosion was more prevalent, that rain tended to run off rather than be absorbed into the soil, and that crop yields in the less-nourishing soil diminished. Fallowing did not replenish soils as efficiently as in times of heavier rainfall, too, so farming villages probably moved more frequently than before. There is evidence of regular movement of Niumi's villages, perhaps of only a few miles at a time, through recent centuries.[7] And decisions about which crops to grow seem to have changed over time. The Portuguese had introduced maize to Senegambia during the wetter sixteenth century, and Niumi's farmers grew the crop to sell to the English garrison on James Island and to the slave ships heading for the Americas. But by the mid-twentieth century it was difficult to find a stalk of maize growing in Niumi. Men and women farmers there today plant almost exclusively one of several varieties of millet, sorghum, or rice. While these grains do not approach the yield of maize when there is sufficient rainfall, millet and sorghum have much greater yields in seasons of low rainfall or drought.[8]

The gradual decrease of seasonal rainfall and changing ecological base also affected the ability of the state's rulers to enhance that part of their military that was based on cavalry. Because the tsetse fly that spreads trypanosomiasis requires thick foliage for coverage, reduced brush associated with drier conditions means healthier conditions for horses, resulting in longer lives for mounts, easier breeding, and more effective crossbreeding. So as rainfall diminished in West Africa through the seventeenth and eighteenth centuries, the zones of horse breeding previously north of the Senegal River moved south. While Niumi never became a place where horses had long lives or where one could breed horses effectively, the sources of horses through overland trade moved closer.[9] When they desired to do so, Niumi's ruling elites could more easily, and perhaps more cheaply, obtain horses from African sources. Such access to horses would be important in the enhancement of Niumi's military aristocracy as the eighteenth century wore on.

The Growth of Mercantile Capitalism and the Expanding Atlantic Complex

The great expansion of the Atlantic economic complex that took place in the seventeenth and eighteenth centuries was part of a larger phenomenon associated with a pulling together of European wealth and its investment in worldwide commercial ventures. All of this led to greater European participation in an expanding global trade.[10]

Through the sixteenth century, Portugal and Spain remained masters of economic complexes that spanned a great portion of the globe, but by the century's end their domination of commercial networks would come under increasing challenge from other Europeans. The Dutch, English, and French rose to be important participants in world trade through the course of the seventeenth century. The Dutch, who were masterful seamen, were the first to encroach on Hispanic monopolies. Individual Dutch merchants could not amass enough wealth to compete directly with Spain, however, so they found ways to pool their wealth for collaborative ventures through the institution of the joint-stock company. With broad investment in a company run by a board of directors responsible to its stockholders, they could mount grand trading expeditions to markets about the world and stick their noses into far-flung Iberian business. Thus, with the resources of its great chartered enterprises, the East and West India Companies (established in 1600 and 1621), Dutch entrepreneurs ventured in trade for spices in the east and worked to wrest a share of the plantation carrying trade of the Atlantic. Of course, only fools failed to arm their merchant ships for protection, so it was a fine line between commercial competition and military encroachment. The Dutch were inclined toward whichever seemed more prudent at the time. Through the first half of the seventeenth century, the Dutch captured Portuguese outposts in East Asia, West Africa, and Brazil, and it was clear they had scant regard for any Spanish notion of monopoly in the Americas. England and France were weaker maritime powers, so their nationals moved more slowly overseas, but by the middle of the seventeenth century they, too, were manning outposts around the world—in India, in West Africa, and on Caribbean islands—where they could gain a greater share of the thriving world trade.

As noted, the slave trade from Africa to the Americas was solidly in place by 1600. In a typical year of the early seventeenth century, some

5,000 slaves would be acquired along Africa's west coast and shipped across the ocean to sugar plantations in Brazil or mining operations in Peru. But the entire Atlantic commercial complex was to expand greatly for the next two centuries. In terms of shipment of slaves, the system would reach a peak between 1740 and 1810, when every year, on average, over 60,000 slaves were imported into staple-producing plantations that stretched from British mainland North America, through the islands of the Caribbean, to Brazil and beyond.[11] It was an intercontinental economic complex on the largest scale and greatest significance yet, for peoples bordering the Atlantic, but also for others about the world.

The biggest stimulation to growth of the Atlantic complex was the increasing ability of English and French traders to accumulate capital and participate on larger and more favorable terms in the expanding world market. "Adventurers" (as the English referred to those who risked capital in commercial enterprises) from England and France settled islands in the eastern Caribbean and then, in the 1640s, turned those settlements toward plantation agriculture on a larger scale than ever before. For the Caribbean it was a sugar revolution, stimulated ironically by Dutch shippers, who cared less about who owned the plantation land and more about profiting from the carrying trade of slaves and cane. To the English and French just settling Caribbean Islands in the first half of the seventeenth century, Dutch carriers gave instruction on the best production techniques and offered to sell machinery and slaves and to purchase sugar. The movement was rapid. On Barbados, the early leader in the sugar revolution, for example, no sugar was produced in 1637, but by 1645 40 percent of the island was planted in sugar, and by the 1670s it was producing 65 percent of all the sugar consumed in England. The English and French Antilles followed Barbados's lead, and once European mariners solved problems of catching appropriate winds for the eastbound, trans-Atlantic voyage, Jamaica and Cuba became big sugar producers. By the start of the eighteenth century the Caribbean was one massive, sugar-producing enterprise, exporting cane and importing laborers and foods to feed them from all about the Atlantic basin.

Essential factors in the growth of the Atlantic plantation complex and the slave trade as part of that enterprise were Europe's population expansion and disease-related demographic factors in the Old and New Worlds. After a setback from the Black Death in the fourteenth century, Europe's population recovered in the fifteenth and began growing more rapidly thereafter. An important element in the Continent's population growth was the importation of new food crops from the Americas. Although relatively free of large animals and many of the diseases associated with them that shortened human life, the Americas were loaded with foodstuffs from which they alone ever had benefited. Coming to Europe over the course of the sixteenth century was a cornucopia of vegetables that included most varieties of beans, squash, tomatoes, and by far of greatest importance, maize and potatoes. Relatively easy to grow and full of carbohydrates and important vitamins, these plants, when combined with European technological improvements and the clearing of more land for agriculture, added greatly to the European diet. With more and better food, Europe's population was in the lead of a worldwide trend toward steady increase. In Europe the number of people went from around 70 million in 1500 to 90 million in 1600, 100 million in 1650, and 180 million by the end of the eighteenth century. There were simply more persons to consume sugar, and do a host of other things, every year.[12]

Furthermore, as wealth flowed to Europe through several centuries of its expanding economy, more people had money to purchase products that heretofore had been luxuries. Sugar was one. And the price of sugar went down steadily because of improved production techniques and cheaper freight rates that were the result of the greater capacity of European shipping. This increased demand even more. Per capita sugar consumption in Britain was only four pounds a year in 1700, but it grew to eight pounds by 1750 and eighteen pounds by 1800. More people wanting more sugar meant the continuing quest to increase production on more cleared land across a greater extent of the tropical Atlantic.

But this alone did not account for the growing demand for African slaves. By 1700 between 1.5 and 2 million Africans had been carried to the Americas, most to work on sugar-producing plantations. With a growth rate reasonable for the time, this population could have provided sufficient labor for the expanding tropical plantations. But it experienced no growth rate at all; in fact, the New World slave population could not sustain itself through procreation. A lack of acquired immunities to some tropical diseases kept death rates of slaves high. Moreover, a notion held by some planters that it was less expensive to purchase a mature slave direct from the Atlantic passage than it was to rear a slave in the Americas (which meant that many planters did not encourage, and often actively discouraged, childbirth among their slaves) led to birthrates among the plantation labor force that were lower than normal. Thus, in a coldly economic sense, the New World tropical plantations consumed manpower. Figures supporting this phenomenon are startling: on the island of Jamaica, 750,000 slaves were imported between 1640 and 1834, when slavery there ended. On the latter date, the island's black population numbered only 350,000.[13] Simply maintaining the labor force required importing a large number of slaves every year, but to meet the increasing demand for sugar, more and more laborers were re-

Box 4. The African Diaspora

In a book focusing on world history and Africa it is appropriate to call
attention to the role Africans played in the settlement and population
of the Americas. For over four and one-half centuries African slaves
were transported to various parts of the New World to work as
laborers. In round numbers, some 10 million Africans arrived in the
Americas and were sold as slaves. Until the beginning of massive
European migration in the last half of the nineteenth century, more
Africans than Europeans crossed the Atlantic each year. The largest
numbers were taken to the islands of the Caribbean and Brazil, but
many also went to lands of the Spanish mainland of Central and
South America and British and French mainland North America. Historians refer to this movement of people outside the African continent and their population of most parts of the New World as the
African Diaspora. In terms of everything from commerce and production to cultural heritage, the African Diaspora is one of the most
important phenomena in the history of the Americas.

When considering simply numbers of slave imports in relative
perspective, British mainland North America (later the United States)
was a lesser part of the Atlantic plantation complex, and of the
African Diaspora, than many other American regions. Fewer than
half a million African slaves came directly from Africa to British ports
on the North American mainland, only about two-thirds as many as
were imported onto the small Caribbean island of Jamaica. But for a
variety of reasons the slave population of the United States grew
more rapidly than elsewhere, so today the country has one of the
largest African American populations in the Americas.

Slaves from around the Gambia River were involved in the Diaspora from its beginnings until early in the nineteenth century. Relatively large numbers of Gambian slaves crossed the ocean in the
first century of Atlantic slaving—they were important in early Spanish mining operations in Peru and sugar production on Hispaniola—
and the numbers did not fall off so much as those from other places
along the African coast grew much larger. Gambian slaves played
important roles in the history of the United States. It may well have
been rice-producing Jola slaves from the river's lower south bank,
for instance, who made rice growing an efficient economic enterprise in colonial South Carolina. And it was along the banks of the
Gambia—a village in Niumi, in fact—where Alex Haley, author of
Roots (see chapter 7), claimed to have found his maternal ancestor.

quired. West and West-Central Africa would continue to be the source for such captive laborers.

Because northern European maritime powers had made a habit of using force in their competition with Spain and Portugal—and eventually with one another—and because the Dutch in particular had already begun seizing Portuguese commercial outposts along the African coast by the 1640s, European governments began seeing to it that their nationals built fortified trading posts to protect their share of the African trade. Ideal spots for such fortifications were easily defended—and for Europeans, marginally healthier—islands near the coast. The Dutch fortified the island of Gorée, off Cape Verde, in 1647, and in 1651 the duke of the tiny Baltic duchy of Kurland sent an expedition into the mouth of the Gambia River with the intention of building a settlement to foster and protect what he conceived to be his land's economic calling in West Africa. The Kurlanders liked the looks of an island twenty-five miles upriver from the mouth, a small, anvil-shaped body almost centered in the river off Niumi's southern riverbank. A Kurland agent negotiated with Niumi's *mansa* for the right to occupy the otherwise useless island and to have access to a small plot on Niumi's riverbank where the island's garrison could gather wood and draw water in return for an annual payment. For the next decade, amid regular threats from rival European privateers (some of which Niumi's boatmen helped deter), the Kurland garrison held the island and traded in the river.[14]

Kurland's chances of keeping its outpost in the face of challenges from larger and commercially stronger European competitors were slim indeed, but they were made slimmer by notions in England that there were mountains of gold up the Gambia River and an abundance of slaves there for the English islands in the Caribbean. In 1661 an English chartered company, The Royal Adventurers of England Trading into Africa, sent an expedition to set up an outpost in the Gambia. Its leaders negotiated with Niumi's *mansa* and then gave the seven remaining Kurlanders on the island a choice between safe passage home or certain death. They took the former. On March 19, 1661, employees of the Royal Adventurers occupied the island, named it James Island for the reigning English monarch, and began an English presence in the river that would be longer lasting than that of any other European nation. In the 1670s the Royal African Company, with a grant of monopoly over Gambian trade from the English government, took over James Island (and on it by then, James Fort) from the defunct Adventurers and attempted to wring profits out of the trade in the river.

But the English would never quite be free of European competition in the

Gambian trade. In 1677, during one of many mercantile wars of the period, the French took Dutch forts at Gorée and on the adjacent mainland, effectively ending Dutch trading interests along the upper Guinea coast. In 1681 the French Compagnie du Sénégal obtained trading rights in West Africa of an older chartered company and then sent an agent to negotiate with Niumi's *mansa* for a plot of land for an unfortified trading post at Albreda, on Niumi's riverbank, straight across from James Island. The French occupied Albreda and stayed there (with some hiatuses) until 1857, and French merchants would remain important in Niumi's ties to the Atlantic trade and the world market for a longer time. Thus, within a generation after 1660, Niumi's rulers became landlords for trading diasporas of the two European nations that would figure most prominently in worldwide commerce for several centuries.

The Long March of Islam

Not all cultural and economic influences on peoples of the Upper Guinea Coast in the seventeenth and eighteenth centuries came from the Atlantic. Some arrived overland, as ever, from the savannas that stretched eastward between the southern edge of the Sahara and the northern reaches of the Guinea forests. For the lower Gambia, these influences included a strong element of Mandinka culture, for the majority of the region's people looked to the Mandinka heartlands along the upper Niger River for a spiritual and cultural home. But over several centuries following the demise of the Mali and Jolof Empires, Islamic cultural influences, particularly from the Senegal River valley, continued to bear, and more heavily still, on the lives of people on all levels of Niumi's society. The period that saw peoples along the Gambia River participating more fully than ever in the Atlantic economy also saw the spreading about of more Muslim merchants, scholars, and mystics, and the slow assimilation of parts of their spiritual outlook by more than just the commercial elements in African societies.

Such a steady assimilation of Islamic cultural practices was hardly unique to Niumi or West Africa; it was taking place across far-flung parts of the Old World. Grand Islamic empires between the Mediterranean and India captured the attention of seventeenth- and eighteenth-century Europeans (and still hold the attention of many historians), but these empires' conquering armies were not the principal agents of Islam's spread through the period. The major purveyors of the Arabic language and a greater Islamic civilization were the lone mystics and scholarly clerics, consumed by spiritual affairs and thus no threat to rulers of states or heads of armies among whom they traveled. These individuals or lineage groups studied the

Qur'an and other bodies of Islamic literature; moved about; settled enclave-like villages; set up informal schools; sold their ability to divine the future, protect persons from harm, and heal bodily ills; and generally created small fountains of an Islamic lifestyle in ponds of foreign culture that were the wonder and envy of the surrounding non-Muslim majorities.

Gradually, some of the Muslims' ways became the ways of others. In specific instances the distinction between who was a Muslim and who was not became blurred. It was not love of Allah and respect for Muhammad that was spreading so much as it was certain ways of life and thought practices of those who loved Allah and revered The Prophet. Some of the culture of the Islamic world, or, in a grand sense, a part of Islamic civilization, was being adopted by peoples who still communicated with deities through their ancestors and sacrificed animals to appease spirits of the soil. This assimilation was a critical part of what African historians call "The Long March of Islam," the slow spreading of Islamic culture and then, ultimately, the Islamic faith among peoples of different ethnic groups of the West African savannas.[15]

This assimilation was manifested in Niumi by Fulbe and Mandinka lineages, who moved to the lower river's north bank in the sixteenth century and after. Commerce brought them to settle in the villages of Juffure, Albreda, and Sika, where they fit comfortably with the Africans and Luso-Africans participating in trade. But by the eighteenth century, Muslim lineages were establishing villages in Niumi away from the river and close to villages of ruling groups, locating themselves where they could benefit from the protection of rulers and, just as important, perform magical and spiritual functions for those in the state with the greatest ability to pay for their services. Rulers whose position of leadership was rooted in ties to traditional spirits and deities began appearing in public with Muslim advisers, wearing charms containing words from the Qur'an, and seeking maraboutic divination before taking major courses of action. Islam's long march was under way through the years of heaviest slave trading, and European observers who kept careful records noticed. They simply failed to pay it much attention.

The Niumi Polity

Elders in Niumi and oral traditionists from around the lower Gambia have a good laugh, mostly, when they tell the story of Nandanko Suntu Sonko. Old Nandanko, the fifth *mansa* of Niumi from the Sonko lineage residing in Berending, tried to stop the flow of the Gambia River. He did it by getting his subjects to throw rocks into the river along the state's southeastern riverbank, near Sika. Something to that effect seems really to have happened. Resident traders on James Island wrote in December 1760: "The king . . . is on a scheme of stopping some Part of the River, in order to prevent large vessels from passing his country & of course to bring the [slave] coffels down. We look upon it as chimerical and what cannot be effected." The reason the English regarded the effort as absurd is the same reason people today shake their heads and chuckle when they tell the story: the river is more than three miles wide at the spot of all the rock throwing. It would take one of the grandest engineering efforts of the modern world to dam the lower Gambia.[16]

But Sonko was not bereft of his senses. At least in a figurative way, or one that would send an appropriate message to European shippers, he was reaffirming his claim to control of traffic that tied the Gambia and its hinterland into the Atlantic complex. Long before the middle of the eighteenth century, Niumi's rulers had institutionalized their method of gaining wealth from the river trade. Shippers wanting to obtain slaves or other commodities—cowhides, beeswax, gold, foodstuffs—had to do so on Niumi's terms. Masters of vessels entering the river had to pay fees for anchorage and for taking on wood or water. Those wanting to sail upriver, where access to slaves was more direct and prices might be more favorable, had to employ extra crew members, brokers, and interpreters from Niumi's mixed populace. And Niumi's rulers collected *ad valorem* duty on all transactions. The wealth that allowed Niumi's ruling families to enjoy their elite lifestyle, to maintain their strategically important cavalry, to dress in finery, eat well, drink spirits of their choice, and marry sons and daughters to other prestigious families about the region and thus maintain collective security, came largely from the river trade. Sonko wanted to make sure everyone knew that Niumi's rulers were serious about keeping control of flow along the river—not of water toward the ocean, as the English accurately noted, but of the river traffic in the other direction.

State Structures

One thing above all others was the key to Niumi's stability and prosperity through the seventeenth and eighteenth centuries: the ability of the state's rulers to control and tax the busy trade between the western savannas and the Atlantic complex that passed along its shores and through the state. Those who controlled political and social functions of the state recognized this and developed institutions to maintain order and ensure state revenues through the period when the slave trade, and the no-less-significant trade of other commodities, was going on all about. By the time of the state's

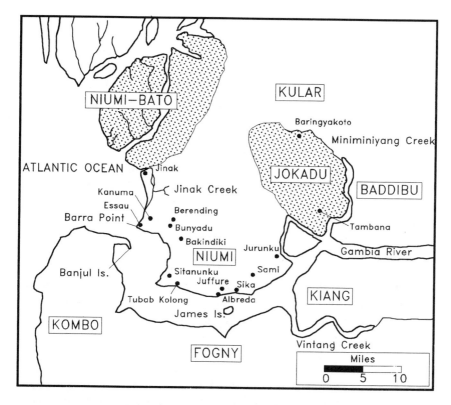

Map 7. **The Niumi State, Seventeenth–Eighteenth Centuries**

thorough incorporation into the Atlantic economic complex, Niumi had developed an efficient, systematic, manageable, and adaptable political apparatus. Its basis was the Mandinka village and state structure long in place across the Mande-speaking savanna world. But Niumi's ruling families gradually altered and expanded elements of the structure to meet the new circumstances surrounding the state's involvement with Atlantic commerce.[17]

The basis of Niumi's administration was the hierarchical system of Mandinka polities involving family, village, and state. People at each level had progressively broadening functions. The nuclear family—a man, his wife or wives, and their children—was a basic social grouping, but several related nuclear families in the same village lived together and operated as a unit. Such extended families varied in size; large ones might make up half or more of one village. Generally, the eldest male of the original family group was the extended family's head. With the advice of other male family elders, he supervised matters pertaining to birth, death, marriage, circumcision, divorce, inheritance, interfamily affairs, and relations with dependents—slaves, visitors, or wards.

A village was a collection of between four and a dozen extended families. Again, one of the eldest members of the village's founding lineage was normally the village head; heads of the other lineages and important and prosperous others served as a council. These men decided collectively when to plant and harvest, how to regulate bush fires and care for livestock, where to locate family compounds, and which plots of land the different families could use. Village leaders also looked after public works—construction and maintenance of wells, granaries, paths, and the like—and they supervised public ceremonies and celebrations. The village head was the principal adjudicator in disputes among the village's lineages. In masked form, to hide symbolically and help eliminate conflicting loyalties involving kin and friends, the village leaders meted out justice. Finally, the village head worked with, though not specifically for, Niumi's ruling lineages in collecting taxes, summoning manpower for military pursuits, policing the village and its approaches, and taking other action that would help maintain peace and security in the state. Village elders gave rulers counsel when asked. The frequency of this depended on the strategic or commercial importance of the village or on the relationship, through marriage, among village families and the ruling lineages.

The state, then, was a collection of lineages in a group of villages. The *mansa,* as head of state, represented the figure of leadership of all the state's separate lineages and the formal link with their collective group of ancestors. People addressed him as "grandfather," the symbolic authority figure of every lineage in the state. He was the spiritual leader of all the non-Muslim residents, and as such he played a key role in the communal worship of Niumi's spirits that resided in the ground and tall trees. And as head of the hierarchy of authority he had a range of responsibilities: keeping order; defending the state, and thus raising armies for defense or deterrence; levying taxes and controlling commercial exchange; and supervising relations with persons from outside the state and with other states.

Beyond his responsibilities, the *mansa* was the embodiment of the state. His well-being and that of Niumi were the same; his actions represented the state. For these reasons, people expected him and those around him to live a life they could speak of in superlatives. When the *mansa* ate, he ate the best food and lots of it; when he drank, he drank the most of the best spirits. When he rode it was upon the finest horse fitted with the best-worked saddle. He owned the most slaves and had the most wives—sometimes more than a score, many from leading families in various of Niumi's villages and other states, with political connections in mind. His granaries were the most numerous, the first filled, and the last emptied. And, literally, his drum beat loudest.

Court Officials

A number of officials in the *mansa*'s court assisted in administration. Most were physically close to the *mansa*—the English called them "the King's people": they included attendants, advisers, and assistants, though some typically were "hangers on." Most were from an entourage built over the years. Among the traditional duties of these officials, Niumi's ruling lineages made modifications to accommodate dealings with the broadening commercial world.

In everyday affairs, Niumi's *mansa* had a chief of staff, frequently his closest adviser. Contemporary Englishmen called him the "King's Key Keeper."[18] His primary duty was to filter visitors. For those not allowed access, he conveyed messages (as the *mansa* often remained in his dwelling or behind a screen) and returned with replies. He also coordinated personnel in the ruling household. This official was selected from among the most trustworthy of the ruling lineage's royal slaves. His rewards were related to how much he could enhance the *mansa*'s position and prestige, and in personal remuneration through receipt of a "dash" when the *mansa* received a gift, rather than social advancement.

Still closer physically to the *mansa* were several bodyguards, called *satalama,* who ensured the ruler's safety and proper treatment. People in Niumi still speak of the two stout bodyguards, dressed in black head ties, who sat on either side of the state's next-to-last reigning *mansa*. "If you wanted to kill Mansa Wali," one man said, "you had to kill them first."[19] Records of the Royal African Company from James Island in the 1680s show a bodyguard in action. The company's chief agent, Alexander Cleeve, came onto Niumi soil to resolve a dispute involving an assault committed by an English trader named Hodges on a Niumi resident. *Mansa* Jenung Wuleng Sonko had seized the company's agent at Juffure and would not release him without compensation for the assault. The haughty Cleeve found Sonko "at the foot of a great tree," records read, surrounded by bodyguards and courtiers. Cleeve strode up and said to Sonko, " 'How now, old Gennow, how is it?' " Quickly, he realized the impropriety of his words and conduct. The record continues: "But one of the grandees, by name Sambalama, taught him better manners by reaching him a box on the ears, which beat off his hat, and a few thumps on the back, and seizing him, disarmed him together with the rest of his attendance, amongst which was Benedict Stafford, commander of the *Margaret,* now in London (who made his escape and ran like a lusty fellow to his ship) and . . . several others, who together with the agent were taken and put into the king's pound and stayed there three or four days till their ransom was brought, value five hundred bars."[20]

The bodyguards were royal slaves also. Their dependence on the *mansa* was the key to their position. If he died they would lose everything—prestige, comfortable surroundings, and perhaps their lives—and gain nothing.

Other court members included bards, diviners, magical practitioners, and royal slaves performing a further variety of tasks. One or more bards accompanied the ruler wherever he went. They announced his presence, communicated with large audiences, spoke for the *mansa,* and regularly sang praises of the state and its ruling lineages. Accounts from James Island at various points in the eighteenth century show gifts given to the *mansa*'s "drummers" and "singing men." Magical practitioners were among the most important court members. No successful person in Niumi would be far from a trusted worker of magic. Such individuals divined the future, practiced healing, interpreted dreams, and made amulets and charms for most conceivable reasons: to protect the individual, to ensure bountiful crops, to help hunters at the hunt or warriors in battle. A special group of practitioners were the intermediaries between the *mansa* and the spirits of the land, normally worshiped or shown respect through icons or fetishes. These men prepared sacrifices—often fowls, or for greater occasion, cattle—and read the spirits' wishes in their acceptance or rejection of the sacrifice. In return for their services, magical workers' families received food and slaves. Successful warfare often brought captives, and the *mansa* would designate some for the diviners who predicted success or the makers of amulets that protected soldiers and horses. Over the seventeenth and eighteenth centuries Muslim clerics—generally called *marabouts*—came to play an increasingly important role in magical practice in Niumi. At least one of Niumi's royal lineages, the Sonko of Berending, had a marabout lineage, the Fati of Aljamdu, just a few miles away, attached permanently to them in a patron-client relationship. Marabouts won a reputation for being the best at certain kinds of magic, particularly at making charms to protect from wounds and for prophesying. They were allowed to lead separate lives and worship as they wished, so long as they assisted the *mansa.* Like others, their rewards were in slaves or booty.

A body of royal slaves—a broadly inclusive term—performed most routine court duties. Some were captives who had proved themselves loyal; some were persons from families in Niumi or elsewhere with whom the ruling lineages had marriage ties, offered to the state for service. Royal slaves cooked, tended children, cared for horses, worked in fields, delivered messages, wove cloth, guarded food stores, and did the hundreds of other things necessary to secure the properties of the ruling lineages and make their households operate efficiently.

Finally, at court were a number of people who appeared in many states about the world as adjuncts to royalty. Foremost were soldiers—some from Niumi's ruling lineages; some young members of ruling families of other states who came to learn the arts of war and effective rule (and to distance themselves from intrigue in their own courts); some itinerant soldiers of fortune who traveled about with their followers in pursuit of the exciting, male-dominated, high-living existence associated with the seats of rule in West African states; and some slaves. Also, forever at the court were persons from Niumi villages seeking the *mansa*'s favors and official and unofficial representatives from the ruling courts of other states.

The size of the *mansa*'s entourage varied with the ruler's reputation and wealth. In the days of heaviest commercial activity, when revenues were large, followings were substantial. When traveling, the *mansa* may have pared his retinue, as in 1702, when Niumi's ruler visited the French frigate *Mutiné* anchored in the Gambia's estuary: only one of his "tributary rulers," his "pope," several marabouts, and a dozen "princes" accompanied him onto the vessel.[21] But English and French officials who visited royal villages found that the *mansa* lived surrounded by larger numbers of people, most finely attired, who added greatly to the splendor of the court.

State Administration

Beyond the ruler's attendants and court following were officials whose major concern was state business. The most important for internal affairs was an official called the *suma*. Each of the royal villages had a special slave family, the head of which was the *suma*. As with others, slave status enabled the *suma* to deal directly with the highest levels of authority without posing a threat to them. It was a primary function of this official to provide continuity during the potentially disruptive transition period between one *mansa*'s death and the investiture of another. The *suma* of the village of the previous ruler took care of state affairs, while the same official of the village of the next *mansa* oversaw selection of the new ruler and his installation. The second important function of the *suma* was the organization of Niumi's fighting forces. Helping him in this regard were several "war leaders," who were members of the ruling family, and a person in charge of Niumi's powerful canoe fleet (to whom the English referred as Niumi's "Admiral"). Royal African Company officials on James Island occasionally sent spirits across the water for "the Comma and King's brothers with the rest of the army to drink."[22]

An equally important group of officials dealing with external affairs were those called *falifo*. In other Gambian states a *falifo* was any prosperous foreigner residing in the state, but in Niumi the position became an institution of state, reserved for members of a family originally from elsewhere whose patriarch had married a woman, or women, of one of Niumi's ruling lineages. They were, thus, "royal nephews." Their status was unique: they had advantages for the rulers, for as outsiders they could not claim political authority; yet, as relatives through marriage, they had state interests at heart more than ordinary foreigners. As a consequence, they were suited to fill positions where the potential to acquire wealth, prestige, and power was great.

These are the primary reasons why a lineage named Tall, initially maternal nephews of the Jammeh royal lineage, settled in Juffure and gained the political plum of being tax and toll collectors at that major locus of trade. From some time in the sixteenth century Juffure's Tall family played a growing role in the administration and control of the waxing commercial and social exchange among Portuguese, Luso-Africans, other Europeans, other Africans, and the people of Niumi. State residents regarded the leader of Juffure's Tall lineage as the "state *falifo.*" In addition to customs and tolls, he collected taxes on exchanges made in Niumi and received foreigners' gifts to the *mansa,* his court, and lesser officials. Yet, no matter how prosperous the Tall family became—and there were times when the "Alcaide of Gillifree" (as the English sometimes referred to the *falifo*) was among the most influential persons in the region—its members remained outsiders, related to the rulers only through marriage and thus no threat to usurp hereditary political authority.[23]

Dependent Territories

Much of Niumi's population lived in about fifteen villages within a mile or two of the ocean or river, where the state's economic interests were focused. Given distances and difficulties of travel through heavy forests, it was difficult for rulers to control people living very far away. Especially independent were people on the state's peripheries, which served as buffer areas with surrounding states. In such regions Niumi's rulers found it advantageous to vest local lineages with state authority. These families administered, taxed, and defended people in the area with Niumi's backing. Europeans called such subrulers "kings" and Africans called them *mansa,* both titles carrying different levels of meaning. It is clear that such individuals in the dependent territories were subordinate to, and invested by, Niumi's ruling lineages.

The area for which there is the earliest evidence of subordinate status is Jokadu, along Niumi's east side. Jokadu was one of the best farming regions along the Gambia. It is likely that it was settled permanently after the middle of the seventeenth century, when families established villages there to grow grain to sell to Europeans at James Island and Albreda and to slaving vessels in the river. Niumi sometimes fought with its eastern neighbor, Baddibu, over control of Jokadu, and after a time the region's population preferred independence from either state so they could benefit from their own production and trade. Niumi maintained a senior-subordinate relationship with Jokadu until the middle of the nineteenth century, when, under altered circumstances, Jokadu succeeded after a long struggle in winning its independence from a weakened Niumi.[24]

Niumi's *mansa* also invested persons with the state's authority in the salt-producing regions northward along the Atlantic coast. This once held more of a central focus for the state, when salt production and shipment eastward, up the Gambia, was its primary commercial activity. But in the sixteenth century, when operations of the Atlantic trade in the river's estuary captured more state interest, Niumi's direct control over the "Salt Islands" waned. Sovereigns of the states of Siin and Saloum to Niumi's north coveted the islands; they were a frequent focus of interstate hostilities. When in control there, Niumi's ruler kept a subordinate in charge. In the 1730s the English gave gifts to "Lassora Sonko, King of the Salt Islands," probably a royal slave of Niumi's *Mansa* Dusu Koli Sonko (r. 1727–36).[25] Niumi maintained greater or lesser control of the area until 1860, when Muslim revolutionary forces decisively defeated Niumi's army there.

A third region where Niumi supported a dependent ruler was around the village of Kular, on the edge of a sparsely populated buffer area between Niumi and Saloum. Eighteenth-century maps show a separate territory of Kular, and English officials noted that Niumi maintained a "tributary king" there through the first third of the nineteenth century, after which people in Kular allied with Jokadu in its effort to secure independence.[26]

Examination of dependent regions underscores that Niumi was less a carefully delineated territory and more the area where people admitted allegiance to Niumi's *mansa*. The state's boundaries were as fluid as its people's social relationships. The social ties and arrangements of reciprocity the state's leading families had with other lineages throughout the lower part of Senegambia were more important than control over sparsely inhabited land. At times these relationships spread widely, making Niumi seem to observers with mindsets about territorial ownership as if it comprised a good-sized piece of land. At other times they were more restricted, or concentrated with different groups (traveling merchant families or Luso-

African traders, for instance) in different directions, making it seem to Europeans as if the state had much narrower geographical confines and was not strong at all.

State Revenues

Niumi's ruling lineages had two primary sources of revenue: the agricultural surplus produced by farmers in the state and the trade that passed along the Gambia River and through the state. By taxing grain and supervising growing their own, and by exacting taxes, tolls, and gifts from a variety of traders, the rulers obtained revenue they needed for the function of the government and the maintenance of their social position. Each was important. If production of commoners and slaves enabled male members of Niumi's ruling class to glorify themselves with personal finery, good food, strong drink, and ostentatious display on and off horseback, and to live the sometimes idle, sometimes dangerously active lives of marauding horsemen, it also supported effective administration and provided for the forces that kept the people in the state reasonably secure from invasion. All elements of society accepted this last aspect as one of the primary reasons for the state's existence.

Agricultural surplus was at the heart of Niumi's existence. The state's ruling lineages obtained surplus grain and cotton through taxation and slave production. Following harvest, village heads supervised collection of about one-tenth of village production and conveyed it to the *mansa*'s village. Farmers recognized their need for protection and knew that when famine or other hard times beset them they could turn to their rulers for food. The ruling lineages used some of the wealth to create and maintain reciprocal ties, mostly through marriage, with wealthy lineages in the region, so they could call for assistance—food in times of famine, soldiers or horses in times of war—when necessary.[27]

Rulers also supervised slave production of grain and cotton; royal fields were reputed to be the largest of any, for they could amass the greatest labor force. A *mansa* could call on the young men's age group to work in the fields at critical times, but slaves did most of the work. Produce from these crops provided food and trading commodities; surplus added to the *mansa*'s wealth.

Of course, a major way to increase state wealth was to increase production, and the only way to do that given the technology of slash-and-burn, hoe agriculture, was to increase the amount of land under cultivation. This required more people to work the land. Every immigrant family, attracted by the protection afforded by Niumi's royal lineages, increased state production and, thus, state revenues. Yet, another way rulers could increase the size of the state's labor force was to purchase slaves (and slaves arriving from inland when demand was low at the river's mouth often sold for less) or to capture persons from outside the state and bring them back to live and work as royal slaves. Male members of the ruling lineages tended to be avid plunderers, inclined to make periodic horse-borne raids that brought in human booty. Some captives could be ransomed and some sold for horses, grain, or other items of value, but the rest joined the rulers' workforce.

The other major source of state revenue was commercial exchange. Merchants passing along or through a West African state customarily paid tolls to assure protection and rights to trade, gather provisions, and take up temporary residence. From as early as there are records, Niumi derived revenue from the passage of salt between the Atlantic and the upper river. With the opportunity of the waxing Atlantic commerce at its shores, Niumi's rulers adapted such requirements as necessary to deal with European merchant vessels.[28] Ships entering the Gambia out of the Atlantic steered for Jinak Point, where large trees marked what old coasters called "The King's Pavillion." There they fired a salute to announce their arrival. The ship's master then dispatched a longboat to Niumi's shore to obtain a pilot, who would guide the vessel past shoals near Barra Point and on to Juffure, where the *falifo* conducted Niumi's business. Masters had to provide gifts for the *mansa,* the *falifo,* and from two to seven or eight other lesser officials. Vessels remained at anchor off Juffure while the *falifo* conveyed the gifts to the *mansa* and returned with word that they were satisfactory. The *falifo* then set a date when the master would be obliged to pay set tolls for anchorage and passage, and for the privilege of taking on wood, water, and provisions. European merchants intending to proceed upriver then had to hire a pilot, several "linguisters" for pending commercial transactions, and a number of crewmen to help with the strenuous work of tacking and rowing against the current. Each of these auxiliaries received a standard rate of pay.

After the English and French established permanent posts on Niumi's riverside, their agents arranged annual customs payments with Niumi's ruling lineages. In return, the *mansa* regularized payments required of company-affiliated trading vessels and speeded proceedings, the latter always a concern for ship masters. Private traders continued to pay higher tolls and charges. These annual customs rose over the years with expanding trade and rising prices. English customs nearly quadrupled in the century after 1665. In addition to providing revenue, they bound and renewed the established relationships of local landlord and European stranger as well as specific agreements on trade.

Greater still than revenues from customs and tolls were rulers' tariffs on transactions taking place in Niumi. The *mansa* might claim one of every ten items exchanged, so caravans of several hundred slaves descending the river's north bank for sale in Juffure or Albreda would bring the *mansa* several times more revenue than he received in annual customs or tolls from trading vessels.

And there were other customary sources of wealth related to trade. By traditional rights, vessels running aground off Niumi's shores became state property. In one instance in 1754 English merchants paid Niumi's *mansa* sixty-four gallons of rum just for the privilege of *attempting* to refloat their own grounded vessel. In another in 1732 the *mansa* berated company officials on James Island for giving aid to a private trading vessel in danger of running aground. He had his eye on the cargo.[29]

Some of Niumi's rulers were masters at ransom and extortion. Well informed of conditions in the foreign enclaves, they would take advantage of European isolation or weakness. In an incident of this kind in 1708, when the James Island garrison staged an unsuccessful mutiny, Niumi's *falifo* sent word from Juffure to the island that the *mansa*'s canoe-borne forces would attack and pillage the weakened factory unless given sizable gifts. Rulers became adept at playing French and English interests against one another too. In 1752 English agent James Skinner lamented that Niumi's *mansa* "comes 2–3 times each month to the Fort & demands spirits &c, which we always give him expecting he would turn the French out of the river, according to his promise. Instead he told the French at Albreda of his plan & likewise got more from them." When Skinner refused to entertain the *mansa*'s entourage on his next visit, the ruler kidnapped an Englishman living in Juffure and charged the English five kegs of rum for ransom.[30]

Ruling elites of Senegambian states seem regularly to have mounted war parties to raid neighboring villages or even some in their own states, capturing persons working in fields or fleeing from a village and enslaving them. They called such activity "horse-running"; it was the combined sport and productive work of the ruling strata.[31] Such raiding satisfied the desires of the elites to demonstrate their warrior capabilities and brought yet more wealth to the state's rulers through ransom, sale, or increased production. Perhaps because of their steadier revenues from external trade, however, Niumi's ruling lineages did not do much marauding and raiding, especially of their own villagers. Only when a *mansa* lost control of difficult warrior elements in his entourage would internal raiding take place. Admittedly vague oral and written evidence suggests that on occasion after the mid-eighteenth century common villagers, including Euro-Africans and Europeans engaged in commerce, suffered increasingly from the depredations of

Niumi's warriors acting beyond the *mansa*'s control. Such activity partly explains the virtual disappearance of Niumi's Euro-African population by 1800; the almost continual revolutionary activity of its dependent territories through the first half of the nineteenth century; and, when combined with the increasing availability of firearms, growing British power, and other economic and social factors, the violent rebellions of the mid-nineteenth century that led to the demise of Niumi's ruling elite.[32]

A Wider Material and Intellectual World

Through its connection to the Atlantic trade, Niumi gained more direct and regular access to a larger material and intellectual world. Back through the years, with their connection to the coastal trading area of Senegambia and upper Guinea, persons in Niumi tapped into useful exchange of regional products—kola nuts, cloth, foodstuffs, cowhides, slaves, and more—and through indirect trade from across the Sahara they acquired products and ideas from a world as far away as the Mediterranean and Middle East—horses, leather goods, metalware, figs, dates, and an acquaintance with Islam and some of the material and intellectual accouterments of the growing religion. But in its manifestations in the Gambia River, the Atlantic trade put Niumi's population in touch with a material and intellectual world that stretched beyond any they had known. By the seventeenth century—or in regard to some things, somewhat earlier—men and women in Niumi were habitual consumers of products from all around the Atlantic and from central and East Asia. Furthermore, although they were not always as receptive to foreign ideas and notions as they were to foreign products, mostly because they neither wished nor needed to be, they were becoming increasingly familiar with different ideas that people had across large bodies of water and vast expanses of land.

Niumi's Changing Material World

Discussion of material goods people in Niumi received in exchange for local and regional commodities, including slaves, leads one to put to rest forever the old "gewgaw myth." Stanley B. Alpern explains that practical cloth and metal goods tended to dominate European imports into West Africa during the Atlantic trade, but that "the range of commodities was so broad that inbound European ships eventually came to resemble. . . 'floating supermarkets.' " Curtin lists a typical sample of goods the Royal African Company exchanged for 180 slaves in the Gambia River in 1740 and 1741; it includes twenty-five different items—five varieties of cloth, five of beads or other decorative items, four of metal or metalware, two of firearms, gunpowder and lead, spirits, silver coins, salt, and paper.[33]

Generalizations about Gambian imports through the seventeenth and eighteenth centuries show changes in African preferences and suggest corresponding changes in ways of life. Items of apparel and personal decoration made up almost half of all imports, with preferences shifting from beads to cloth. Metals and metalware constituted another third, iron bars being more important in the seventeenth century and silver becoming more so in the eighteenth. Weapons made up from 10 to 25 percent of imports—swords through the seventeenth century and firearms, increasingly, in the eighteenth. And holding steady were imports of spirits, with tobacco entering the picture toward the end. Throughout the period, African demand was the primary determinant of what European shippers brought to trade, just as European demand for gold, slaves, hides, or beeswax led Africans to produce those commodities.

Items of apparel and decoration remained the greatest import into the Gambia throughout the years of the Atlantic trade and beyond. (In fact, even today one cannot walk down major streets in The Gambia's capital or visit markets around the country without noticing the ubiquity of imported cloth, clothing, and items of adornment for sale at nearly every turn.) Dress and personal decoration were the major way many West Africans displayed their wealth or indicated their social status. Clothing, jewelry, and beads served this function, and the Atlantic trade supplied all three. Waist girdles were one of the most popular adornments for persons of both sexes, from rulers to commoners. Gambians had access to beads before the Atlantic trade, but the multicolored glass beads coming out of Austria, France, Germany, and Holland, along with crystal, pearls, coral, and semiprecious stones from various distant parts of the globe, brought new possibilities in personal decoration. Most of the beads, purchased by the ton in Venice or Amsterdam, were inexpensive to Europeans, and for some the markup in the Gambia was considerable. But Alpern argues, "the vital measure of personal ornaments is surely the pleasure they give, the charms they set off, not their cost of production. To call cheap but pretty beads rubbish is to see them through the eyes of a Western sophisticate, not those of an African consumer." Furthermore, not all glass beads were inexpensive for Europeans and some (like the carnelians that came from Bombay and became especially popular in the Gambian trade), along with Mediterranean coral and crystal, were not cheap at all.[34]

Cloth was a different story. Residents of Niumi had access to good cotton cloth from the savanna lands east of the Gambia. People there had grown cotton since Muslim traders had brought the cloth and seeds across the Sahara from North Africa in the first millennium, and they spun cotton thread, wove sturdy cloth, and exchanged it for other products they wanted but did not produce. There had long been a steady movement of cotton cloth east and west across West Africa's savannas. As early as the eleventh century Muslim travelers noticed cotton cloth in use as currency along the Senegal River, and English trader Richard Jobson early in the seventeenth century reported that cloth in the Gambia River was "the staple commodity to pitch the price upon, to value other things by."[35] When Europeans began importing beads, they too fit into the currency structure, so that eventually cloth (or in some cases silver coins) served as the large units of currency and beads were the equivalent of small change.[36] Cotton producers inland from the Gambia were eager to exchange cloth for the salt they needed from Niumi's Atlantic coast. Through the 1600s, little European cloth interested consumers in Niumi—they did not like the designs of the European material, it was more expensive, and did not hold up under local laundry methods—though Europeans did find profit in buying African cloth in the upper Gambia and using it along the Atlantic coast to acquire foodstuffs or slaves. In the 1680s, when beads and semiprecious stones made up about 40 percent of European imports in the river, textiles constituted only one-tenth as much. But as English and French traders got easier access to the finely woven, brightly colored Indian textiles that were passing through Liverpool or Marseilles, and as some of the Indian imports gained elite status among West African consumers, the Europeans began to import cloth that appealed to Gambian consumers.[37] Northern European producers also imitated Indian cottons (though most Africans continued to prefer the real thing), and they made increasingly fine woolens and linens and such useful items of clothing as kerchiefs, hats, and caps. Thus, cloth and clothing imports rose steadily after the seventeenth century as beads and semiprecious stones declined in relative terms.

All of this enabled people in Niumi to adorn themselves more colorfully, more fully, more comfortably than before. With increasing frequency, wealthier people dressed up with more clothing, wrapping linens and woolens around cotton garments, and wrapped themselves in more layers on chilly dry-season nights. Brightly colored wraps covered the heads of prominent women in public; men wore long gowns with various wraps and more hats and caps; cotton sheets covered things appropriately kept from sight—corpses at funerals, brides at weddings, the future *mansa* in an inauguration ceremony. In the Muslim enclave villages, religious men had an easier time dressing like their North African models, in long, loose-fitting gowns.

But the importation in great quantities of personal decorations and cloth had a social effect that went beyond the aspect of wearing one's wealth. The

major use of cloth currency was in social exchange: men who were inclined
to marry needed cloth to provide to the family of the prospective bride. This
compensated the woman's family for its loss of a productive member—the
amount was related to the economic, social, or political position of the
bride's family—and it symbolized the mutual obligations each family had
to its in-laws. Cloth, and to a lesser extent items of personal adornment, all
easily stored items that retained their value, became standard payments for
bride wealth. The more and better cloth and beads one had, the more wives
one could marry from larger and stronger families from a wider region. And
the more marriage ties one had with such families, the more one had strong
and prosperous outsiders on whom to rely in times of need—famine, especially, or physical threat. In time, male members of the wealthiest and most
influential families in Niumi came to have dozens or scores of wives—often
women from wealthy and powerful lineages all around the lower Gambia.
Likewise, women from Niumi married prominent men from a wide area.
These interfamilial ties were the essence of security in the lower Gambia,
and the Atlantic trade increasingly provided the wealth and goods for
Niumi's prosperous families to create and maintain such relationships. Records of Royal African Company gift giving in the first half of the eighteenth century give evidence of the connections of Niumi's prominent
lineages—African and Euro-African—and of those with lineages in other
states throughout the region. They suggest, as well, the obligations families
had to their in-laws, responding to tragedies, attending funerals, or sending
men to fight in neighboring wars—obligations, incidentally, in which English and French traders became involved as well.[38] The political and social
stability of the lower Gambia and a greater region of Senegambia was based
on the mutuality of interests of the region's leading lineages.

Metals and metalware also made up a significant portion of Niumi's
imports out of the Atlantic trade. "Without iron and alcohol one cannot live
there, much less trade," wrote Abbé Demanet after a visit to Niumi in
1764. Niumi had blacksmiths, but they worked iron rather than produced it.
Long before Europeans arrived in the river, Niumi obtained iron from West
Africa's interior, and local smiths turned it into useful products—farm im-
plements, weapons, utensils, chains, gongs, and other things. But by the
seventeenth century so much iron was entering the lower Gambia via the
Atlantic that the "bar," based on a standardized piece of flat wrought iron
common in the lower Rhine and early brought to West Africa by the Dutch,
became the Gambia's standard unit of currency. Iron imported from the
Atlantic partially replaced imports from the eastern hinterland, and this iron
continued to make up a third or more of Gambian imports through the
seventeenth century. Then iron imports declined steadily, replaced partly by

silver and metalware in the 1730s. By the end of the century, metals and metalware (not counting cutlery and weapons) were an insignificant part of the trade. The ability to obtain high quality, inexpensive iron was good for Niumi's smiths, farmers, and soldiers. Moreover, as more metalware in the form of copper basins, brass pans, and pewterware entered the region, one suspects that the women's art of pot making declined. Metal tools and utensils must have made their way into the lives of wealthier people in Niumi's villages.[39]

Weapons of one sort or another were important elements of European trade into the Gambia River until recent times. Swords and cutlasses were major imports into the eighteenth century; firearms and gunpowder grew slowly in volume throughout the period. Metal swords and spears were the weapons of choice of Niumi's horsemen; use of firearms in warfare was slow in coming. Before the nineteenth century, Africans around the lower Gambia seldom used guns to fight with because they were slow to load, inaccurate, undependable, and cumbersome. They used firearms, instead, for hunting, for keeping predatory animals from crops, for noise making at celebrations, for ceremonial functions (Niumi's *mansa* returned salutes from arriving vessels), and as symbols of royal prestige and power (for in most instances only the ruling lineages could afford to keep guns in significant numbers).[40] So before 1800 firearms affected Niumi's population in surprising ways: through controlling dangerous and predatory animals and thus enhancing crop production, and providing another way for the ruling lineages to display their wealth and status—as a form of conspicuous consumption.

Spirits (normally in the form of brandy or rum) were another commodity in steady demand in Niumi, especially among the ruling lineages. European traders had to include rum or brandy as part of the *mansa*'s annual custom (he received half his customs in rum, twenty gallons, in 1726); ships entering the Gambia had to give gifts of spirits in Juffure; and, generally speaking, some form of "cordial water" was oil for the wheels of commerce throughout the region. "Without brandy there is no trade," wrote the chief factor at James Fort to the Royal African Company in 1680. Over the last quarter of the eighteenth century, as British and French traders had their attentions drawn to revolutionary and military matters in other colonies or at home, American traders worked the Gambia trade and brought copious quantities of rum. The ruling families were the greatest consumers of brandy and rum, not only because they were the wealthiest elements, but because part of the worshiping ceremonies of the traditional religion involved libations for the spirits (and the practitioners) and because the lifestyle of young male lineage members involved an element of abandon on horseback and unpredictable behavior in public, all of which alcohol enhanced. The availability of strong spirits played a role in what seems to have been the growing militancy, and predatory nature, of Niumi's rulers and their entourages. By the mid-eighteenth century the warrior groups surrounding the *mansa* were making life hard for European traders; by the early-nineteenth century they were making it hard for their own subjects. Only the Muslim lineages in the state and those unable to afford a draught of "bumbo" now and then remained outside Niumi's culture of alcohol.[41]

Finally, Niumi obtained from the Atlantic trade small, but not insignificant, amounts of paper. The literate Muslim elements in Niumi's society used the paper, largely for the manufacture of charms containing writings from the Qur'an. Its continuing importance is an indictor of the persistence of Niumi's Muslim enclaves. Once those enclaves began to expand and more people began converting to Islam in the mid-nineteenth century, requirements for paper would increase.

Niumi's Changing Social and Intellectual World

Niumi's main riverside villages—Juffure, Albreda, and Sika—were quite the cosmopolitan places in the first half of the eighteenth century. A visitor to Niumi at this time might notice several villages inhabited partly by black Christians bearing Portuguese surnames and dressed in long gowns with crucifixes around their necks. Living nearby might be matriarchal women of considerable influence, wealthy in their own right (rather than their husband's), from their prominent positions in regional trade. None of this would be typical of West African societies inland and any distance from the Atlantic trade; yet, Niumi's society still had a number of elements similar to those in grand states like Mali and Kaabu. These included a strong, at times parasitic, group of rulers who increasingly identified more closely with distant lineages of their elite class than with the lower-class elements in Niumi, and a body of apolitical Muslims, some living detached from others but growing in influence because of their importance in trade and the reliance of others on the Muslims' work with supernatural forces. These characteristics existed because Niumi's society, while based on the traditional Mandinka model, changed over its long contact with persons and institutions involved in Atlantic and Sudanic trading and broadened social structures to include new elements that were useful for the functioning of the cross-cultural trade.

Luso-Africans

The two centuries of Niumi's history under study were a time of steady Luso-African rise among the state's commercial elite, followed by a relatively rapid decline.[42] Filling a niche in the water-borne trade by connecting settlements near the Atlantic with merchants bringing goods from beyond the Gambia's headwaters, these offspring of Portuguese traders and African women grew in importance through the middle of the seventeenth century and beyond. When northern Europeans became firmly established in the river in the 1660s, Luso-Africans were the dominant middlemen in the trade between the Atlantic and the head of navigation. The first ledger of the English outpost on James Island, begun in January 1664, lists thirty-one different persons with Portuguese surnames trading for or with goods of the Royal Adventurers. Some amassed considerable wealth and had ties through marriage to ruling lineages of the Gambian states. In the 1730s, enough Luso-Africans resided in Sika, east of Juffure, that a priest from the Cape Verde Islands visited there twice each year to administer the sacraments.[43]

A good number of the prominent mulatto traders were women. At the start of the eighteenth century one of the most influential persons in the intercultural commercial relations of the lower Gambia was a daughter of Niumi's *mansa,* who had been married to several Luso-African traders (and who, through her father's rights, had inherited their property when they died). "Signora Belinguere," she was called, and according to the director of the Compagnie du Sénégal, who met her in Juffure in 1700, she was literate in French, Portuguese, and English; she resided in a square "Portuguese house" with white walls and a vestibule; she had a network of sources that provided her with excellent commercial intelligence; and she could secure credit for nonaffiliated traders. According to another Frenchman, she also was "the reef upon which many whites of several nations have foundered."[44] English records from the 1730s list several "señoras" as prominent persons in trade in Niumi, and a generation later one Señora Llena, who lived in Juffure, owned a number of slaves whom she hired to work on European vessels as linguists and boatmen. Llena was married to Haly Sonko, brother to Niumi's next *mansa,* and he interceded on her behalf when her economic interests brought her into conflict with Niumi's ruling elite and probably others.[45]

Yet, it would be wrong to assume that all of Niumi's mixed Euro-African population were wealthy entrepreneurs. The largest number seem to have been *gromettas*—auxiliary boatmen, interpreters, and other sorts of commercial and cultural intermediaries. In the mid-seventeenth century some of the English Royal Adventurers employed "Lopeez the Grometta" and hired "Dom do Aldea" to tend their cattle. In 1729, five of the seven Royal African Company linguists and messengers had Portuguese names. Five years later the company hired Philip Gomez, Emanuel Vos, and Barnaby Lopez to man provision "factories" at various locations in Niumi.[46] And

some of Niumi's Luso-Africans were slaves. Royal African Company accounts from the 1730s contain references to António Gomez, a "Castle
Slave," who ran errands for the company, and Superanca Vas, who had
"belonged to" Robert Plunkett, governor of the James Island establishment.
One Luso-African, Diogo Gomes, was in the special category of slaves of
the ruling lineages. Indeed, Gomes was the head slave of *Mansa* Alimaranta
Sonko in the 1720s. During Sonko's reign, Gomes carried on trade on his
master's behalf, and he continued a prosperous commerce of his own after
Sonko died in 1725. His master's death did not alter his status: a decade
after Sonko's death the English were still identifying Gomes as "the late
King of Niumi's head slave."[47]

Neither prosperity nor ubiquity in records of the river's trade were characteristics of the Luso-Africans for good, however. Niumi's Luso-African
population declined steadily after the middle of the eighteenth century. The
cultural hybrids had been able to sustain themselves and, in some cases, to
prosper by performing commercial functions on the Gambia beyond the
inclinations of others. But as French and British interests in the river began
to compete and English factors at James Fort determined to send their own
traders up the river to obtain more commodities at better prices, they undercut and gradually displaced the Luso-Africans. Muslim merchants in Niumi
may have been hurt by the same actions, but they had their work with the
supernatural to fall back on for their primary livelihood. Luso-African
Christians did not come from so much of a magical/supernatural tradition—
or at least one that incorporated the making of protective charms that fit so
well into traditional African practices. Niumi's rulers hurt the Luso-Africans,
too, with their tendency to insist on customary rights of inheritance from
foreigners dying on Niumi soil—and regardless of where they were born,
the Luso-Africans remained a foreign group in this regard—or of all persons tied to the ruling lineages in relationships of dependence. As the latter
half of the eighteenth century wore on, some Luso-Africans probably
melded into Niumi's African population and disappeared from the record;
some drifted off to areas of more promising trade south of the Gambia. By
the late 1750s there are no longer Portuguese names in the English ledgers.
Those who remained on Niumi soil into the 1760s and beyond clung to
relationships with French traders in Albreda. A French clergyman noted in
1764 that Niumi's "Portuguese Christians" were something of a sad lot,
having not seen a priest in twenty years. By the end of the century there no
longer was a noticeable Luso-African presence in Niumi, unless, of course,
one counts the cultural remains of square houses with white walls, *pirogues*
carrying much of the trade goods along the lower Gambia, and a trade
language of the region with many words rooted in Portuguese.[48]

Muslims

While Niumi's Luso-African population was moving toward its eventual demise, Muslims in the state were very much holding their own. Like their counterparts throughout central parts of the Old World, followers of Islam along the lower Gambia River benefited from their association with the material goods of trade, the supernatural elements of their beliefs, and their own accommodationist leanings that enabled them to fit pre-Islamic beliefs and objects of worship and veneration into manifestations of the Islamic faith. As more wealth came into Niumi through the growing regional commerce, Muslim lineages prospered, either through their own trading or through remuneration for their protection and divination. A good part of their wealth came to be in slaves, which were vital to both facets of their work. With slave labor growing crops to sustain the family, men of the lineage were freed to travel for trading or to study through the early years of their lives and then to practice their "Muslim works."[49] European observers had typical contempt for the religion of "the Mohammedans," so they failed to recognize the level of scholarship and learning that West African clerics achieved. But in the eyes of others, such men were part of a body of scholars and mystics who were advancing Muslim religious thought throughout the realm of Islamic civilization. Learned Muslims in Niumi in the eighteenth century may have been making the pilgrimage to Mecca, but they more clearly were involved in traveling widely to attend schools of Islamic scholarship and mysticism. Some Niumi marabouts carried the title of Fodé, an indication that they had mastered some of the most advanced religious texts.

Eighteenth-century Niumi was thus a society with a visible and valuable Muslim presence. One can recognize the importance of Muslims in the trade of the lower Gambia in the 1730s from examination of records from James Island listing gifts and payments rendered in hopes of facilitating English trade. A portion of the Royal African Company's largess went to "Oil for the Mahometans," to the "Great Mohamedan priest of Sika, on having lost his slippers," and to the "great priest's son that is with the King." The same records show that Muslim clerics were retained by Niumi's rulers and most prominent traders to work as advisers and protectors: Company payments go to "Seca Scaroe, Bushreen [marabout] of Niumi," to "Bram Bojan to go to the great Priests to get their opinion for the best place for the new King of Niumi to make his town," and to "the Bishreen attendants of Sr. Antonio Vas." At least one of the state's royal lineages, the Sonko of Berending, and probably more had a Muslim lineage permanently attached as clients. Elders of the Fati lineage of Aljamdu say they built their settlement in the last quarter of the seventeenth century just a few miles from Berending, at the request of *Mansa* Jenung Wuleng Sonko, so they could be near enough to work for him.[50] And, of course, the Tall lineage of Juffure, who provided the *falifo* of Niumi, the person through whom Europeans dealt and to whom they paid customs, was not only a Muslim but, by the 1760s, a recognized cleric.[51]

There is no indication that ideas of militant Islamic revival that were spreading through the Muslim world, or even influences from movements of religious reform and revolution that had taken place not too far north and east of Niumi from late in the seventeenth century and even more strongly in the eighteenth century, had spread among Muslims of the state.[52] Niumi's commercial and clerical lineages went about their trading, scholarship, and supernatural work in the same pacific way, to their benefit and that of those among whom they lived and worked. These lineages would be well placed in the middle of the nineteenth century, when reformist movements against non-Muslim or partially Muslim rulers were spreading across Senegambia, to take up the banner of reform and lead a growing number of followers against Niumi's ruling lineages.

The Soninke

By those mid-nineteenth-century years, more people in Niumi than the Muslim clerics would consider their rulers in need of reform. Niumi's ruling lineages were typical of those throughout Africa's western savannas: they considered themselves privileged, lived off the produce of their slaves and the nonroyal families in their states and off the trade that passed through their territories, had minimal constraints on their behavior, and did what they needed to maintain their elite status. This may have been the case from the time of consolidation of Niumi's ruling groups in the sixteenth century. After all, the predatory *nyancho* elite of Kaabu, from whence came several of the ruling lineages in Niumi, was the reputed model for aristocratic privilege and uncontrolled, despotic behavior. There is no reason to believe that they were not this way from the start. It may be that Senegambian rulers became more oppressive after the ending of Atlantic slave trading than they were a century earlier, but evidence does not exist to support the claim. The ruling groups of West Africa's savanna states never were simply benevolent protectors. Such was not the nature of statehood at the place and time.

Still, over the eighteenth century changes were happening among the ruling elites. Across West Africa's grasslands, ruling groups were beginning to identify more with others in their class and less with peasants in their ethnic or political units. Eventually, ruling lineages of most of the

Senegambian states were related to one another, sometimes indirectly, through marriage. They formed a tightly knit group—a surclass of restricted membership that transcended political boundaries—connecting across a wide area those elite lineages with interest in common political and social goals. As such, they formed a kind of "interlocking directorate" of the states. Sometimes they disagreed and quarreled over trading rights or inheritance; sometimes their disagreements resulted in fighting between individual states or among groups of states; but none of their fighting was totally destructive. Like family feuds, these quarrels ended short of serious damage because, although living in separate states, they shared the interests of an expanded family. Solidarity and stability remained uppermost in their minds. As long as they controlled the fighting resources of the region—in soldiers on horseback, canoe-borne forces, and iron-tipped weapons—and practiced a form of collective security, calling on powerful related lineages in other states when threatened, no one from outside or below could mount an effective challenge to their supremacy and control.[53]

Among Mande speakers, members of the ruling elite came to be known as *Soninke*. Formed partly in apposition to the spreading acceptance of elements of Islamic culture, the *Soninke* identity included possession of political authority, glorification of the attributes of the horseback warrior, worship of the traditional pre-Islamic spirits, showy manifestation of wealth in dress and material goods, and consumption of alcohol with attendant unpredictable behavior. *Soninke* tended to keep aloof, preferring to marry persons of their class from other states than local persons from lower classes.[54] Increasingly, rulers stuck with rulers, warriors stuck with warriors, and the more numerous peasants, artisans, and slaves in their midst could fare as they wished, as long as they supported the ruling strata.[55] If that support was not forthcoming and especially if it was being diverted elsewhere—toward Muslim mystics, for example, or toward the acquisition of wealth by lineages of the lower classes—rulers were positioned to take what they wished in a fashion that peasants, traders, clerics, and others would consider oppressive. In time, the lower classes would seek ways to end their oppression.[56]

The Changing Nature of Dependence

Still other changes in the eighteenth century had ominous portent for people on all levels of Niumi's society. Curtin renders a judgment about Senegambia during the century following 1740 that bears on the depth and nature of the region's dependence on the world market. Over this period, he writes, the region's "foreign trade increased enormously because Senegambia sold more to Europe at higher prices. But the returns in the form of imports may not have been those best calculated to increase Senegambia's own productive capacity."[57] He arranges Senegambian imports from the Atlantic trade into three groups—raw materials (iron and silver), consumer goods (brass and copper ware, pewter, textiles, beads and semiprecious stones, and paper), and nonproductive goods (arms and powder, spirits, and tobacco)— and notes that the importing of raw materials dwindled to almost nothing over the eighteenth century while that of consumer and nonproductive goods rose steadily. Had the region brought in more raw materials for productive use and fewer consumer and nonproductive goods, it might have created "a greater capability of further growth." As it was, the region generally, and Niumi specifically, became more and more dependent on items its wealthy ruling strata desired—items they enjoyed and made use of for social and political purposes, but not items that enabled them to become productive over the long term. For these consumer goods and nonproductive items, they exported slaves, gold, and raw materials that others around the Atlantic basin used in productive ways.

And this may not have been the only way in which Niumi's dependence was growing. Scraps of evidence suggest that at least by late in the period of Atlantic slaving, people living in Niumi had grown dependent on the connection to the Atlantic economic complex for items critical to their survival. This was not always the case. For a part of the sixteenth century Niumi's rulers were dependent on foreign traders for horses, and from early in the state's participation in the Atlantic trade its larger population had become reliant on imported iron for tools and weapons, imported cloth for clothing and symbolic wealth, and more. Yet, approaching the middle of the eighteenth century Niumi seems to have remained largely self-sufficient in foodstuffs and even an exporter of grain. The Royal African Company regularly bought "country corn" from the *mansa* and others in Niumi for the garrison on James Island, and from late in the seventeenth century the company stationed factors in certain of Niumi's villages to buy provisions for the island and waiting ships. Niumi villagers were selling grain to English agents as late as the 1740s.[58] As long as Niumi remained self-sufficient in foodstuffs, growing enough millet and rice to feed its population, it could withstand fluctuations in demand and periodic disruptions of the Atlantic trade.

But a series of about a dozen years after the mid-1740s that were disastrous for agriculture across Senegambia seem to have ushered in a period of change for Niumi. The result of drought and swarms of crop-devouring locusts, the crop failures, followed by regular recurrences, seem to have altered Niumi's agricultural self-sufficiency and, at least for a time, turned it into an importer of foodstuffs from different ecological zones to the east and south. No records from James Fort after 1741 refer to purchases of grain in Niumi. From the 1740s the English began having to look to the river's south bank and farther upriver for grain. More important, within a generation of that time Niumi itself was importing foodstuffs, exchanging salt or merchandise it received through Atlantic trading for grain. Interesting letters out of James Fort from the 1760s and 1770s suggest how the English could get the upper hand with Niumi's *mansa* and stop having to "pay as much in liquor as we get in water." They call for acquiring armed sloops to cut off Niumi's canoes "from the higher parts of the River, from whence they draw their chief supply of Corn."[59] The English factors never got their armed vessels, and they abandoned James Fort for good only four years after the last of these letters was written in 1775. But that those in charge recognized Niumi's vulnerability in its dependence on grain imports shows that by the last third of the eighteenth century the state had a different, more dependent relationship with the trade of the Atlantic and its Senegambian hinterland. At least some of the wealth the state was getting from the Atlantic trade was passing on elsewhere, so people in Niumi could have enough to eat. This was dependence of a different nature—dependence on trade for an absolutely essential commodity rather than a desirable one or a luxury good. From that time on, such dependence would be a recurring theme in Niumi's history, and soon there would be an even greater world economy on which to be dependent.

Notes

1. J.B.L. Durand, *A Voyage to Senegal* (London: Printed for Richard Phillips, 1806), 40.

2. Philip D. Curtin, *Economic Change in Precolonial Africa: Senegambia in the Era of the Slave Trade* (Madison: University of Wisconsin Press, 1975), 309–11.

3. Hugh Trevor-Roper on the program "Listener," November 28, 1963, cited in J.D. Fage, *On the Nature of African History* (Birmingham: Birmingham University Press, 1965), 1–2.

4. John M. Gray, *A History of the Gambia* (London: Frank Cass, 1940), 326–27. Gray refers to Niumi's *mansa* as a "king," but to indicate that the ruler was hardly a sovereign in the European sense, he encloses the title in quotation marks each time he uses it.

5. Compare Sharon E. Nicholson, "Climatic Variations in the Sahel and Other African Regions during the Past Five Centuries," *Journal of Arid Environments* 1 (1978): 3–24, with George E. Brooks, *Landlords and Strangers: Ecology, Society, and Trade in West Africa, 1000–1530* (Boulder, Colo.: Westview Press, 1993), ch. 1.

6. James L.A. Webb Jr., *Desert Frontier: Ecological and Economic Change along the Western Sahel, 1600–1850* (Madison: University of Wisconsin Press, 1995), 5–9.

7. Prior to the twentieth century, it was commonplace for residents of an agricultural village in West Africa to move the village. Reasons for such movement were numerous,

but mostly they had to do with declining fertility of farming land, decreasing healthfulness of the site because of accumulation of waste or growing presence of disease factors, or general depletion through use of the resources in the neighborhood of the village. Such natural events as fire destroying a village, which occurred with frequency in a land where dry-season burning of brush was the first step in the annual agricultural cycle, or a fierce storm leveling a portion of a village, often precipitated a decision to move. Regular movement was expected, and houses thus were constructed more as temporary dwellings than as permanent structures.

8. Webb, *Desert Frontier,* 8.

9. In his diaries and quarterly reports from colonial Gambia's North Bank Province in the 1920s, Commissioner Emilius Hopkinson regularly commented on the difficulty of keeping horses alive in Niumi.

10. This segment relies heavily on Philip D. Curtin, *The Rise and Fall of the Plantation Complex* (Cambridge: Cambridge University Press, 1989), chs. 6 and 7.

11. Philip D. Curtin, *The Tropical Atlantic in the Age of the Slave Trade* (Washington, D.C.: American Historical Association, 1991), 265–66.

12. Alfred W. Crosby, "The Potato Connection," *World History Bulletin* 12 (1996): 1–5; Alfred W. Crosby, *Germs, Seeds, & Animals: Studies in Ecological History* (Armonk, N.Y.: M.E. Sharpe, 1994), 92 and ch. 9.

13. Philip D. Curtin, "The Slave Trade and the Atlantic Basin: Intercontinental Perspectives," in *Key Issues in the Afro-American Experience,* ed. Nathan I. Huggins, Martin Kilson, and Daniel M. Fox (New York: Harcourt Brace Jovanovich, 1971), 90.

14. The early chapters of Gray, *History of the Gambia,* are a detailed account of early European activities in the Gambia River.

15. Richard M. Eaton, *Islamic History as Global History* (Washington, D.C.: American Historical Association, 1990), 27–29; 40–41; Nehemia Levtzion, "Patterns of Islamization in West Africa," in *Conversion to Islam,* ed. Nehemia Levtzion (New York: Holmes & Meier, 1979), 207–16.

16. The English reference to Nandanko's activities is in Joseph Debat and Robert Coulton to the Committee, James Fort, December 8, 1760, T 70/30, 388.

17. There are difficulties inherent in discussing the way things were, a long time ago, in African societies. Most of the evidence pertaining to state structures and functions is from oral tradition, which, at its best, presents a formalized ideal rather than an accurate sense of a state's workings. Furthermore, precolonial African states were far from static. They changed over time to enable rulers to deal with changing economic, social, and political circumstances. It is almost impossible to discuss with any precision the evolutionary nature of a state's governmental apparatus some time into the past because evidence for gradual institutional change does not exist. One must infer a good bit to make the descriptive comments that follow. In addition to oral data, they are based on contemporary European accounts and anthropological studies. Specific citations to these are in Donald R. Wright, "Niumi: The History of a Western Mandinka State Through the Eighteenth Century," Ph.D. dissertation, Indiana University, 1976, ch. 4.

18. This official's title in Niumi was *bukenek.* There was no such official in states located in more central parts of the Mandinka areas, but Wolof polities had such an official. The *bukenek*'s existence in Niumi suggests the kind of borrowing and assimilation that went on over time—in political structure and most other cultural manifestations—where ethnic groups mixed and mingled.

19. Interview with Landing Jammeh, Brikama, Kombo Central District, The Gambia, December 13, 1974.

20. William Wilkinson, *Systema Africanum; or a Treatise Discovering the Intrigues and Arbitrary Proceedings of the Guiney Company* (London: 1690), 11–12, quoted in Gray, *History of the Gambia,* 96.

21. M. St. Vendrille, Commandant of the frigate *Mutiné,* to ?, River Gambia, September 20, 1702, B₄23, 391.

22. Minutes of Council, James Fort, November 18, 1722, Rawlinson MS, C-745–7, 580; Gambia Castle Charge Book, 1736, T 70/1452.

23. See, for example, Journal for the Factory on James Island in the River of Gambia, January 9, 1664, T 70/544; Gambia Journal, James Island, Aug. 31, 1693–Nov. 30, 1699, T 70/546; Account-Ledger, Gambia, 1728, T 70/838; Gambia Castle Charge Book, 1737, T 70/1452.

24. Gambia Journal, James Island, Aug. 31, 1693–Nov. 30, 1699, T 70/546; Gambia Castle Charge Book, 1737, T 70/1452; M. Blain to Commandant Particulier à Gorée, July 18, 1846, 13₆317, 51.

25. Accounts and Charges, James Fort, 1734, T 70/1451.

26. Francis Moore, *Travels into the Inland Parts of Africa* (London: Edward Cave, 1738); Gambia Castle Charge Book, 1736, T 70/1452.

27. Evidence of the importance of regional marriage linkages is mostly from oral traditions, but some contemporary written evidence is informative. In 1737 and 1738 payments appear in Gambia Castle Charge Books to "Jay Sunco," apparently one of the *mansa*'s daughters, who is identified as "a great Fidalgo and Head Wife of the late King of Bursally [Saloum]." The Charge Books are in T 70/1452–3.

28. A considerable body of evidence describes the process a European vessel had to go through to enter and trade in the Gambia River. The requirements changed over time, of course. See, for example, Abbé Demanet, *Nouvelle histoire de l'Afrique françoise,* 2 vols. (Paris: Duchesne, 1767), 1:133–34; Thomas Weaver to Royal African Company, James Island, May 4, 1704, T 70/13, 78; or A.&P., 1789, LXXXIV (646a), pt. 1 (Privy Council Report), Captain Heatley, quoted in Roger Anstey, *The Atlantic Slave Trade and British Abolition, 1760–1810* (Cambridge: Cambridge University Press, 1975), 20.

29. James Skinner et al. to the Committee, James Fort, March 12, 1754, T 70/30, 76; Anth. Rogers and Thos. Harrison to Royal African Company, James Fort, Feb. 12, 1732, T 70/7, 192.

30. John Snow to Royal African Company, Gambia, May 8, 1708, T 70/18, 21; Skinner et al. to the Committee, James Fort, Jan. 28, 1752, T 70/29/34.

31. Jack Goody, *Technology, Tradition, and the State in Africa* (London: Oxford University Press, 1971), ch. 2.

32. Oral traditions contain considerable information relating to such activity, though without a sense of when it took place. Information in "Details sur l'établissement des française dans la rivière de Gambie et sûr le caractere de quesques rois de ce pays," c. 1776, C₆17, leads one to believe that the depredations of rulers and their entourages began earlier, perhaps in the middle of the eighteenth century.

33. Stanley B. Alpern, "What Africans Got for Their Slaves," *History of Africa: A Journal of Method* 22 (1995): 6; Curtin, *Economic Change,* 172.

34. Alpern, "What Africans Got," 23; Curtin, *Economic Change,* 315–19. Demanet, *Nouvelle histoire,* 1, 242–50, is a discussion of merchandise in demand along Africa's Guinea Coast by a man who spent time in Niumi.

35. Richard Jobson, *The Golden Trade* (London: Dawsons of Pall Mall, 1623), 113.

36. Andrew Watson, *Agricultural Innovation in the Early Islamic World: The Diffusion of Crops and Farming Techniques,* 700–1100 (Cambridge: Cambridge University Press, 1983), ch. 6; Marion Johnson, "Cloth as Money: The Cloth Strip Currencies of

Africa," in *Textiles in Africa,* ed. Dale Idiens and K.G. Ponting (London: Pasold Research Fund, 1980), 193–202.

37. B.W. Hodder, "Indigenous Cloth Trade and Markets in Africa," in Idiens and Ponting, *Textiles in Africa,* 205–6.

38. In addition to showing such interesting items as the *mansa* of Niumi's sister being married to the ruler of sometime-enemy Saloum, these records offer evidence that the *mansa* had wives and children residing about the state and beyond, and that the *mansa*'s "people" helped the "Emperor of Fogny," across the river, fight against his neighbors. English letters attest to the importance and pervasiveness of marital obligations. David Francis wrote to the Royal African Company on August 30, 1715 (T 70/6/22), "The French . . . at Albreda . . . are married to the Chief women of the country, who having canoes & boats up the river, prevent the merchants coming down with their trade." And Thomas Rutherford wrote to William Knox from the African Office in London, Sept. 23, 1778 (CO 267/17), "The Castle Slaves [employed by the English on James Island] are so closely connected with the People of the Country by Marriages and other Social Ties, that an Attempt to remove any of the former would infallibly occasion very great Disturbances and Insurrections among the Natives, and render the Safety of the Forts and Settlements highly precarious, as their Defense depends more on the Attachment of the Slaves than on the feeble Force in Civil and Military Servants."

39. Curtin, *Economic Change,* 207–15, 240–41, 312–14; Alpern, "What Africans Got," 12–16; Demanet, *Nouvelle histoire,* 1: 242.

40. R.A. Kea notes similar use of firearms on the Gold and Slave Coasts in "Firearms and Warfare on the Gold and Slave Coasts from the Sixteenth to the Nineteenth Centuries," *Journal of African History* 12 (1971): 185–213. A controversy continues over uses of firearms and their role in the enslaving process, as indicated by J.E. Inikori, "The Import of Firearms into West Africa, 1750–1807: A Quantitative Analysis," *Journal of African History* 18 (1977): 339–68. Alpern, "What Africans Got," 18–22, contains useful discussion of firearms, as does Curtin, *Economic Change,* 324–25; Demanet, *Nouvelle histoire,* 1:249, reports that guns are "only for the Kings and the big men of the court."

41. Information on payments of alcohol to officials and traders is in James Island journals and log books, T 70/544 and 550. The factor's letter is Alexander Cleeve to Royal African Company, James Island, Aug. 24, 1680, T 70/20, 53. See also Curtin, *Economic Change,* 323; and Alpern, "What Africans Got," 24–25. The availability of so much strong spirits must have had an adverse effect on Senegambian society. Moore offers evidence in *Travels,* 85:"The King [of Saloum] and all his Attendance profess the *Mahometan* Religion, notwithstanding they drink so much Strong Liquors; and when he is sober, or not quite fuddled, he prays."

42. Useful studies of this group are Jean Boulègue, *Les Luso-Africains en Sénégambie, xvie-xixe siècle* (Lisbon: Instituto de Investiga, cao Cientifica Tropical, 1989); Curtin, *Economic Change,* 95–100; and Brooks, *Landlords and Strangers,* 188–96.

43. Ledger for the Factory on James Island, begun January 9, 1664 by Capt. John Ladd, T 70/827; Moore, *Travels,* 55.

44. Labat, *Nouvelle relation,* 5:377–78; Prosper Cultru, *Premier voyage de Sieur de la Courbe fait à la coste d'Afrique en 1685* (Paris: Emile Larose, 1913), 196.

45. Frequent mention of Luso-African women in the 1730s is in Accounts and Charges, James Fort, and Gambia Castle Charge Books, 1733–8, T 70/1451–3.

46. Ledger for the Factory on James Island, 1664, T 70/827; Journal of the Factory on James Island, 1665, T 70/545; Natives Employed as Linguisters and Messengers, James Fort, 1720, T 70/1450; Accounts and Charges, James Fort, T 70/1451.

47. Accounts and Charges, James Fort, 1733, T 70/1451; Relation veritable de Jean Baptiste Benoist cy dessous Commandant en Gambia en 1723 et 1724, May 10, 1720, C₆29; Gambia Castle Charge Book, 1735, T 70/1452.

48. Curtin, *Economic Change,* 100; Boulègue, *Luso-Africains,* 66–67, 87; various Accounts and Ledgers, James Fort, 1758–9, T 70/582, 868; Demanet, *Nouvelle histoire,* 1:122–24.

49. Nehemia Levtzion, "The Eighteenth Century: Background to the Islamic Revolutions in West Africa," in *Eighteenth-Century Renewal and Reform in Islam,* ed. Nehemia Levtzion and John O. Voll (Syracuse: Syracuse University Press, 1987), 28.

50. This is from an interview with Afang Seku Fati in Aljamdu, Upper Niumi District, The Gambia, December 14, 1974. Fati said that *Mansa* Jenung Wuleng Sonko asked his ancestors to settle near Berending to work for them. Other information indicates that Sonko reigned in the 1680s.

51. "The Minister of the King of Niumi is named Faudé, is a Marabout—or a Mohammedan Priest." M. Poncet de la Riviere à Government, Gorée, May 25, 1764, C₆15.

52. Philip D. Curtin, "Jihad in West Africa: Early Phases and Inter-Relations in Mauritania and Senegal," *Journal of African History* 12 (1971): 11–24; Levtzion, "Eighteenth Century: Background."

53. The argument in this paragraph is one I make in "The Epic of Kelefa Saane as a Guide to the Nature of Precolonial Senegambian Society—and Vice Versa," *History in Africa: A Journal of Method* 14 (1987): 307–27. It is possible that similar relationships existed among elite lineages of the Kaabu Empire some time earlier and that, as with much else, Kaabu influenced forms of elite society along the Gambia.

54. Kathryn L. Green describes the formation of a Mande-speaking group of Soninke (Sonongui) in northern Cote d'Ivoire in the eighteenth century in "Dyula and Sonongui Roles in the Islamization of the Region of Kong," in *Rural and Urban Islam in West Africa,* ed. Nehemia Levtzion and Humphrey J. Fisher (Boulder, Colo.: Lynn Rienner, 1987), 97–117.

55. Most of the evidence for heightened class solidarity and identification is from oral traditions, but there is corroboration in contemporary written records. In 1734 a "great warrior," Toggomoi Fall, who was the "Prince of Biole" [Baol, a Wolof state immediately north of Niumi's northern neighbors, Siin and Saloum] and a brother to the ruler of Kayor, on Baol's north, paid a visit to James Island. Coming in his company were Maunkey Njie, "a Jelleware [Guelowar, the Wolof equivalent of Soninke] of Colar [Kular]" and the "King of Niumi's people" to make proper introductions. It appears to have been a delegation from the ruling strata of a significant part of western Senegambia. Accounts and Charges, James Fort, 1734, T 70/1451.

56. This argument does not agree with the ideas of historians who believe the Senegambian ruling elites became predatory with their subjects only after the Atlantic slave trade ended, thereby reducing royal revenues. See, for example, Boubacar Barry, "Senegambia from the Sixteenth to the Eighteenth Century: Evolution of the Wolof, Sereer, and 'Tukulor,' " in *General History of Africa, vol. 5, Africa from the Sixteenth to the Eighteenth Century,* ed. B.A. Ogot (Paris: UNESCO, 1992), 262–99; or Martin A. Klein, "Social and Economic Factors in the Muslim Revolution in Senegambia," *Journal of African History* 13 (1972): 419–41. Curtin argues that Royal revenues did not decline with the ending of the Atlantic slave trade in Senegambia and that evidence is not sufficient to postulate increased slave raiding and lawlessness on the part of the ruling groups in "The Abolition of the Slave Trade from Senegambia," in *The Abolition of the Atlantic*

Slave Trade: Origins and Effects in Europe, Africa, and the Americas, ed. David Eltis and James Walvin (Madison: University of Wisconsin Press, 1981), 83–97.

57. Curtin, *Economic Change,* 325–27.

58. Gambia Journal, July 1–Dec. 31, 1741, T 70/576. Various Account and Charge Books from the James Island outpost provide evidence for grain purchases. These are in T 70/545 and 1451–2.

59. Charles O'Hara to Lord of the Treasury, Fort Lewis, Senegal, September 15, 1768, CO 267/14; Matthias McNamara to Earl of Dartmouth, James Fort, June 8, 1775, CO 267/16. Corn here refers to millet or sorghum.

Part III
THE MODERN PERIOD, 1800–1996

Kolimanka Manneh was Niumi's *mansa* from about 1815 to 1823. When he began his reign, European ships entering the Gambia still had to come near Niumi's Atlantic shoreline and fire a multigun salute to the *mansa,* which he ordered returned from his village of Bunyadu, six miles in from Barra Point. The vessels then had to sail twenty-five miles upriver to Juffure, where masters had to pay customs and take on local boatmen and translators before proceeding to trade. When in 1816 the English wanted to reestablish an outpost in the Gambia to stop slaving and encourage legitimate trade, they ended up selecting Banjul Island, connected to the river's *south* bank, rather than their old post on James Island. Part of their reasoning was that Manneh, whose armed vessels patrolled the surrounding waters, would not take lightly to losing his customs payments on slaving vessels. They wanted distance between their new outpost and Niumi's *mansa.* Even on Banjul (which they named Bathurst), five miles across the river and claimed by another Gambian ruler, the English paid Manneh an annual custom for allowing them to settle there. He was indeed one of the last rulers of Niumi to exercise power far outside the confines of the state.

Seventy-four-year-old Jerre Manneh is Kolimanka's great-great-grandson. He lives in a middling-sized compound in Kolimanka's old village of Bunyadu, which today is in Lower Niumi District, The Republic of The Gambia. Through his twenties and thirties Manneh worked as a telephone linesman around Bathurst, and he dabbled in local politics, but for nearly forty years he has been a peanut farmer. Today, he is not doing very well. His peanut harvest last year was small; his annual income is under 2,000 dalasies ($200); his sons have moved to the city; and he spends days quietly in his house. He is regarded locally as a good and wise man, but his influence barely extends beyond his compound.

The fall from power of the Manneh lineage, as seen in a comparison of the lives of these two men, is only one personal manifestation of a broad range of changes that came to the lives of everyone living in Niumi in the nineteenth and twentieth centuries—an era one might call the "modern period" of Niumi's history. Reasons behind the sweeping, fundamental changes in the way Niumi residents led their lives are many, but overriding elements include early encounters with the much more powerful, industrializing, core nations of western Europe, followed by full incorporation on the periphery of a world system that was restructuring, broadening, and strengthening to include nearly every region of the globe. By 1850, only a quarter century after Kolimanka Manneh's death, the Niumi state was greatly weakened and most Niumi villagers were becoming involved in producing peanuts for export to the world system's core; by 1900, when most people in Niumi were struggling to produce peanuts and stay ahead of debts incurred to provide imported food, Niumi's dealings with the British government and the world economy were institutionalized in a formal, colonial relationship; and by 1965 Niumi was part of a newly independent country, The Republic of The Gambia, whose common citizens were locked into an exchange relationship—still peanuts for foodstuffs and other commodities—that was the basis of the country's economy and its political stability. When, by the 1990s, drought, pests, low world-market prices, inept government actions, and rapidly altering social conditions cut peanut exports, weakened The Gambia's financial basis, and altered slightly the nature of its relationship with the world system, the country's government toppled.

This would not mean much for Kolimanka's great-great-grandson, however. Like most Niumi residents, Jerre Manneh's life had long been one restricted by the bounds of poverty and narrow options. Heading into his seventy-fifth year, he did not know how he was going to plant a reasonable peanut crop, nor pay his taxes, nor provide for the twenty-odd people in his compound. Reasonable solutions to his problems simply did not exist.

5

A TIME OF TRANSITION IN NIUMI, 1800–1897

I account for this disparity to the terrible enfield rifle. I saw no less than three men inside the stockade fall before one discharge, so thick were the warriors they never moved after. I would not allow the soldiers to bayonet the bodies of such brave foes.

> —Col. George A.K. d'Arcy, 1866, after storming a Niumi village and finding 350 dead, no wounded, out of a force of 800[1]

Owing to the failure of the ground-nut crop from want of sufficient rain and the destruction of their food crops by locusts, the natives began to feel the pinch of famine early in the year. Their position was made worse from the fact that the merchants, who in former years had given out credits of rice, to tide the people over the rains, decided to discontinue the practice. Already the people had begun to hunt in the forests for roots and berries, and to pawn and sell their clothing, many being reduced to wearing rice-bags as their sole covering.

> —Traveling Commissioner's Report, North Bank Province, 1901[2]

Historians who concern themselves with expansion of the world economy, dependence, and related matters do not agree on when different parts of Africa became dependent on the world market or, using Wallerstein's terminology, became fully incorporated into the modern world-system. It was natural to look at the colonial period in the first half of the twentieth century as the time when European nations established a formal, superior-subordinate relationship with their African colonies. Yet, a quarter-century ago some began to consider the roots of dependency and underdevelopment in the dealings Africans had with European shippers in the seventeenth- and eighteenth-century Atlantic slave trade.[3] Still others, Wallerstein perhaps foremost among them, believe much of Africa went through a "process of incorporation" between 1750 and 1900, when the capitalist world economy needed "new areas of low-cost *production,* as part of the general expansion of its level of economic activity and rate of accumulation."[4] Examination of Niumi's history supports this last belief more than the others. As noted in the previous chapter, evidence exists that makes one wonder if, in their

137

reliance on European imports to exchange for foodstuffs in the last third of the eighteenth century, Niumi residents were not then moving toward a new form of dependence on the growing world market. But in terms of becoming one of the areas of low-cost production for the expanding world economy, Niumi clearly made the change between 1835 and 1850. The happening was related to the industrialization of Western Europe; it resulted in great social and political upheaval that brought about a changing of old ways and, by 1900, the demise of the Niumi state. The nineteenth century is, thus, a true turning point for Niumi's history.

Following a French sacking of the fort on James Island in 1779, the English abandoned the outpost, leaving the Gambia without a seat of British authority for the next thirty-seven years. The French supported a tiny group of traders at Albreda until 1804 and then left as well. During this time, when the British and French were experiencing revolution abroad and at home, followed by wars that involved most of Europe, independent traders remained busy in the Gambia; English, French, and American merchants, as before, came to the river for slaves, hides, beeswax, ivory, and small amounts of gold. The British Parliament's outlawing of the slave trade after 1807 did not slow traffic in the river. Then, in 1816, largely to bring about closing of the Gambia to slavers, the British reestablished a formal presence in the river, not on James Island but on a sand spit called Banjul Island, nearer the river's mouth. Over the period between its abandonment of James Island and its establishment on Banjul, Britain experienced the early phase of the Industrial Revolution. This is largely why, in terms of power, confidence, intent, and ability to do as it wished on foreign shores, it was a different group with which rulers and traders in Niumi had to deal after 1816. Fuller territorial acquisition was not a British goal and would not be for another two-thirds of a century, but commercial control was. Already it was clear to some in Britain that Europe's poorly paid industrial labor force would not consume all that manufacturers were producing. Africans and Asians could help fill the consumption gap. What was necessary for this to happen was the elimination of obstacles to free trade so that merchants armed with inexpensive British manufactures could extend the market beyond rulers and traders to the foreign masses.

So, fairly quickly, using gunboat diplomacy, the British set out different terms for its commercial relations with Niumi. Moreover, as the leading state of the industrializing West, Great Britain would grow ever stronger in relation to Niumi, a typical polity that was not industrializing and increasingly outside the core of states in a central position in the world economy. The small Gambian state would soon fit into a niche in the world system as

---

Box 5. Burungai Sonko

In the minds of people who tell stories about Niumi's past, the state's *mansa* from 1823 to 1833, Burungai Jeriandi Sonko, will remain forever a scoundrel. Sonko usurped the seat of power from the chosen *mansa,* a close relative, first by threatening to expose the intended as an adulterer (after an episode of what one might call "entrapment") and then by threatening to blow up everyone at the installation ceremony with a pile of gunpowder if they did not name him as the next ruler. But while perhaps extreme, such intrigue was not different from what others before him had done to gain political authority. People today remember Sonko's evil exploits partly because he had the misfortune of serving as Niumi's *mansa* at the time when Great Britain decided to use its burgeoning power to break Niumi's lock on river traffic. The British pressed Sonko into ceding them Niumi's entire riverbank for a mile inland, offering him paltry quarterly payments in return for the land and rights to exact tolls on shipping that had long belonged to Niumi's rulers. As he weighed the offer, Sonko had to stare out onto the nearby river at a heavily armed British man-of-war and the first steam fighting vessel ever to churn up West African waters, both with big guns trained on his village of Essau. Then, when Sonko organized a force to oust a British garrison from a new fort on Barra Point, in sight of Essau, he faced troops from various corners of Britain's Atlantic empire, French forces on land and sea, and mounted soldiers from African states on two sides whom the British lured into the fray with promises of payments and spoils. By a final treaty in 1832, Sonko and his headmen had to declare "their sorrow for the outrages they have committed" in "an unjust and cruel war" against the British, and had to confirm their loss of sovereignty over the state's riverbank. After Sonko's pivotal reign—he died within a year of signing the treaty—Niumi's royal lineages began a steady slide toward oblivion. In the face of growing British power to enforce their will and Muslim reformers' inclination and ability to stand against the armies of the state, the royal lineages saw their once strong position weaken steadily. After the 1850s only the ironic support of the same British who had begun the decline kept the *mansa* in charge of state government, and by the end of the century the collapse of the Niumi state in the face of formal British takeover went almost unnoticed. Thus, it was simply being the *mansa* at the beginning of the end rather than his methods of gaining power that left Burungai Sonko unpopular in the hearts of the state's oral traditionists.

---

a supplier of raw materials—in Niumi's case it would be peanuts—and a consumer of manufactured goods. By the end of the century it would be so weak economically and politically, and so dependent on its relationship to the world economy, that Niumi would forfeit its sovereignty to Great

Britain's colonial juggernaut with little fanfare and almost no effective opposition.

Over the same period of British absence from the Gambia, on either side of the turn of the nineteenth century, events were taking place in the Islamic world that would have equally lasting effects on the people of Niumi. For centuries, Muslims in West Africa had been pragmatic merchants, intent on finding accommodation with the rulers and village heads among whom they traveled and lived. They demanded little of their hosts and, when individuals in Niumi converted, accepted a form of worship that included pre-Islamic rites and practices. But reform efforts that had been moving about in the Islamic world since late medieval times began to appear in West Africa, first in a religious hotbed along the middle Senegal River as early as the seventeenth century and then in several locations across West Africa's savannas at the beginning of the nineteenth. Seemingly content with their mutually beneficial *modus vivendi* with the state's *Soninke* rulers into the 1770s, Niumi's Muslims nevertheless were aware of successful reformist *jihads* in West Africa, some not so far away. The growing desire to purify the Islamic faith, to move from accommodationist religious practice to one where Islamic law governed the behavior of all residents of the state, would spread to serious Muslims around the lower Gambia and make Niumi ripe for religious reform at the very time when other social, political, and economic changes were sweeping into the state, so that the traditional ruling lineages were finding it harder and harder to maintain control. Thus, the world outside, from greater distances away, would make itself felt with increasing strength in Niumi, in old ways and new ones.

Revolutionary Change in the West

Global issues were critical for the beginning of western Europe's Industrial Revolution.[5] Worldwide population growth after the seventeenth century, partly the result of the dissemination of American food crops, created more laborers for industrial production, more consumers, and more producers of raw materials. Encounters with new plants, animals, people, and stars in voyages about the globe helped set sixteenth- and seventeenth-century European minds to revolutionary thinking about science. The growing global commerce on which western Europeans were thriving brought in necessary capital and raw materials as it connected them to vast markets. Some of this wealth helped seventeenth-century monarchs turn old sovereignties into more powerful nation-states. Capital, management, labor, government policies that favored risking capital, and entrepreneurs participating in the world economy came together in Great Britain after the middle of the eighteenth century to begin a process of industrialization. In its simplest essence, this involved harnessing new forms of power to machines that produced more, and less expensive, goods in factories.[6] The factories were the places of production; from them soon radiated transportation networks that connected to the world's resources and a global market. This process of change was so dramatic that it has come to be called a revolution—the first real change in the way humans tapped energy and produced goods since the agricultural revolution 10,000 years earlier. Practical invention of new machines to spin and weave cotton were symbolic of Britain's Industrial Revolution into the early nineteenth century.

Because of these changes, the Britain of the 1820s already was dramatically different from the country half a century earlier—in wealth, productive capacity, military capacity, commercial inclination, and attitude. Other countries in western Europe and North America industrialized in England's wake—France, the United States, Germany (after its unification in 1871)—competing to apply science to production, work with new and stronger metals, discover new sources of energy, and perfect mass production. The same spirit of invention that automated textile production by the 1780s provided the railroad and steamship for rapid world transportation on land and sea by the 1830s and brought firearm technology from the flintlock musket to the breech-loading rifle and machine gun by the 1880s. The Industrial Revolution was the major factor in the rise of the West to worldwide economic and political dominance in the twentieth century.

Accompanying the early phase of the Industrial Revolution in western Europe were new thoughts about old human issues. Lumped together, we refer to the body of fresh ideas entering the realm of Western social and political thought after the middle of the eighteenth century as the Enlightenment. Through application of scientific method to consideration of society, government, and economy, European thinkers began to question such previously accepted institutions as slavery, divine-right monarchy, and mercantilism. By the end of the eighteenth century, intellectual forces were in motion in western Europe and North America that eventually would end the slave trade and slavery, give greater consideration to fundamental rights for humans, make steady efforts toward broader participation in government, and open the marketplace to all without government interference.

Thus, in addition to forces and products of industrialization, it was political and social results of the broad, new liberal ideology that enhanced European power in the nineteenth century. Political change at home enabled European states to tap more fully the resources of their populations and to extend their control of trade in foreign areas; then an intensification of national rivalries brought the industrial European nations into intense economic and political competition around the world. The French Revolution unleashed the forces and ideas of Europe's growing middle class, especially the credo of liberalism, which provided the basis for governmentally insured freedoms to act, trade, and prosper. It also brought forth an ideology of nationalism that united peoples of one country across classes and enabled them to mobilize their growing populations in efforts deemed of national importance. Through the middle of the nineteenth century, under policies of laissez-faire economics, such national competition was largely a private affair around the arena of world trade. But in the second half of the century, as England, France, Germany, and the United States continued industrializing at an ever-greater rate, the nations began to recognize that national competition might require the force of government intervention. A series of economic depressions after 1870, created by overproduction of Western industries, led Europeans to believe their long-term economic well-being might require return to rigid mercantile principles. What followed were efforts on the part of European nations to peg out areas of the nonindustrial world as preserved markets for the future and sources of raw materials needed for industry. The result, by the last two decades of the nineteenth century, was a rush of the strongest and wealthiest nations at the core of the world economy to incorporate territory in Africa and Asia into formal empire.

The desire for markets and tropical products was only one reason for western Europe's "scramble for Africa" between 1880 and 1900. All are related to the Industrial Revolution. Medical advances, especially the identification of the malaria suppressant quinine, enabled Europeans to live longer in the tropical environment—long enough for soldiers with superior weapons to conquer and officials with bureaucratic formalities to administer; advances in the technology of firearms and new methods of producing inexpensive steel, from which the weapons were made, gave Europeans novel advantage over the less-well-armed Africans; and faster steamships and new telegraph lines enabled European governments to manage affairs better around the world.[7] Such industrial and technological advancement gave Europeans a sense of superiority over others that was utterly out of touch with any sense of the past, yet that fact did not matter. And because northern Europeans were light skinned and Africans and Asians dark, the former ascribed their superiority to "race." In a corruption of Charles Darwin's ideas of evolution, many Western intellectuals by the 1890s were interpreting recent global events as a struggle among humans for social supremacy that whites were winning and darker peoples were losing because of the latter's lack of fitness to survive. If Africans were to avoid social regression and ultimate extinction, Social Darwinists argued, Europeans had to take them over and "civilize" them. It was a burden, poet Rudyard Kipling would inform the English-speaking world, to bring along these "new-caught, sullen peoples," who were "half devil and half child," but one that whites had to bear.[8] This fit well with arguments missionaries had been making for governmental assistance in efforts to save black souls. And industrialists realized that "civilized" Africans living more like Europeans would want more of the goods European industries turned out and might be able more efficiently and inexpensively to produce raw materials the Western industries required. The new circumstances of the West's industrial existence, with the ideology that was evolving that combined Christianity, philanthropy, and self-aggrandizement, all fit neatly into a rationale for taking political control of territories around the world where previously Europeans had traded freely with Africans, Asians, and Americans. Niumi would be only one very small place in Africa, and Africa just one of several great land masses lying mostly south of the Tropic of Cancer, that would be affected by these changes in western Europe and the world economic system it dominated.

Islam's Militant Strain

Central parts of the Muslim world experienced political decline in the seventeenth and eighteenth centuries. The once-mighty Ottoman, Safavid, and Mogul empires of central Asia either were gone or declining by 1800. Muslims around the world could look about and see not only European interests steadily gaining an upper hand in world trade but also Europeans physically encroaching on Muslim territory. Napoleon's foray into Egypt between 1798 and 1801 exposed the weakness of the Ottomans and made more than a handful of Muslims wonder if they had strayed too far from The Path or, indeed, if the path they were on was leading in the proper direction. Steady Western influences on age-old Muslim lands from southeastern Europe to southern India—at first through trade and related technological and cultural exchange—heightened Muslims' search for a proper response to Western forces. As early as the mid-eighteenth century, followers of Abd al-Wahhab on the Arabian Peninsula attempted to revive Islam by a return to its purer practice. By the nineteenth century, similar purifying reform movements were springing up in various parts of the Islamic world, from Sumatra and India to the Caucasus and lower Nile. Islamic revolutions that swept across West Africa's grasslands in the nineteenth century thus fit into the broad theme of reformist movements in greater Islamic history.

But the more one knows about the spread of Islam in West Africa, the more one recognizes that the fit with the broader efforts at reform across the Muslim world is not tight—that a strain of militancy, probably not unique but not shared widely, existed among some West African Muslims for a long time in the past and that West Africa's Islamic revolutionary leaders, while worldly enough to know of, and be affected by, the currents of reform existing elsewhere, were social revolutionaries with political ends as well as religious reformers. Some scholars trace a continuity in Islamic militancy in West Africa back to the Almoravid movement, an eleventh-century Berber effort at reform in the western Sahara.[9] After the Almoravid decline, a group of Berber scholars, the Zawāyā, kept the tradition of Islamic purity and learning alive in western Sahara religious centers, and these scholars were important in passing along their ideas to a group that originated in the Futa Toro region of the Senegal River valley, the Torodbe. Not so much an ethnic or lineage grouping as a body whose members held similar deep beliefs and shared ascetic ways, the Torodbe were, in John Ralph Willis's words, "slaves or descendants of slaves from a broad spectrum of Sudanic society. Any believer willing to disdain the despised crafts and embrace a sedentary existence which espoused the cultivation of Islamic learning" could enter the fold. It was not kinship, ethnicity, or territorial ownership that held them together, but the brotherhood of Islam.[10] From the Senegal valley, Torodbe scholars took their ideas of religious purity (and perhaps a sense of a heritage of militant reformism) and spread about West Africa, some all the way across the drier savannas to northern Nigeria, some along the middle Niger and upper Senegal, and some southward toward the lower Gambia. If Jahanka lineages kept alive Islamic scholarship and magico-spiritual works between the middle-Gambia and Senegal, it was Torodbe clerics who did the same in the states between Futa Toro and the lower Gambia, and pacificism was not dyed so deeply in their cotton cloaks as it was for the Jahanka.

Zawāyā and Torodbe clerics began showing their militant side late in the seventeenth century. What vexed them was not so much that rulers of the states in which they were residing were not Muslims—quite a few were, of sorts—but that Islamic religious practices in the states were heavily mixed with traditional rites and that the rulers were a long way from enforcing the *Shari'a,* the Islamic law that Muhammad dictated for peoples living in the realm of Islam.[11] In most cases the reformers followed proper form by attempting to foster change through peaceful means (*jihad* of the tongue and hands) and then purifying themselves (*jihad* of the heart) before resorting to religious war (*jihad* of the sword). The Mauritanian cleric Nāsir al-Dīn may rightfully be regarded as the source of much of the subsequent Islamic militancy around Senegambia and beyond. In the 1660s he began preaching conversion and reform, and he sent missionaries to move and spread the word among peoples south of the Senegal River. This *toubenan* reform movement, as the French on the Senegal knew it, gained popular support among persons in the Wolof states and further afield. Nāsir al-Dīn's political uprising against traditional rulers in Futa Toro and Jolof in the 1670s did not last long after his death in 1674, but a militant *jihad* soon broke out in Bondu, farther up the Senegal, in the 1690s, and then in the highland area of Futa Jalon to the south. The states formed from these efforts quickly moved away from reform and became similar to the old secular polities, but the *toubenan* spirit never quite cleared from the air south of the Senegal.[12]

In the middle of the eighteenth century the West African leader of the Qadiriyya brotherhood began espousing reform, and his ideas spread widely from a center north of Timbuktu. A second *jihad* in Futa Toro was short-lived, but in the early part of the nineteenth century Torodbe reformers led movements to purify Islamic societies on a larger scale and with greater success: Usuman dan Fodio, a local Qadiriyya leader, led a successful *jihad* in the Hausa states of northern Nigeria in the first decade of the century, creating the Caliphate of Sokoto that would last into the twentieth century; and Ahmadu Lobbo overcame non-Muslim rulers along the middle Niger and formed the fundamentalist Caliphate of Hamdullahi. News of such activity reverberated around West Africa's Muslim world, especially among clerics who were disaffected with their own rulers.

Thus, Niumi was on the edge of an area long buffeted by currents of Islamic reform. Muslim lineages in the state, relatives of some of the oldest and strongest Torodbe reformers in Senegambia, long carried the idea of *jihad* in their intellectual baggage. They would be good candidates to pick up the spirit of *jihad*, the prescribed effort to purify the faith, when it entered the region with a handful of individual reformers in the decades after 1850.[13] In this vein, they would make a prolonged effort to unseat Niumi's non-Muslim *Soninke* lineages, and would leave in their wake a weakened state unable to mount any kind of effective resistance to British takeover in the last decade of the century.

Weakening of the Niumi State

It was not the decline or eventual halt of Atlantic slaving that brought about a crisis for Niumi's ruling elite. Slave exports via the river remained on a relatively steady, high plateau through the first two-thirds of the eighteenth century, averaging between 1,000 and 1,500 per year. The trade fell to about 800 per year in the 1770s, to 300 per year in the 1780s and 1790s, and then to 150 per year in the first decade of the nineteenth century.[14] It came to a halt soon after 1816. But Niumi's ruling families and their entourages received their wealth not from the capture and sale of slaves so much as from the tolls they charged passing commerce—*any* commerce. So it is important to recognize that as the slave trade was declining over the half century after 1770, other trade (termed "legitimate" trade by the anti-slave-trade forces in England) was taking up the slack, and its purveyors continued to provide Niumi's rulers revenue from tolls on shipping. Hides, beeswax, ivory, gold—all were in demand internationally and all could be obtained in the Gambia for fair, albeit rising, prices. Niumi's rulers taxed the movement of such trade across its boundaries and, more importantly for state revenue, continued to charge tolls, duties, and fees to shippers plying the legitimate trade as it had done for those coming to the river primarily for slaves.[15]

What seems most to have brought about the start of a long decline of Niumi's ruling class and served as a trigger for the start of sweeping political, social, and economic change in the region was not the waning slave trade but the new attitude Britishers brought with them when they returned to the Gambia following the Napoleonic Wars. Always before, trade in the river was on African terms. British garrisons on James Island since 1660 were so dependent on the good graces of residents of Niumi for food, water, and cultural mediation to facilitate trade that it could not have been otherwise. Customs that traders in the river had respected for a century or more brought Niumi's ruling lineages the tolls and fees that enabled them to maintain their sizable retinues and their elite lifestyles. But the British who resettled in the Gambia in 1816 were a different bunch, separated from the previous group by a long generation that had seen the effects of early industrial technology and two decades of warfare. These men commanded greater power relative to Niumi, held different attitudes about trade and about who was in charge, and in a broad sense tended to recognize a greater cultural, social, and technological distance between themselves and the Africans among whom they came to reside.[16] This would not bode well for the toll collectors residing along the north bank of the lower river.

As an act of war against their French enemies in 1800, the British had taken Gorée Island, and for fifteen years English, Africans, Anglo-Africans, Franco-Africans, Luso-Africans, and a host of others conducted coastal trading from the rocky Atlantic outpost nestled just below Cape Verde. When they returned the island to France a year after the Treaty of Vienna in 1815, the British resettled the Goréean community on Banjul Island, eight miles up the Gambia from its Atlantic entrance at Cape St. Mary's. The low, sandy island had no regular inhabitants. For some years prior to its British occupation, women from Niumi had made residences there during the rainy season for growing rice and cotton.[17] The British named the island Bathurst after the British colonial secretary, the Earl of Bathurst. The trans-

---

Box 6. Niumi and the Settlement of Bathurst

From a late-twentieth-century perspective it is clear that Britain's deci-sion to locate its principal Gambian city and port on the *south* side of the river was one of the most damaging acts imaginable for the subse-quent history of Niumi. Not only did all trade soon come to focus on Bathurst, but almost all colonial and postcolonial investment in develop-ment occurred there. Today, Banjul (the former Bathurst) and Kombo–St. Mary's (the adjacent region on the river's south bank) are far and away the most populous, prosperous, developed sectors of The Re-public of The Gambia. The country's major medical, educational, bank-ing, and commercial institutions are located there. Along paved streets and roads residents obtain safe water from spigots under the illumina-tion of streetlights. A forty-five minute ferry ride across the river, Niumi is a different world. It has one paved road, electricity only in the vicinity of Barra Point and a handful of locations where individuals or groups own diesel generators, no water purification, minimal sanitary facilities, one major (since 1988) and one minor health center and a couple of dispensaries staffed by technicians, and no banks. Before 1995 it had no secondary school. People in Niumi who have business to do have to cross the river to do it, an effort that takes a full day. It was not that way two centuries ago, but the focus of power and wealth switched sides of the river, away from Niumi, over several decades after the British es-tablished their commercial, strategic, and (eventually) colonial head-quarters on Banjul Island. Nothing in Niumi has been the same since.

---

planted merchants believed there was sufficient trade in the river to justify expenditures on the new outpost, but the British government had another reason for Bathurst's existence. In a climate of growing humanitarianism, Parliament had outlawed the slave trade as of 1808, but most people famil-iar with the trade knew that legislation alone would not halt the centuries-old traffic. Big guns at the Bathurst settlement would be a major step toward stemming illegal slaving in the Gambia, by this time carried on mostly by Americans in vessels under the Spanish flag.

Standing between the Bathurst merchants and commercial profit, how-ever, was the centuries-old custom of shippers paying tolls and excises to the traditional master of the river's trade: Niumi's *mansa*. The small British expedition that reconnoitered in 1815, prior to resettling the traders from Gorée, was in no position to dictate new terms. The expedition's leader, Captain Alexander Grant, was careful to assure *Mansa* Kolimanka Manneh that he could continue to collect the same tolls. (Grant did explain that vessels conducting slaving in the river would be seized without payment.) So, for a brief time, entering vessels continued to fire salutes to the *mansa* and then sail to Juffure, where their captains notified the state's *falifo* and paid their dues. But after June 1817 it became apparent that the Bathurst merchants were not ones to follow old ways. Because of vague charges of "misconduct on the part of the king and his people," Grant advised captains entering the river to pay but half of Niumi's ordinary duties and fees. Early in 1820, when ship masters complained of the time it was taking to visit Juffure for customs payments (one vessel having to lay by for ten days as someone went to the royal village to fetch the absent *falifo)*, Grant began having the Bathurst customs officer collect the *mansa*'s due and deliver it to him. Such an arrangement continued until July 1822, when, at the behest of Bathurst traders, administrator Charles MacCarthy simply began paying values considered roughly equal to Niumi's traditional tolls out of revenue accumulating from Bathurst's own import duties. Within half a dozen years it was apparent that old relationships in the river no longer held. Soon the British would begin pressing their new superiority in the relationship. Once they did, gunboat diplomacy, rather than careful negotiation, would characterize their actions toward Niumi, and it would remain that way for the next half century.[18]

The British saw clearly from Bathurst's early years what they had to do. Their outpost rested on shifty ground both in a literal sense—Banjul being little more than a good-sized sandbar backed by swamps and mangroves— and a fiscal one. Costs of maintaining the settlement came from import duties worth in the neighborhood of £40,000 into the 1820s, but Niumi's customary tolls added to shippers' expenses, and they passed all of these along to the merchants at Bathurst. The latter grew increasingly disturbed. Then, when Manneh sensed he was not receiving his due, he made bellicose gestures that threatened the poorly garrisoned British settlement. "The King has frequently crossed over and levied contributions on the Merchants," reads one retrospective critique of Grant's years in charge, "and one very disgraceful transaction took place. . . . The King . . . went to Government House and told the Commandant that he would take the place and burn his house if he did not give him what he wanted, and I am sorry to say that he succeeded in intimidating the Commandant."[19]

To exasperate the British further, at the same time they settled Bathurst the French had reestablished themselves at Albreda, twenty-five miles up-river on Niumi's riverbank. Bathurst merchants suspected that French goods were entering the river duty free, giving their rivals commercial advantage. A way for the British to act toward solving all these problems and to gain firmer command of shipping in the river and thus clamp down more strongly on the slave trade was to take control of the strategic river-bank across from Bathurst—territory that had been Niumi's since before Europeans knew there was a Gambia River. Ceding its riverbank and control of shipping was not something Niumi's rulers would do lightly.[20]

In 1823 Kolimanka Manneh died. As on most occasions when political authority in the state moved from one lineage and village to another, there was a period of disruption. The British took the occasion to press Niumi to cede its riverbank. Once installed, the new *mansa*, Burungai Sonko, refused such a request, recognizing that giving up its territory along the Gambia would be tantamount to committing strategic, financial, and political suicide. But the British brought in a show of force aboard the HMS *Maidstone*, one of the cruisers of the British African Squadron patrolling the coast for illegal slaving, and the *African*, the first British steam vessel in African waters. Each was armed to a degree never before witnessed in Gambian circles. Under such pressure, the British offer of quarterly payments of 400 Spanish dollars (about £87) in exchange for cession of a strip of Niumi's riverbank a mile wide and "the sole right to the navigation of the River Gambia with all claims and demands for customs or dues of whatever sort to which they have been entitled and have received from time immemorial" (excepting whatever tolls Niumi's rulers wished to charge French vessels visiting Albreda) did not appear to be such a bad deal. On June 9, 1826, Sonko signed the treaty. It was symbolic of the altered circumstances from a decade earlier, of the new power relationship with the British and the new commercial circumstances in which Niumi found itself with the end of a demand for slaves for the Atlantic trade. Although Niumi's rulers could not have realized it at the time, it was symbolic also of the beginning of the decline of Niumi's sovereignty and of a way of life for its ruling groups that had enabled them to live as elites among peoples of the region for several centuries. Thereafter, change would come with increasing speed, and for the *Soninke*—the old ruling class of the Gambia—it would not be for the better.

If the traders and administrators in Bathurst thought that Niumi's rulers were going to sign away their livelihood with nothing more than foot drag-ging, the next half dozen years proved how wrong they could be. As effects of the new treaty, especially of the loss of their traditional shipping customs, became evident, a general malaise settled among Niumi's ruling families. When the British almost immediately began construction of a fort on Barra Point in the Ceded Mile (as the British began calling their newly acquired territory along Niumi's riverbank), followed by erection of a bat-tery of guns in the fort and stationing there of a garrison of thirty troops from a force sent to the Gambia from Sierra Leone, Sonko and his entou-rage made their discontent known. One British official in 1827 labeled

Sonko "an insane drunkard, who has always been troublesome, and can only be restrained by fear."[21] Reports circulated around Bathurst in 1829 that the *mansa* was "sorry he ever ceded any part of his territory," and early in 1830 Sonko's men seized part of the cargo of a British coasting vessel that ran aground at the river's mouth, as was his traditional right, and preferred losing half of his annual payments from the British to returning the cargo. Thereafter Niumi's ruler was "frequently troublesome."[22]

Events came to a head in 1831, triggered by what now seems to have been part arrogant aggression and part cultural ignorance on the part of Bathurst's settlers.[23] An English agricultural society wanted to establish a colony of pensioners and liberated slaves on Dog Island, off a point of land on the Ceded Mile, to experiment with the growing of hemp. They did not realize that Dog Island was where residents of one of Niumi's seven royal villages, Sitanunku, harbored their most precious fetishes and animist spirits.[24] No one was to reside there, let alone foreigners. Within a matter of weeks, Sitanunku villagers had run off the Dog Island settlers and Niumi's *mansa* had closed all paths to trade and stopped canoes from going to Bathurst with supplies. Bathurst authorities reinforced the garrison at Fort Bullen. On August 22 and 23 a large force from Sonko's village burned a British settlement of discharged soldiers outside the fort's walls, engaged the fort's garrison, and forced it to flee for safety across the river. The British reacted quickly and showed Niumi just how far reaching were their resources. They organized a blockade of Niumi's coastline to cut the state from supplies of food and munitions, sent an influential African trader to the states surrounding Niumi to arrange for its isolation by land (and to persuade one of the states to threaten attack on Niumi's eastern border, forcing Sonko to send some of his force to the other side of the state), called for more troops from Britain's colony in Sierra Leone, and asked the French on Gorée for assistance. Wanting to protect the interests of the traders at Albreda, France sent a warship to bombard Essau and harass the soldiers there over ten days. The governor of Senegal followed with eight officers and forty-five men to bolster the British force.

On November 11 a well-armed unit under British command—451 officers and men, backed by the heavy cannon on two armed colonial vessels—assaulted Barra Point and retook Fort Bullen from a Niumi force that "could not have been less than 2000." Six days later the combined British and French force marched on Essau and engaged the Niumi army in a five-hour fight that ended in a standoff. Eleven in the colonial force were killed and fifty-seven wounded. Niumi may have experienced greater casualties. The colonials kept up a daily fire on Essau for the next month, and it was wearing. On December 19 the *mansa* of Kombo, the state on the south side of the river, went to Bathurst and, speaking for Niumi's ruler, asked the British for peace. He suggested that the people of Niumi were "so reduced as to consent to any conditions." The Bathurst colony's lieutenant governor, George Rendall, assessed the situation at the end of January 1832: "The people of [Niumi] have suffered so severely from the strict blockade kept upon their coast, and by the kings of Salum and Baddibu who closed their communications on the landside that I am induced to hope they will be very quiet for some time to come."[25]

The formal result of the "Barra War" was a humiliating treaty, signed on January 5, 1832, by Sonko and seventeen other Niumi officials, the provisions of which abridged the sovereignty of the state. Those from the Niumi side, "having publicly declared their sorrow, for the outrages they have committed, and given their solemn promise never to offend again," had to deliver hostages from each royal lineage for their "good faith," ratify again the 1826 treaty ceding a mile of the state's riverbank, agree to seek the consent of the lieutenant governor of Bathurst before selecting a new *mansa,* indemnify residents of Barra Point and Dog Island for losses sustained, turn over all pieces of ordinance in Essau, and promise "to hold peace and friendship with the subjects of His Majesty the King of Great Britain for ever."[26] After at least three centuries of maintaining Niumi's sovereignty in the face of warfare, slave raiding, and threats from within and without, the state's ruling lineages had met their match.

New Systems of Production and Exchange: The Peanut Revolution

Just a year before Niumi's soldiers ran the British garrison out of Fort Bullen, in 1831, British traders had sent a few baskets of locally grown peanuts to the British Institute for Tropical Agriculture in the West Indies. They had been looking for primary products in world demand they could obtain along the banks of the Gambia in exchange for the consumer goods being manufactured in western Europe in ever-greater quantity. This time they found one.

Although the Portuguese brought peanuts to West Africa from Brazil as early as the sixteenth century, farmers in Niumi never paid them special attention—nor did anyone else along the Gambia River for quite a long time.[27] Over two centuries and more, peanuts had become just one more of a host of crops grown for local consumption, mainly as a hedge against failure of the grains. When people were *really* hungry, they would eat peanuts. Ruling elites had their slaves feed the tops of the plants to their horses and some believed this made the mounts stronger and likely to live longer than horses that did not have peanut tops in their fodder.

But peanuts in the Gambia would have their day. Through the first third of the nineteenth century, demand grew steadily in Europe for vegetable fats and oils that could be used in candles, cooking oils, lubricants, and soap. For soap in particular, it was a time when people around the Western world were becoming aware of the relationship of personal hygiene to good health. A popular tropical oil in use for soap production since the latter part of the eighteenth century was palm oil, obtained along the forested coasts of lower Guinea. England's Lever Brothers combined palm oil with olive oil and turned out the famous Palmolive brand that sold briskly. In addition, French cooks had begun using peanut oil as a cheaper substitute for olive oil, and soon there were experiments with its use in soap manufacture. Four years after the initial British testing of Gambian peanuts, 213 baskets of the product left the Gambia and ended up at Forster and Smith, the London firm that was to become Britain's leading peanut importer. Forster and Smith had experience in the West African trade; they were importers of palm oil, rice, beeswax, and mahogany. In 1835 the firm built a mill in London to crush peanuts and render their oil, and the demand for peanuts was under way.

Other factors relating to the world market aided the rise of peanut pro-duction for export in Niumi. In Europe of the 1830s factory workers and common laborers made paltry wages, so there were not masses of people with disposable money for the purchase of industry's large and growing output. This was especially true for Britain's leading industry: textiles. In-dustrialists saw African consumers as possible candidates to fill the con-sumption gap. To entice a broader range of Africans to consume European goods, British and French traders offered liberal credit to almost anyone, including many who previously had been outside the commercial network in the Gambia River. Large numbers of people with fewer means and less influence in Niumi found it possible to obtain imported goods for trading. Once peanuts proved to be a major item in demand, common peasants had a clear way to pay their debts and obtain still more inexpensive European manufactures that they increasingly desired. After the 1830s a much broader segment of Niumi's population became involved in the market, eventually acquiring more products on credit and paying off their debts with peanuts.

Gambian peanut exports grew for a time with unprecedented speed. A market for Gambian peanuts blossomed in the United States after 1835, and soon three-quarters of the Gambian peanut crop was crossing the Atlantic and ending up for sale in New York and New England, at fruit markets and newsstands and at American circuses and shows. A restrictive American tariff in 1842 all but stopped such imports momentarily, and then they fluc-

tuated wildly. But France stepped in as the major buyer of Gambian peanuts, and with the exception of lean years caused by revolution and war, it
would remain such for a long time. The initial reason for French interest
was that, unlike British consumers, the French did not take to the yellow
palm-oil soaps. Until the soap industry could find a method to remove the
yellow, such soaps had a small market in France. But after experimentation,
Marseille soap makers found they could make a blue marble soap with
peanut oil as a major ingredient, and not long afterward the rush for the
small legume was on. Marseille imported a ton of peanuts in 1841, 205 tons
in 1845, 5,500 in 1854.[28]

As European demand grew, farmers along the Gambia responded. By the
1850s Gambians, who never had exported a nut before 1830, were exporting, on average, over 10,000 tons of peanuts a year with a value in some
years of over £130,000; by the end of the century it was 30,000 tons at
£200,000.[29] Providing additional incentive were the falling prices of European manufactured goods, the result of great increases in productive efficiency. Between 1817 and 1850 the price of British textiles dropped by 75
percent, for instance, prompting Niumi's growers of cotton and weavers to
buy imported cloth, with profits from peanut sales, rather than to produce
their own. With world prices for peanuts holding firm in spite of the increased African production, entering the market for a number of years was
simply smart economics.[30]

Like other regions of coast-wise Senegambia, Niumi quickly became a
region of large-scale peanut exporting. Its male farmers made the transition
to export production over a short time and remained the state's major peanut producers thereafter. They did so, argues economist Jan Hogendorn,
largely because of particular circumstances of the time and place. Hogendorn believes that such farmers had surplus land and wanted a variety of
reasonably priced European products at the very time the world market
beckoned. They were able to clear additional land, interplant peanuts with
food crops, and produce nuts for export while for a long time continuing to
grow sufficient food for their regular consumption.[31] The continuing existence of slavery all about the region played a role too. By the 1840s captives from wars who once might have been marched toward the coast for
sale and shipment across the Atlantic could be taken to centers of export
production like Niumi and sold there. Slave laborers were important elements in Niumi's peanut production; the numbers and proportion of slaves
in Niumi grew through the middle and late nineteenth century.

But another phenomenon added considerably to Niumi's peanut exports
and became an important part of seasonal life and the workings of Niumi's
peanut-based economy since the 1840s: what locals call "strange farming."

This involved persons from elsewhere, often some distance away (the strangers), migrating to Niumi before the beginning of the rainy season, taking up temporary residence in a village, making a peanut crop, selling it, and returning home with cash or goods.[32] The roots of strange farming may extend back even earlier, to the eighteenth century, when the Atlantic slave trade was at its height. Dealers who marched slave caravans down to Juffure in the dry winter months for sale to Europeans there might encounter low demand, and thus low prices, on arrival. One option they had to selling cheaply was to rent land and put the slaves to work growing a crop, which they would sell once harvested and then hope that prices for slaves were better. It is possible that at the same time small handfuls of farmers from the region of the upper Senegal and Gambia Rivers moved down toward the Gambia's mouth for a season of farming nearer points of exchange with European merchants. These early strange farmers sold their crop for trade goods and then marched inland with them and became traveling merchants themselves over the dry season.[33]

Once Niumi's farmers began growing peanuts for cash, the banks of the lower river lured persons from as far away as modern Guinea and Mali, intent on bettering their social and economic position at home in ways that involved possessing some wealth. A number of young men went strange farming for one or several seasons to acquire bride wealth for marriage. Aware of traditional requirements to share wealth with needy kinsmen, they recognized the benefits of improving one's personal economic position some distance away from family demands. Niumi had the advantage of having farming land near the river (meaning transportation costs could be low), coupled with a relatively light population. The prospective strange farmer would come to one of Niumi's villages between late April and early June and inform the village head that he wanted to make a crop with the coming rains. The village head either would assume the role of the individual's landlord or would designate another villager to serve in that position. In either case, the village head collected a custom payment from the stranger, a portion of which went to Niumi's *mansa*. The landlord would provide a dwelling for the stranger, see to it that he had sufficient food for the farming season, designate a plot of land for the stranger to farm, and make sure the stranger had tools and seed. The stranger would be required to work for part of a week, normally three or four days, in his landlord's fields, and he would give the landlord one-tenth or a little more of the peanuts he produced.[34] The stranger would be gone soon after the sale of his crop, but one strange farmer might return to the same village several years running if the experience was profitable. In this way, the land of Niumi produced more peanuts than its regular, small population could grow.

The merchant populations at Bathurst and Albreda and British officials up and down Africa's west coast encouraged the migration of distant farmers or anything else that would increase peanut production and trade in Niumi. Supplying peanuts for the European market for oils was a worthy engagement for Gambian merchants, but every bit as important were issues related to colonial revenue. British outposts along Africa's coast—like Bathurst—were proving expensive. The troops, gunboats, colonial steamers, constables, and administrators cost money, and it was money for which British taxpayers did not want to be the source. The key to having funds for such settlements was a bustling commerce. British port authorities at Bathurst levied duties on goods imported; as the quantity of imports rose to exchange for peanuts, so did Bathurst revenues. Then, in 1863, as indigenous warfare threatened trade and production up and down the river and made the British administrator ponder expensive military operations, Britain's administrator in Bathurst imposed an export tax on peanuts.[35] It was not a large tax, but one that brought in greater revenue as peanut production climbed toward the century's end. Its historical importance was great, however, for taxes on peanut exports of one sort or another would become an important part of Gambian revenues from that time on, through the period of formal British control of its Gambia colony and through the early decades of independence.

There were more reasons for common folk to grow peanuts. Always a supplementary crop for the peasant, the peanut normally was of minor significance and thus was outside the realm of taxation by the ruling elites of African states. Niumi's rulers might get a tenth of a peasant's millet crop, but if they took anything of the peanuts that common farmers grew, it was only the tops of the plants (for fodder), which farmers did not want anyway. Now, with demand for peanuts at the waterside expanding, peasants could grow peanuts and trade them to European buyers and thus, seemingly for the first time, gain access to a significant source of wealth all their own. With such wealth they soon were able to acquire commodities that previously only the ruling elites could afford—metalware and cloth, decorative items and luxury goods, and especially weapons, in this case firearms and gunpowder. These last items turned out to be of particular importance, for such weapons would enable the peasantry at first to resist their frequently oppressive *Soninke* rulers, and then, as peanut exports and firearm imports continued to mount, to rise and attempt to overthrow them for good. This seems to be what happened in Niumi over the half century following 1830, when the region experienced one of its most disruptive periods ever: a time of far-reaching political, social, and economic change that Gambians know as the era of the Soninke-Marabout Wars.[36]

The Soninke-Marabout Wars

Before the nineteenth century, Muslim elements in Niumi tended to be apolitical and peaceful. They were distinct minorities among Niumi's common villagers, who were bound to the soil, tied to their ancestors, and intent on placating the spirits of both. The pragmatic Muslims embraced an attitude of compromise that brought them to accept traditional African elements in their religious practices. They could perform divination and supernatural work for non-Muslim rulers and live in a land ruled by infidels because they held to a pacificism that counseled removal from affairs of state and accommodation where necessary or practical. This was not unique for Muslims in Niumi: it was the case across much of West Africa before the eighteenth century.

But militant Islam with roots extending deep in West African history began to have its effects on Niumi around the middle of the nineteenth century. The human catalyst for Muslim-led uprisings along the Gambia was a member of a Futa Toro lineage named *Shaykh* Umar Tal. Umar may have been a typical itinerant Torodbe cleric through his early life, but on a pilgrimage to Mecca in 1830 he was made head of a new Islamic brotherhood, the Tijaniyya, which through its ritual and enhanced mysticism had greater appeal to common people. When Umar returned he was not just another Muslim pilgrim and mystic, but head of the Tijaniyya in West Africa and a scholar of considerable repute. Moreover, he burned with the reformist fire that previous Torodbe clerics had kindled in Futa Toro. After two decades of travel and teaching, Umar launched a *jihad* around the headwaters of the Senegal and then marched north and eastwards, overcoming large chunks of territory under non-Muslim authority. Before his death in 1864, his empire extended all the way to Timbuktu and contained thousands of square miles of West Africa's grasslands.[37]

Niumi's connection with *Shaykh* Umar and its ties to Islamic reform were through a Torodbe cleric residing in the state of Baddibu immediately east of Niumi. His name was Maba Diakhou.[38] Maba's father moved to Baddibu from Futa Toro around the beginning of the nineteenth century and established a Qur'anic school there. As was typical, Maba studied away from home through early adulthood. In 1850, not long after he had returned to live and teach in Baddibu, *Shaykh* Umar visited him, acquainted him with the Tijaniyya, and blew on the embers of Islamic revival that already may have been glowing within Maba.

The glow probably existed because the lower Gambian states were prime targets for political, social, and religious reform. By mid-century the ruling lineages of the states, the *Soninke,* had become weak and ineffective. Like

Niumi's rulers, most had difficulty controlling the warriors in their midst. The *Soninke* drank excessively, took what they wanted from peasants, flaunted their non-Islamic worship of spirits, and lived off the rest of the population at a time when the rest no longer needed the protection the *Soninke* offered. *Mansa* Demba Sonko of Niumi, whom the British described not long after he gained the position in 1834 as "very well disposed and sensible, anxious for peace," did not wear well. Twenty years later the British administrator in Bathurst, Luke Smythe O'Connor, described Sonko as "a man of unwieldly frame and indolent habits . . . much changed in appearance, depressed, attended by few adherents, and in reality holding a shadow of power in his dominions."[39] Sonko had turned increasingly to mercenaries to prop up his authority, and some of them were out of control. They rustled cattle, plundered traders, and harassed Muslims in their enclave villages. When Jokadu rose in 1853 in the same quest for independence from Niumi it had been attempting for the better part of a century, Sonko employed a Serahuli warlord, Ansumana Jaju, to put down the rebellion, giving Jaju one of his daughters in marriage and three of his sons as warriors in the transaction. Then Jaju would not leave. Instead, he and his mercenaries did as they pleased. O'Connor believed they "had almost unlimited sway" and were the "main cause of aggressions" in Niumi.[40]

What is more, the recent rise of peanut production for export gave Niumi's peasants the means to fight against their oppressors. Income from the sale of peanuts went mostly to the growers and merchants who transported the nuts to the riverside. With the new income they acquired firearms, which British and French merchants were importing in enormous quantities, and with the weapons they took on their oppressive rulers.[41] Through the 1840s and 1850s, states like Niumi had to use more of their resources to keep dependent areas like Jokadu in check. By 1860 reform and rebellion were ripe along the entire lower Gambia's northern bank, and Maba was well placed geographically, spiritually, and militarily to lead the movement.

Maba led a rapid and successful *jihad* against the *Soninke* rulers of Baddibu in 1861, and this effort encouraged Muslims in Niumi. In April 1862, after nearly three decades in power, Demba Sonko died in Berending. In the disorder that followed the transition of power, 700 Niumi Muslims rose and stormed Jokadu, forcing its Niumi-backed *Soninke* ruler to shave his head (signifying capitulation to Islam). They then called on Maba for help in a war against Niumi's ruling lineages. Maba sent his brother, Abdu, with a large force and together the Muslims swept across Niumi. Through early May they burned *Soninke* villages and generally had their way. At Berending they burned the town and exhumed and desecrated Demba

---

Box 7. **Kelefa**

Up and down the Gambia and across a larger area from Senegal to Guinea, the most popular tale sung and told by *griots,* society's bards, is the epic of Kelefa Sanneh. Its popularity is due partly to the music—it is a strapping good tune—but also to Kelefa's symbolic significance: he was the last of the great *Soninke* warriors.

Kelefa was a member of a royal lineage in a state south of the Gambia. By young adulthood he had a reputation as one of the fiercest warriors alive. On horseback, with spear, he would take on anybody and fight for any noble cause. His contempt for fear and death was legendary. When Niumi's *Mansa* Demba Sonko faced rebellion in Jokadu, he sought help from various *Soninke* warriors. As Jokadu's success mounted, Sonko turned to Kelefa. In spite of warnings of doom from seers and advisers, Kelefa rode to Niumi to join the battle. He was leading Niumi's royal forces toward victory, riding about and using his spear with more effectiveness than ever, when he met his symbolic fate. A soldier of Jokadu paid a Muslim diviner to bless a bullet for his gun, climbed a tree with his weapon in hand, and just as Kelefa was raising his spear to thrust it at another Jokadu fighter, the gunman fired and hit Kelefa in the chest. Fighting from a distance with a firearm, rather than face to face, was the height of cowardice in the eyes of the *Soninke,* but it did not matter. The tide of battle turned in Jokadu's favor, Kelefa left the field and eventually died in Juffure, and the glory days of the *Soninke* warriors were numbered. Hearing the story of the death of the greatest of these warriors, at the hands of a Muslim-inspired gunman who was hiding in a tree, reminds Gambians of the end of *Soninke* rule in the Gambian states and the demise of an elite lifestyle that had existed for several centuries.

Sonko's corpse. Then they pushed on toward Essau, where the state's traditional war leader, the *suma,* had drawn the remaining *Soninke* behind a stockade for a final stand.

In dire straits, the *suma* asked the British for assistance. As fate would have it, the administrator of the small colony, George A.K. d'Arcy, was an ardent anti-Muslim. As a colonel with the Third West Indian Regiment, he had formed his low opinion of Muslims during service in India. He considered Gambian Muslims "crafty, ambitious and sensual, besides being given to slave labour and dealing." His opinion of Niumi's ruling lineages and their retainers was not a great deal better—they were "warlike drones"; yet d'Arcy rationalized that at least "from this wild unthinking people the kings had been hitherto elected," and he seemed intent on keeping it that way. So with Niumi's *Soninkes* under siege, d'Arcy sent members of the Gambia Militia to beef up West Indian Regiment troops at Fort Bullen on Barra Point, where several hundred *Soninke* women and children sought protection. One six-pound field piece, two howitzers, and two rocket guns pointed out over Essau's stockade at the Muslim lines, 1,000 yards east of the fort. Inside the stockade d'Arcy could see the *Soninke* army, "all dressed in the death-colour, yellow, and sounding their fetish bell," readying a "desperate stand."[42]

The big British guns deterred the Muslims for the time, but it could not thwart the spirit of their leaders. At a meeting convened at Albreda between Muslims and the state's rulers, d'Arcy made known his displeasure at the Muslim actions and forced a cease-fire and Muslim recognition of a new *Soninke mansa* for Niumi. But the reformist urge among Muslims was strong and the next decade witnessed repeated attempts to overthrow the *mansa*. British authorities had to use more troops and gunboats to prop up the weak ruling lineages. On one occasion in 1866, d'Arcy led 140 West Indian troops and 100 members of the Gambia Militia on an expedition to burn and drive Muslims out of four of Niumi's river villages. At Tubab Kolong, which d'Arcy considered the Muslims' main "fetish and maiden fortress," a British man-of-war bombarded the village and then a colonial force stormed it, leaving 350 dead among the Muslim force of 800.[43] A year later Muslims sacked the *mansa*'s village, Bakindiki, killing the ruler and driving stragglers south toward the river, and in the early 1870s Maba's successor in Baddibu was frightening traders along Britain's Ceded Mile by rebuilding stockades in the Muslim villages and threatening to attack the ruling lineages once more. Under such circumstances, the rulers rounded up their herds and possessions and headed for Barra Point and English protection at Fort Bullen. This remained enough to enable them to continue to install a *mansa* through the last decades of the century, though his authority and control never again would approach what it had been only a few generations earlier.[44] By the 1880s Niumi's population was mostly Muslim and just waiting for the moment when the old ruling lineages would give up the ghost.

Formal British Takeover

The ruling lineages never recovered from the episodes of civil war. The British government in Bathurst effectively discouraged Muslim reformists from raising the banner of *jihad* in the state after the early 1870s and provided enough support to enable the ruling elites to continue naming a *mansa* in the regular rotational pattern. The ruler continued to receive an annual subsidy from the British and to levy tolls on cattle passing through

Niumi to the markets in Banjul; slaves and retainers continued to work the royal fields and keep a few horses alive for pomp and ceremony. But by the last quarter of the nineteenth century, Niumi's rulers were powerless in the face of British will.

Ironically, it was not the British who would hasten the process of ending the Niumi state. By the 1870s Niumi was so much a part of a wider world that political events taking place on other continents could have serious implications for its population. Between July 1870 and January 1871, Prussia humiliated the French army in a short war, and in the ensuing peace treaty took portions of French territory for the new German state. Barely a year later France joined the rest of western Europe in experiencing an economic slump—a fall of consumption, a glut of manufactured goods, industrial slowdowns, and fears of a sharp downward economic spiral. French planners began thinking that state expenditure on railroads, roads, and canals might pull the nation's economy out of the slump, and such expenditures overseas, particularly as they might tie into a quest for empire in North and West Africa, would bring the army to conquer peoples over vast amounts of territory and thus help France regain the honor lost to Germany. Moreover, wise economists seem to have realized that once persons in the newly acquired empire began consuming French-made products it would be a further step toward solidifying an outlet for French industrial production and a hedge against future economic slumps. So France expanded into West Africa, beginning construction of a railroad between Dakar and Bamako on the upper Niger in 1879 and proclaiming protectorates over ports along West Africa's coast in 1882. German fears following the economic downturn and a perceived need to counter British occupation of Egypt in 1882 prompted Otto von Bismarck to announce German protectorates over territories in West and Southwest Africa, and then the European "scramble for Africa" was on. Most Western nations met in Berlin over the winter of 1884–85 to rationalize and justify the takeover of Africa that was under way. Within a decade, one or another European state would lay claim to almost the entire African continent.[45]

With so much territorial acquisition going on—with gold discovered and pioneer columns forging northward out of South Africa, with King Leopold II staking a personal claim to central African territory that was fifty times the size of his native Belgium, with the French Foreign Legion chasing resisters around the Niger's headwaters and Britain's Royal Niger Company consolidating the palm oil territories along the lower Niger under British protection—Gambia, its trade, and its affairs raised little interest in European colonial circles. For a time in the 1870s French and British officials discussed a trade, the British leaving the Gambia River to the French in exchange for a few French possessions farther down the coast where Britain might have uninterrupted control. But the protests of British traders in Gambia to their members of Parliament helped nix such a trade. Then, as France gained most of the territory surrounding the Gambia, the two countries set themselves to negotiating bilaterally just who might claim what. Representatives met in Paris in 1889 and agreed to delineate boundaries giving the British control along about 200 miles of the river. It took another fifteen years for a succession of joint surveying teams to set the exact boundaries—generally a series of straight lines and neatly scribed arcs that limited British territory to an area seldom more than ten miles in from either bank.

So it was that with the shake of hands, the scoring of a long, straight line on a map, the hollers and waves of surveyors, and the pounding of boundary stakes in 1891, the greater part of what once had been the Niumi state got separated from a lesser part that included the salt-producing islands north of Jinak. The former became British territory and the latter French.[46]

No force in Niumi was strong enough even to hassle the survey team, let alone resist the extension of British authority. By the 1890s most residents were caught up in the monotonous annual cycle of the peanut. Their concerns were more with rains, locusts, and market prices than with who claimed the land that was the key to their livelihood. Following the suicide of *Mansa* Wali Jammeh in 1883—an act symbolic of the frustration and humiliation felt by Niumi's once-proud rulers—Maranta Sonko of Essau assumed what was left of political authority in the state. In April 1893 the Gambia's British administrator agreed not to "interfere with any homage, deference, or respect" that Sonko was accustomed to receive and to continue paying him £110 annually in return for cession of all Niumi territory between the Ceded Mile and the new boundary with Senegal to the north, an agreement to collect no tolls, and a pledge of loyalty and obedience to the colonial government. Indicative of how much the British had Sonko in their pocket was his request in February 1896 for British protection. Parties met and negotiated a treaty to that end in January 1897. The British administrator named Sonko Niumi's first "Head Chief," and until his death in 1910 he would represent colonial government in what used to be the Niumi state.

A Deepening Dependence

In the second half of the nineteenth century, as peanut exports from the Gambia were rising steadily, more and more men in Niumi were becoming involved with peanut production. Even those who had other primary occupations—blacksmiths, leather workers, bards, clerics, traders, even one-

Box 8. The Death of *Mansa* Wali

On January 12, 1881, Niumi's *Mansa* Wali Jammeh showed up on horseback, with an entourage of forty men, to see the British-appointed police constable, Nbye Buss, in Berwick Town on the British-controlled Ceded Mile of Niumi's territory. Jammeh was seeking one of his wives, who had run away and was residing with Buss's wife. When Buss refused to turn over the runaway, Jammeh pointed a gun at him; when Buss fended off the weapon with his sword, it discharged, killing an onlooker. Since the incident took place on territory that was nominally British, Gambia's administrator, Gilbert A. Carter, called for a formal inquiry and a coroner's jury found Jammeh guilty of "willful murder." The administrator issued a warrant for Jammeh's arrest, but instructed police not to enforce it so long as the *mansa* remained in the part of his territory that was outside British control.

On June 9, 1883, however, Jammeh visited Bathurst—in spite of warnings from his own people and the administrator—and shortly after he arrived, he was apprehended and sent to jail. Jammeh apparently had anticipated the events: he left directions for the care of his children and snuck a penknife into the cell under one of his loose garments. On the evening of June 11 the *mansa* used the knife to sever the arteries in his neck and cut a deep gash in his abdomen. He lay back on the bed in the cell and quietly bled to death.

"The deceased appears to have been exceedingly unpopular among his subjects," reports Carter, "which fact was strikingly evidenced by the whole of his male followers deserting him. [T]hree of his wives and as many children alone remained to see to the disposal of the body which eventually was buried at the expense of the colony."[*]

---

[*]G.T. Carter to The Administrator-in-Chief of Sierra Leone, Bathurst, June 14, 1883, CO 1/68; Francis Pinkett to Earl of Derby, Sierra Leone, June 30, 1883, CO 87/120.

time royal cavalrymen—planted a peanut crop so that they could obtain commodities they wanted, with various ends in mind: accumulation for marriage, acquisition of some newly designated necessity, conspicuous consumption to heighten status, or a host of others unique to the individual. Young students at the growing number of Qur'anic schools in the state grew peanuts for their teachers; slaves of wealthier lineages, or, increasingly, some not-so-wealthy lineages, spent much of their time growing, harvesting, winnowing, or hauling peanuts. Just after the century's end Niumi's first colonial commissioner, J.H. Ozanne, estimated that "practically the whole of the male population is engaged in ground-nut production eight months of the year."[47] Such had been the case for several decades. What also had been the case was the steady declining in the ability of people in Niumi to grow enough grain to feed themselves—something they were having difficulty doing even before men were devoting more of their labor to producing peanuts—and the related importing of rice from distant markets, with merchants providing that rice to Niumi residents on credit. Precisely when this change to increasing dependency on the merchants and the expanding world market occurred is difficult to determine, but the late 1850s seems to have been a critical time. As noted, food was sometimes scarce in earlier times: as early as the mid-eighteenth century Niumi's residents needed to import grain from the Gambian hinterland to carry them through the "hungry season" until their own millet or rice was harvested. But a century later the situation was worse. Gambian Administrator O'Connor wrote in 1857 that "natives until the present year have cultivated enough grain for their own subsistence, but an alarming scarcity of food-stuffs have [sic] this year struck considerable parts of the river." Rice imports cost £6,007 that year, £19,351 the next, and £28,208 in 1859. The era of reliance on food imports from the world market was upon Niumi's populace.[48]

The nature of peanut farming was part of the problem. Unlike most other crops that Africans turned to produce for export in the nineteenth century— such commodities as palm oil, cocoa, coffee, and rubber—the peanut is a crop grown in the same rainy season and parallel to food crops. With the limited labor supply along the Gambia River, when men began growing peanuts it meant that they grew less millet, sorghum, and rice. At the end of the harvest they would have less grain, but more goods or cash (cloth and silver coins remained current) to use in exchange. They could obtain imported grain to substitute for the decrease of production. But worldwide technological conditions were right at the time, too, to allow for such importing from much farther away than ever before. The tentacles of world shipping were stronger and reaching farther: larger and faster vessels were finding it profitable to carry bulkier items (like rice) over much longer distances. Fast sailing vessels and steamers could bring rice from Asia, Europe, or the Americas to the Gambia River, where merchants were eager to get the rice into the hands of peanut growers.

But there was a problem of timing that made a simple cash-for-rice transaction impossible. People needed rice at a time of year when they lacked ready cash. At the end of the harvest season, around the end of the calendar year, they had food to eat and, once they sold their peanuts, cash. They purchased the commodities they desired during the "trade season,"

Box 9. **Women's Changing Roles**

Some of the economic and social changes that altered the lives of all residents of Niumi in the nineteenth century had particular effects on the role of women in society, not necessarily beneficial ones. Although early cultural patterns are difficult to determine, it seems that prior to the rapid move to peanut exporting in the middle of the nineteenth century there were no generalized, absolute gender divisions of labor in Niumi—men and women worked in the household unit growing the same crops: millet, sorghum, rice, and around the compound in kitchen gardens an assortment of vegetables. Both contributed roughly equally to the household food supply. Once peanut exporting took hold, however, men became the sole producers of peanuts, planting them instead of some of the food crops they were used to growing. Women concentrated their efforts at making up the food shortage through more extensive growing of rice. "Over the past 20 years men have been growing groundnuts and leaving the much heavier work of rice to women," reads the Annual Report from Gambia in 1880. Men ceased growing rice altogether; it became "women's crop"; and by the century's end it would be taboo for a man to set foot in a rice field. (During times of upheaval, young men would attend women traveling to and working in rice fields for protection, and in normal times they would carry bundles of rice back from the fields, but they would not touch the growing rice or do any work in the rice fields.) By becoming controller of the household's cash-crop revenues, which were the major revenues, men's power within the family increased at women's expense. Men could fulfill their obligations for household food supplies by purchasing imported rice. If household members needed other things, it was to the men that they went for the wherewithal to purchase.

Thereafter, nearly all colonial policies designed to promote agricultural development focused on cash-crop production—on the peanut, man's crop. Introductions of higher-yielding seeds, improved tools, fertilizers, and better marketing operations had the effect of increasing men's incomes and their power in the household. In spite of growing dependence on rice imports, little was done to improve women's ability to grow more and better rice until after the middle of the twentieth century. Only recently, after studies revealed women's importance to household food production (and after peanut exports have fallen in importance in family and state revenues), have development projects focused on women's work and brought them some improvements.

The spread of Islam after the mid-nineteenth century may have led to increased male control and female subordination. That, too, is difficult to determine. Muslim men exert strong social and economic control over

Box 9 *(continued)*

their wives and daughters. What is not clear is if men exerted such firm control in Niumi prior to Islam's growth within the society. A reasonable premise is that they did not—to the same extent.

Sources: Jennie Dey, "Gambian Women: Unequal Partners in Rice Development Projects," *Journal of Development Studies* 17 (1981): 114–15; Ken Swindell, "African Food Imports and Agricultural Development: Peanut Basins and Rice Bowls in the Gambia, 1843–1933," in *Agricultural Change, Environment and Economy: Essays in Honour of W.B. Morgan,* ed. Keith Hoggart (London: Mansell, 1992), 163.

between December and April. By the time the summer "hungry season" set in, when food from the harvest was running low, cash was in short supply. But merchants turned out to be willing to advance family heads enough rice to get them through until the next harvest, with payment for the rice, at interest rates that eventually approached 100 percent, coming half a year later, when the farmers sold their next year's peanut crop. In this way, in the 1860s and 1870s, people of Niumi got bound up with what geographer Ken Swindell calls "chains of indebtedness." The local merchants who bought their peanuts and sold them guns, cotton goods, spirits, or tobacco connected them to the European firms, which, writes Swindell, were "the ultimate creditors from whom all goods originally flowed." By the end of the century, Ozanne would be calling favorable attention to the merchants: "[They] have come to the assistance of the Natives by supplying whole towns with rice at 16/- a bag (90 lbs. each) delivered at the traders' wharves, payment to be made with groundnuts next season." Such indebtedness locked Niumi's farmers into the world market. It would turn out to be a hard-and-fast connection. By the latter part of the nineteenth century, people in Niumi were dependent not only on the natural elements and the world market price of peanuts but on the world price of rice and the rates of interest they might be charged.[49]

Of course, such dependence did not have to result in hardship. After all, some modern Arab states are entirely dependent on exporting petroleum and importing almost everything they consume, and their standards of living are among the highest in the world. In a year when the local peanut crop was strong, world market prices for peanuts were high, and the price of rice was low, people in Niumi could get along fairly well: there would be enough to eat, men could acquire wealth for marriages, people could dress well and even accumulate a stack of cloth or a bag of coins. But in Niumi these circumstances did not often obtain, and it would not take long for the down side of the dependent situation to rear its head. Falling peanut prices related to the worldwide depression of 1873 led Niumi's farmers to join others in calling for a *tong,* a refusal to sell until prices rose. In the late 1880s another downturn in prices resulted in another *tong* and refusal to repay debts, prompting merchants to suspend trade. It was a situation that would go from threats and tension to harmful action. Ozanne described the situation in the first year of the twentieth century:

> Owing to the failure of the ground-nut crop from want of sufficient rain and the destruction of their food crops by locusts, the natives in the Protectorate began to feel the pinch of famine early in the year. Their position was made worse from the fact that the merchants, who in former years had given out credits of rice, etc., to tide the people over the rains, at the close of which the first corn is ripe for gathering, decided to discontinue the practice. Already the people had begun to hunt in the forests for roots and berries, and to pawn and sell their clothing, many being reduced to wearing rice-bags as their sole covering.[50]

Rice bags for clothes and roots and berries for dinner would become commonplace. As we shall see, during the first half of the twentieth century, which was the heart of British colonial rule in the Gambia, a series of world events—wars and economic depressions, mainly—on top of their involvement on the periphery of the now-globe-encompassing world system would keep people in Niumi from gaining much from the political economy managed by their new British rulers.

Notes

1. D'Arcy to Major Mackey, Bathurst, July 5, 1866, CSO 1/13.

2. CSO 9/134.

3. Walter Rodney, *How Europe Underdeveloped Africa* (London: Bogle-l'Ouverture, 1972); Basil Davidson, *Black Mother: Africa and the Atlantic Slave Trade,* rev. ed. (Harmondsworth, England: Penguin, 1980).

4. Immanuel Wallerstein, "Africa and the World-Economy," in *General History of Africa, vol. 6, Africa in the Nineteenth Century until the 1880s,* ed. J.F. Ade Ajayi (Paris: UNESCO, 1989), 23–39. Similarly, J. Forbes Munro points to the period between 1800 and 1870 as a time when "older connexions with the international economy were cast off and new ones evolved," and when "new systems of production and exchange" brought a greater extent, and a different kind, of "African integration into the international economy," in *Africa and the International Economy: An Introduction to the Modern Economic History of Africa South of the Sahara* (Totowa, N.J.: Rowman and Littlefield, 1976), 41.

5. Peter M. Stearns, *Interpreting the Industrial Revolution* (Washington, D.C.: American Historical Association, 1991), ch. 5.

6. Vaclav Smil, *Energy in World History* (Boulder, Colo.: Westview Press, 1994), ch. 5 and passim.

7. Daniel P. Headrick, *The Tools of Empire: Technology and European Imperialism in the Nineteenth Century* (New York: Oxford University Press, 1981).

8. Michael P. Adas, *Machines as the Measure of Men: Science, Technology, and Ideologies of Western Dominance* (Ithaca: Cornell University Press, 1989), ch. 5 and passim. "The White Man's Burden" is in Rudyard Kipling, *Complete Verse: Definitive Edition* (New York: Doubleday, 1940), 321–23.

9. John Ralph Willis, "Introduction: Reflections on the Diffusion of Islam in West Africa," in *Studies in West African Islamic History, vol. 1, The Cultivators of Islam*, ed. John Ralph Willis (London: Frank Cass, 1979), 1–39.

10. Ibid., 2.

11. By the mid-nineteenth century at least some members of Niumi's ruling elite were Muslims, though perhaps not good ones. In January 1834 the ruling lineages put off the installation of Demba Sonko as the new *mansa* because it was the holy month of Ramadan. (Rendall to Hay, Bathurst, Jan. 17, 1834, CO 87/10.) Three decades later, an English official called the *suma* of Essau, who was leading Niumi's *Soninke* forces against Muslims from Niumi and Baddibu, "a Marabout-Soninke," because he claimed to be a Muslim and said his prayers, but did not want to give up political control to the Muslims. Of course, nearly all of Niumi's *mansa* and their entourages drank heavily. Nineteenth-century British officials believed that the most obvious trait separating non-Muslims from Muslims was the latter's abstinence from alcohol.

12. Philip D. Curtin, "Jihad in West Africa: Early Phases and Inter-Relations in Mauritania and Senegal," *Journal of African History* 12 (1971): 11–24; Boubacar Barry, *Le royaume du Waalo: Le Sénégal avant la conquête* (Paris: François Maspero, 1972), 137–42 and pt. 2, ch. 2, passim. Barry contends that the *Toubenan* was an Islamic uprising against slave trading of the traditional ruling elites.

13. A good summary of this argument is Nehemia Levtzion, "Patterns of Islamization in West Africa," in *Conversion to Islam*, ed. Nehemia Levtzion (New York: Holmes & Meier, 1979), 207–16. Levtzion provides other information relevant to the discussion that follows in Nehemia Levtzion, *Islam in West Africa: Religion, Society and Politics to 1800* (Aldershot: Variorum, 1994), 1–38.

14. These figures are from Philip D. Curtin, *Economic Change in Precolonial Africa: Senegambia in the Era of the Slave Trade* (Madison: University of Wisconsin Press, 1975), 164, table 4.3. Curtin divides the numbers into French and British exports. I have assumed that most of the British exports listed are from the Gambia River. Because British traders obtained slaves from elsewhere in Senegambia, my average figures are high, especially for the 1760s and 1770s. Nevertheless, they show trends from one decade to another.

15. Philip D. Curtin, "The Abolition of the Slave Trade from Senegambia," in *The Abolition of the Atlantic Slave Trade: Origins and Effects in Europe, Africa, and the Americas*, ed. David Eltis and James Walvin (Madison: University of Wisconsin Press, 1981), 85–92.

16. Lucie G. Colvin, "Interstate Relations in Precolonial Senegambia," paper presented at the annual meeting of the African Studies Association, Syracuse, N.Y., 1973.

17. Col. A. Grant to Gen. McCarthy, St. Mary's [River Gambia], June 24, 1816, CO 26/42.

18. Much of the detail on customs payments is in "Extract from a letter from Lt. Col. Alexander Grant to R.W. Hay, Esq., Under Secretary of State," November 25, 1825, CSO 1/2, 297–302.

19. Gov. Turner to Earl of Bathurst, July 4, 1825, Freetown, CSO 2/2; Alexander Grant to Earl of Bathurst, Oct. 26 and Nov. 26, 1820, CO 267/51.

20. Paul Mbaeyi, *British Military and Naval Forces in West African History, 1807–1874* (New York: Nok, 1978), 71–73.

21. Sir Neil Campbell to Earl of Bathurst, Freetown, Aug. 3, 1827, CSO 2/2.

22. Col. Alexander Findlay to R.W. Hay, Bathurst, March 1, 1829, CO 87/2; Lt. Gov. Rendall to R.W. Hay, Bathurst, April 28, 1830, CO 87/3.

23. A summary of events leading up to, and taking place in, what the British called "The Barra War" is in letters from Rendall to Lord Viscount Goderich, Bathurst, Aug. 24–Jan. 30, 1832, CO 87/5, 46–60.

24. Niumi residents know that Dog Island has always been the location of Sitanunku's spirits. This explains why villagers were adamant about having no one settle on the small island that appeared to have no particular value.

25. Rendall to Goderich, Bathurst, January 30, 1832, CO 87/6.

26. This treaty is in CSO 1/4.

27. Discussion of the history of early peanut production along the Gambia River is based on George E. Brooks, "Peanuts and Colonialism: Consequences of the Commercialization of Peanuts in West Africa, 1830–1870," *Journal of African History* 16 (1975): 29–54; and Ken Swindell, "African Food Imports and Agricultural Development: Peanut Basins and Rice Bowls in The Gambia, 1843–1933," in *Agricultural Change, Environment and Economy: Essays in Honour of W.B. Morgan,* ed. Keith Hoggart (London: Mansell, 1992), 159–79.

28. Martin A. Klein, *Islam and Imperialism in Senegal: Sine-Saloum, 1847–1914* (Stanford: Stanford University Press, 1968), 36–37; Hazel R. Barrett, *The Marketing of Foodstuffs in The Gambia, 1400–1980* (Aldershot: Avebury, 1988), 37.

29. Barrett, *Marketing of Foodstuffs,* 36–39; Curtin, *Economic Change,* 14, 231; Charlotte A. Quinn, *Mandingo Kingdoms of the Senegambia: Traditionalism, Islam, and European Expansion* (Evanston: Northwestern University Press, 1977), 77; Gambia Ground-Nut Trade Statistics, CSO 54/157.

30. Munro, *Africa and the International Economy,* 45. Historians continue to argue related points. See John Thornton, "Precolonial African Industry and the Atlantic Trade, 1500–1800"; responses to Thornton by Ralph A. Austen, Patrick Manning, J.S. Hogendorn and H.A. Gemery, and E. Ann McDougall; and Thornton's rejoinder; all in *African Economic History* 19 (1990): 1–54.

31. Jan S. Hogendorn, "The 'Vent-for-Surplus' Model and African Cash Agriculture to 1914," *Savanna* 5 (1976): 15–28.

32. Ken Swindell, "Serawoollies, Tillibunkas and Strange Farmers: The Development of Migrant Groundnut Farming along the Gambia River, 1848–1895," *Journal of African History* 21 (1980): 93–104.

33. Curtin, *Economic Change,* 171, 230.

34. Extracts from Annual Reports, 1894–1920, CSO 9/134; Swindell, "African Food Imports," 162.

35. Anonymous [Col. George A.K. d'Arcy], "Gambia Colony and the Civil War," *Colburn's United Service Magazine,* Nos. 419–420 (1863), 405.

36. Martin A. Klein, "Social and Economic Factors in the Muslim Revolution in Senegambia," *Journal of African History* 13 (1972): 419–41; Curtin, "Abolition," 83–97.

37. David Robinson, "Abdul Qadir and Shaykh Umar: A Continuing Tradition of Islamic Leadership in Futa Toro," *International Journal of African Historical Studies* 6 (1973): 286–303; Robinson, *The Holy War of Umar Tal: The Western Sudan in the mid-Nineteenth Century* (Oxford: Clarendon Press, 1985).

38. Charlotte Alison Quinn, "Maba Diakhou and the Gambian *Jihad,* 1850–1890," in Willis, ed., *Studies in West African Islamic History,* 233–58.

39. H. Ingram to Lord Stanley, Bathurst, Dec. 2, 1841, CO 87/28; O'Connor to Secretary of State for Colonies, Bathurst, Aug. 28, 1854, CO 85/57.

40. O'Connor to Secretary, Dec. 2, 1841, CO 87/57; O'Connor to H. Labouchere, Bathurst, Jan. 12, 1857, CO 87/64.

41. British Blue Books from Gambia show that in the decade of the 1830s, for example, nearly 100,000 firearms and 23,000 barrels of gunpowder passed through the customs post at Bathurst. CO 90/4–13.

42. D'Arcy, "Gambia Colony," 238.

43. Residents of Tubab Kolong will still show visitors the massive, old silk-cotton tree with the gouge in the side made by a British cannon ball. Perhaps it is just an ordinary gouge in an old tree, but it is impressive. Evidence for the "Tubab Kolong War" of 1866 is in letters and reports from d'Arcy to his superiors—he was quite the publicist of his efforts—in CSO 1/12 and 1/13.

44. Mahmood Bah to the Queen of England, Powas, Baddibu, June 20, 1871, CO 87/100; W. Boreham to Henry Fowler, Fort Bullen, April 24, 1871, CO 87/99.

45. Michael Adas, *"High" Imperialism and the "New" History* (Washington, D.C.: American Historical Association, 1995), is a concise treatment of recent thinking on causes and effects of imperialism at the end of the nineteenth century, including the takeover of Africa.

46. The negotiations between Britain and France are described in Harry A. Gailey, *A History of the Gambia* (New York: Praeger, 1965), chs. 5 and 6.

47. Extracts from Annual Reports, CSO 9/134.

48. Swindell, "African Food Imports," 163. Swindell bases his chronology on A.A.O. Jeng, "An Economic History of the Gambia Groundnut Industry, 1830–1924," Ph.D. thesis, Centre of West African Studies, University of Birmingham, 1978. O'Connor's statement is in O'Connor to Labouchere, May 31, 1857, CO 87/63.

49. Swindell, "African Food Imports," 164; Traveling Commissioner's Report, North Bank Province, 1898, CSO 60/1. Information on the operation of the export-import and credit systems is in various of the early annual reports of British commissioners. See, for example, Traveling Commissioner's Report, North Bank Province, 1893, CSO 60/1.

50. Swindell, "African Food Imports," 165; Traveling Commissioner's Report, North Bank Province, 1901, CSO 9/134.

6

NIUMI IN THE COLONIAL ERA, 1897–1965

Get out of your rut or get under. Progress called for all over
the world. We are backward and bushmen too much. Work.
Keep yourselves, feed yourselves, improve yourselves!
　　　—Advice to Niumi farmers from Emilius Hopkinson,
　　　Commissioner, North Bank Province, 1921[1]

[I]n this bad year a little hunger must be expected and borne with.
　　　—Hopkinson, 1929[2]

Maranta Sonko is one of the sad figures of Niumi's history. In the only photograph of him, seated with twenty-seven other colonial chiefs at their initial meeting with Gambia's British governors in Bathurst in 1897, he stares at the camera without a hint of expression on his narrow, angular face. His hair is thin and short, his beard gray, his eyes are tired. From the looks on his and the other chiefs' faces, it seems clear that neither the photograph nor the meeting was their idea. The last in the line of Niumi's rulers that stretched back half a millennium, Sonko became *mansa* following his predecessor's suicide in 1883 and found the position empty of almost all traditional power and authority. He was surrounded by Muslims, the vessels that carried salt toward the upper river paid no tolls, and lineage slaves who once tended horses for his state's cavalry now busied themselves growing peanuts. There were only half a dozen horses left in the territory anyway. He had reason to be sad.

In 1893 Sonko signed a treaty with Gambia's British administrator, giving up rights to collect tolls and taxes and pledging his loyalty and obedience to Her Majesty's Government in England in exchange for a £110 annual payment. Four years later Sonko signed a subsequent document, this one placing Niumi under British protection and limiting the annual payment to £83/6/8.[3] It was then that the colonial government named him Niumi's first "Head Chief" and brought him across the river for the chiefs' meeting.

Sonko never took to his new position. In 1902 the government divided Niumi into two administrative districts, leaving Sonko as chief only of "Lower Niumi," not half the region his ancestors ruled in former days. But it mattered little to the old man. The commissioner admonished Sonko for

170

inactivity, after which records show he got "a good deal smarter," but soon he withdrew again from colonial affairs, leaving chief's duties to his son. The younger man grew into the situation in ways his father could not. Official reports bear evidence of the old chief's decline: in 1903 his influence was "nil"; in 1905 he was "getting infirm—and very deaf"; in 1908 a visitor noted that "he seldom moves from his yard"; and the commissioner's report of 1911 reads simply: "Maranta Sonko died during the rainy season of last year."

Soon after his death, the commissioner convinced residents of Sonko's village, Essau—the place where his ancestors had lived when they controlled the river's trade and where, half a century earlier, the remaining *Soninke* had stood boldly behind their stockade, clanging the "death bell," ready to die in defense of their way of life against Muslim reformers—to tear down the village and relocate it half a mile to the southeast, on higher ground. The old place was a "miserable site . . . on the edge of a mangrove swamp infested by tse tse," the commissioner argued. Now they all would be better off.[4]

In contrast to Sonko was J.H. Ozanne, the first British commissioner for Gambia's North Bank Province, which included Niumi. In the photograph with Sonko and the other chiefs, Ozanne is dressed in a white tunic over black pants. From underneath a white helmet, he glares sternly at the camera's lens with a look of confidence. It was a tall order Ozanne had faced in 1893 when he hopped over the boat's side, waded through a few inches of salty water, and set foot on Niumi's reddish-orange soil. He was the administrator who was to establish British authority, and with it bring peace, order, prosperity, and the benefits of "civilization" to peoples living along a strip of wooded savanna 150 miles long and 10 or 12 miles wide— land that contained no roads, only foot paths and horse paths connecting villages and peoples who had been engaged in social upheaval and civil war for two-thirds of a century. He should have felt overwhelmed.

But it appears he did not, and his smug countenance speaks of the confidence in Africa's new rulers that was the result of their coming from the industrialized West, the core of the world economy and center of world politics of the time. Several centuries of involvement with world-spanning commercial capitalism and a century and a quarter with steam-spouting, steel-producing, railroad-building, risk-taking, mass-producing, sometimes mind-boggling industrial capitalism had affected Europeans. Blind self-confidence was one of the personal manifestations.

With such confidence and optimism so widely shared among peoples in the strongest nations of the Western world, it must have been shocking for many, then, to find that the first half of the twentieth century was a period

172

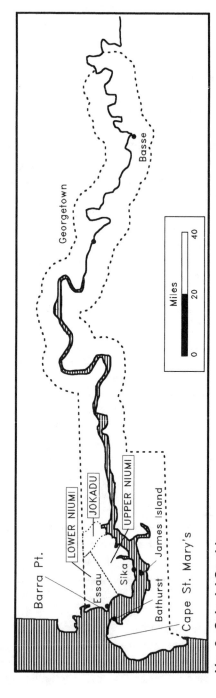

Map 8. **Colonial Gambia**

of mixed fortunes for the world they dominated—a time that brought repeated episodes of political crisis for those at the center of the world's
nation-state structure and hard times for peoples about the globe operating
in the world economy. By 1900 most of the world was divided into nation-
states or colonies subordinate to more powerful nation-states, and was integrated into a vast economic network in which people residing in the
individual nations participated unequally. This is Wallerstein's modern
world-system, resting not so much on political control by colonial rulers as
on the economic relationships, especially the unequal division of labor, in
the still-spreading capitalist economy. People in the industrialized core nations produced manufactured goods (and financed production, controlled
transportation and communication, and managed vast military power),
while those in the peripheral areas worked to subsist and produce raw
materials (at prices the core nations were willing to pay) and consumed
some of the core's industrial production (at prices the core nations could
charge). At the heart of relationships among the core nations was intense
competition, sometimes benign but often rabid, that would play a major role
in bringing about two world wars and a long economic depression in the
first half of the twentieth century, all of which set back the world economy
and set reeling those involved in it. In the end, after the second of the world
wars, a movement toward colonial independence would come alive among
many of the world's peoples. Those in Niumi would get caught up in all
these activities.

Had he known what was on the horizon, Ozanne might have allowed
himself momentary pause, for there was more to make his task daunting.
Somehow, amid the trading and competing and warring that would be going
on about the world, while the European colonies in Africa and Asia were
bringing economic benefit to their mother countries, at a minimum by leveling out the spikes and dips in international trade, the European authorities
were supposed to "develop" their colonies—to find ways to improve the
lives of persons living there. It was a tall order, and Ozanne was at the very
beginning of what was to be a long process of change through a difficult
period. Perhaps he could have accomplished more under different circumstances. As it was, he contracted blackwater fever and died not quite a
decade after he had taken on the task.

The Unsettled Twentieth-Century World

Just as with modern political, intellectual, and social history, for economic
history and study of the modern world economy there is something pivotal
about the beginning of World War I. Before the war, colonial order was

descending on Africa, and peoples long outside the world economy were gradually becoming participants. At the same time, Japan and China apparently were moving toward greater participation in the global economy and world affairs generally. Western forecasters as late as 1912 or 1913 could reasonably conclude that the economy was in sound shape and that people living in the center of industrial production and world trade would have smooth sailing for some time to come. With a long run of reasonably good commodity prices, some believed that the colonial world also might be moving toward a stronger economic position that would eventually result in better lives for its millions. World War I turned the lights out on that vision and set the world on a long course of political and economic instability.[5]

Although the war began in central Europe in August 1914 and involved initially the most powerful nations of the industrialized European world, it did not take long for people in Europe's colonies to realize that this was an event of global proportions. Young men from various parts of European empires were placed under arms and shipped about to participate in the fighting. Over a million African soldiers fought in campaigns in Africa or Europe, and still more African men, women, and children were convinced or coerced to serve as carriers for one or the other armies. Over 150,000 Africans lost their lives in the war effort.[6] In parts of Africa, people would begin to ask why.

Important intellectual currents emerged from the war that would come to affect the world's colonized peoples, too. It was a colossal war for the Western nations—a war to end all wars, people said—and to ensure that it was, various changes were necessary in the way nations did their business. American President Woodrow Wilson brought to the peace table his famous Fourteen Points, among which was the notion of "self-determination"—that peoples have the right to determine who governs them. Neither Wilson nor leaders of the European colonizing powers believed this doctrine need apply to African and Asian colonies, but in the establishment of a League of Nations Mandates Commission to deal with the former German and Ottoman colonies, taking them on as "a sacred trust to civilization" and looking to points in the future (however distant for most African colonies) when the colonies might be able to handle their own affairs, the peace settlement brought to the fore the notion of colonial independence. The war hurt European prestige among colonized peoples, too, and began to erode the psychological dominance colonizers had maintained into the first decades of the twentieth century. Combining these elements, one can see the roots of a movement to end colonial rule and grant colonies their independence that would blossom after World War II, a quarter of a century later.

Of equal or greater importance, World War I disrupted the world economy. A good portion of world production focused on the war effort; patterns of trade changed; wartime inflation appeared and spread; and at war's end the once-dominant nations of western Europe found themselves in debt to the United States, whose economy was largely self-sufficient and whose interests in colonial Africa and Asia were minimal. What in the wartime economy hurt colonial peoples most was the opening and steady widening of a gap between wholesale prices in Europe and import prices in the colonies. Large import and export firms found it a time for enormous profits, while European governments, caught up in the war effort and clinging to the free-trade mentality of the previous century, failed to take preventive action. The terms of trade for producers of raw materials and importers of manufactured goods continued their decline into the 1920s. The gap narrowed only slightly in the late 1920s and then widened again with the onset of the worldwide depression of the 1930s. Thus, many colonized peoples experienced depression and worsening standards of living for the better part of a generation before the onset of the so-called Great Depression. For many African colonies, in economic terms the period between 1914 and 1945 was simply one long, bad time.[7]

But the Great Depression of the 1930s made the previous era seem bountiful by comparison. Triggered by a sudden collapse of the stock market in the United States and subsequent retrenchment in the American economy, the Great Depression showed how thoroughly integrated into a global economy were most of the world's people. The dramatic downturn dragged nearly everyone into a downward economic spiral. Within four years of the October 1929 stock market crash, world trade dropped by almost two-thirds and industrial production by a third. Core demand diminished for most raw materials, so prices for primary products fell and remained low. The effect of these depression years on Africans was uneven; there were mild recoveries in some places in the middle and late 1930s. Still, it would remain for World War II, and the productive efforts of the major countries involved, to jar the world out of its worst economic crisis. And, of course, other ramifications of the war would not be positive.

Economic matters were not the sole reason why the most powerful nations in the world squared off after 1939—one never can discount Hitler's notions of racism and geopolitics, nor his personal psychosis—but Japan had a position at the core of world economics in mind when it fought to create its "East Asian Co-prosperity Sphere"—its own world system, or subsystem, one might argue—and the worldwide political economy was at the center of thinking in the major warring nations. Japan's rapid takeover of much of the Pacific Rim by early 1942 showed the European world how important colonial production was to its economic and material well-being and its ability to wage war. Raw materials and foodstuffs that once flowed in from Java or Cambodia now had to be obtained elsewhere, and it was this rapid rise in demand for primary products that stimulated the economies of colonies from India to West Africa. For many colonial producers the war meant boom times, though a sudden European urge to manage colonial economies more closely, coupled with rising prices of imported goods and the inability to acquire many products long imported, partially deadened the boom.

This war involved fighting on a grander scale than ever before by many more of the world's peoples. Hundreds of thousands of troops from British and French colonies in Africa and Asia fought for the Allies against Nazi forces in Europe and North Africa or Japanese in East Asia. Recruits from British West Africa ended up as part of the 81st or 82nd Division of the West African Frontier Force and spent much of the war in the campaign to reclaim Burma from the Japanese.

For most of Africa and much of Asia, World War II was most important in its role of moving the colonial world more rapidly toward independence. It is true that World War I cracked the facade of European invincibility and introduced ideas of the right of self-determination. It is true, too, that educated Africans had picked up on the Pan-Africanist spirit in the Americas in the 1920s and 1930s and already were agitating for improved conditions in the colonies before the war began. But it all would have been slow in coming had it not been for the dramatic impetus provided by World War II. Many war-related events simply raised colonial people's expectations. British Prime Minister Winston Churchill and American President Franklin D. Roosevelt met on a cruiser off Newfoundland in 1941 and signed an agreement on war aims, the Atlantic Charter. One of those aims was for "the right of all peoples to choose the form of government under which they will live," an item that Churchill did not consider applicable to all peoples in Britain's colonies (later barking, "I have not become the King's First Minister in order to preside over the liquidation of the British Empire"[8]), but one that colonized peoples the world over saw applying to themselves. Then, the millions of African and Asian soldiers, who had served outside their colonies, came home with a fresh outlook. They had witnessed the vulnerability of Europeans—many had killed some, in fact; they had seen how differently others lived and even had fraternized with women and men, who recognized them as friendly forces and treated them accordingly; they had learned languages and new skills; and they had risked their lives for their rulers with expectations of concessions leading toward lives that were materially and emotionally more satisfying in return. But it was not to happen with the speed they had envisioned.

The postwar economic position of the colonial powers stifled such desires. Europe needed to rebuild, and Europeans, naturally focusing on their own hardships during the war years, were starved for everything from clothing to automobile tires, so the products of postwar manufacturers, consumer goods especially, went to purchasers at home rather than to those abroad. Furthermore, England owed massive amounts of money to the United States, had almost nothing America wanted, and was dangerously low on sterling. In dire need of dollars, the British government initiated tight policies at home and with the colonies that prevented importing American goods, which were about the only goods available. Colonial subjects, who had gone without for as long as anyone, were rightfully annoyed. Many, including ex-soldiers, had more money than ever before, yet they could not buy—not even the fine cloth that would constitute the bride wealth for a long-delayed marriage. Disaffection with such things economic brought about agitation to alter things political—a movement that led persons in Britain's colonies to look for leadership in those more politically aware. Such individuals were among the earliest products of an overseas education and were influenced by the milder-speaking nationalists of a generation before.

Britain after the war was under growing pressure to develop its colonies and provide them with the basis for independence. The United States and the Soviet Union emerged from the war as the world's great powers, and as they competed with one another for allies around the world in what would turn into a long Cold War, they recognized the popularity of their anticolonial positions. With its massive industrial production and need for raw materials, America was now the great advocate of free trade—the antithesis of colonial economic relationships. The *idea* of decolonization did not cause Great Britain's newly victorious Labour Party real problems, but the timing did. In the end, colonial peoples took care of that. India already had exacted a pledge of independence during the war and the United Nations trusteeships (the lineal descendants of the League of Nations mandates) in the Middle East were moving rapidly toward independence soon after. It was in this postwar milieu that Kwame Nkrumah of Britain's Gold Coast colony in West Africa stepped forward and speeded the movement for all sub-Saharan Africa. Relying on ideas garnered from schooling in America and London and methods of political organization acquired from left-wing associates through those years, Nkrumah organized Africans to push the British into rapid movement. Once Britain committed itself to independence for one of its colonies—Ghana (the former Gold Coast) in 1957—the others were not long to follow.

Little Gambia was dragged along toward independence in the rush. Gam-

bian development lagged, fewer Gambians were educated, political development and constitutional reforms were slower; still, on February 18, 1965,
Britain gave up its ties to its oldest African possession and The Republic of
The Gambia was born. The existence of Gambia as an independent nation
would have been to the absolute surprise of all those involved in establishing colonial rule there some two-thirds of a century earlier.

Establishment of Colonial Rule

The year 1893 is not the date when Great Britain began to administer a
Gambia colony. Since the foundation of Bathurst in 1816 it had done so, and
over time a handful of land outside Bathurst was added to the colony—the
area between Bathurst and Cape St. Mary's, Niumi's Ceded Mile, MacCarthy
Island 190 miles upriver, and other bits and pieces. This amalgam constituted the Gambia colony that for most of the nineteenth century was administered from Britain's more important possession to the south, Sierra Leone.
But 1893, four years after its agreement with France, is when Britain added
to the tiny colony and accepted administrative responsibility for lands on
either side of the river for 220 miles inland. All this territory was not equal
in British eyes, however. Bathurst and Kombo–St. Mary's, some thirty
square miles where virtually all expatriate government officials and traders
resided, remained *colony;* all the rest, over 4,000 square miles, populated
almost entirely by Africans, was *protectorate*—to be governed separately,
brought along more slowly (as was considered necessary given its less
advanced state), and generally treated as a weak stepsister to the area
around Bathurst. Niumi was in sight of the capital across the river, but was
part of the protectorate.[9]

Any notion that British authorities were feeling their way blindly through
the 1890s in search of policy for governing some of the African territories
they recently had acquired is wrong.[10] The British were old hands at admin-
istering foreign possessions; they had perfected the practice of ruling
through indigenous political systems in India—"indirect rule," they called
it—and never doubted its necessity in Africa. In fact, the British Colonial
Office had a number of strict policies that its officials on the ground knew
well. The most important—literally the bottom line—was that the colony's
budget must balance. British taxpayers had no desire to be paying to administer, let alone develop, some far-flung corner of the empire, so revenues
taken in by the colonial government had to equal or exceed expenditures.
Since revenues were normally thin, colonial administration had to be done
on the cheap, and development would be a luxury beyond the reach of many
colonies in most years and for a long time. This alone dictated indirect rule:

fewer British officials meant fewer European-sized paychecks. The policy worked sufficiently well where there had been strong state structures, and Niumi was one such place.

Gambia had an advantage over a number of Europe's African colonies in that already it had a way of generating revenue. Many adult Gambians were involved in growing peanuts for export, for which they received the equivalent of cash. With their cash they were eager to buy imported goods. From Bathurst's beginning, the government levied duties on imports and since 1866 it had been charging an export tax on peanuts. The government, trading firms, and private traders passed all of these taxes along to the producer and consumer, so Gambian peanut growers received considerably less for their peanuts than they sold for in Europe or America and paid a good bit more for their cloth or sugar or rice or matches than sellers got for them in England, Cuba, India, or Burma.

Such ways and means of raising revenue were part of established policy, and that was good for the new colonial administration. Immediately on commencing formal control of colony and protectorate in 1893, the government enhanced its intake with two ordinances, one establishing licensing fees for traders (thereby ending the practice of African rulers or village heads charging traders fees to operate in their territory) and the other placing a tax on strange farmers (rendering to the government fees that the farmers previously paid to heads of villages in which they resided). Then in 1895 the government enacted the Protectorate Yard Tax Ordinance, the linchpin of its economic policy. Simply put, it required the head of each compound, or "yard," the extended-family divisions of villages, to pay a tax, initially one shilling for every dwelling in the yard. The tax was not onerous, possibly less so than traditional payments people had to render when a *mansa* headed the state, but the method of paying and obtaining payment were different and difficult. Niumi's *mansa* had collected in kind—a portion of whatever families produced, usually grain, sometimes livestock, metal weapons or tools from blacksmiths, and so forth. But the new rulers wanted specie—cash—rather than produce or the cloth that served as a currency, and that would require changes. Ozanne informed Sonko, who passed along the word to village heads, that the way to obtain the cash for the Yard Tax was to grow peanuts and sell them to French traders, who would pay in five-franc pieces during the next "trade season." So common farmers and their families and retainers, students of Muslim clerics, visiting strange farmers, and slaves of the more prominent families grew peanuts, some of which, at least, found their way to French buyers, who paid in the five-franc pieces that Gambians called "dollars"; before long, English buyers started paying in cash too, using the same French currency mostly; and little by little money began circulating. Ozanne was happy to report only minimal difficulties in collecting the Yard Tax the first year it was due.[11] All of this had the effect the British wanted: getting more Gambians to produce peanuts for the world market so that they could consume imported goods. Ozanne wrote in 1899: "Since the introduction of direct taxation, the area of cultivation under groundnuts increases considerably every year, whilst that under corn, cotton and indigo is decreasing proportionately, as the natives now even more than in the past prefer to grow groundnuts for which they can get cash to pay the taxes and then as has been the practise buy other things."[12]

Simply establishing an apparatus to collect this tax was not easy, of course, and that was but one of a number of difficult tasks that faced the colony's first administrators. Gambia's elongated shape made it an administrator's nightmare, and since the British were perpetually concerned about costs, they necessarily were thin on the ground. A governor (with an initial budget totaling less than £25,000), two traveling commissioners (Ozanne for the river's north bank and F.C. Sitwell for the south bank), and one battalion of the West India Regiment made up the advanced guard of British authority. Ozanne's initial encounters with men and women in Niumi were sometimes awkward, but not what one would call hostile. A later administrator recalled, "The natives did not appear to resent the presence of the Commissioners in the country but looked upon them apparently with amusement, a frequent remark on their part being, 'Whatever are those monkeys walking the country for?' "[13]

Once the monkeys took away village heads' traditional revenues and then imposed a Yard Tax, some of the amusement turned to resistance. Maranta Sonko joined ten other chiefs in 1897 in informing the government that "they were all too poor to bear taxation," and over the next two years family heads in Niumi balked at paying. Early budget figures belie commissioners' pronouncements that they were collecting tax without difficulty, but most forms of passive resistance disappeared early in the new century when the government showed what backed up its authority.

The incident that prompted the new government's first show of considerable force was a tragic event in 1900 in a village along the river's south bank. Commissioner Sitwell and seven members of his entourage were ambushed and killed while investigating a land dispute between neighboring villages. In response a large and well-armed expeditionary force, with units of the King's African Rifles brought in from British East Africa to join companies of the West India Regiment from Sierra Leone for the occasion, marched on the villages in January 1901 and either executed or captured and deported as many of the perpetrators as it could turn up. The force then marched up and down the rest of the entire protectorate. In a village just a few miles from Niumi, where a village head had talked threateningly to Ozanne, prompting the commissioner to sneak out of the village under the cover of night, the force marched in with weapons ashoulder, collared village leaders and made them beg forgiveness, levied a fine that required residents to give up their cattle, rounded up all firearms (mostly old flintlocks), and left with a warning devoid of all subtlety about future relations. Word of the incident got around fast. Ozanne noted, "The presence of so large a body of men has had a most wholesome effect, the Protectorate resuming its normal peaceful condition in a very short time."[14]

Common people in Niumi encountered the new government in a variety of other ways. Many answered a summons by a village head and found themselves escorting the commissioner on treks about the province, carrying what seemed an inordinate amount of goods for one man, or clearing roads. Roads, indeed, proved an obsession with commissioners, and this may have been rightly so in their eyes, for until villages were reachable by government authorities they could hardly be expected to contribute to the colonial economy or the government that economy supported. Another factor was that roads were readily measurable, their conditions easily monitored, and as such they became effective yardsticks for colonial "progress." At one time or another, nearly every Niumi chief felt the hot breath of colonial authority on his neck because of a weakened causeway, a washed-out bridge, or a road rendered otherwise impassable by the rains. Chiefs had to provide labor to construct and maintain the roads. This did not sit well with the young, especially.[15]

People in Niumi might also encounter colonial rule through the new legal system that the British established, but the difference from former legal constraints was neither great nor always apparent. As part of their indirect-rule theory, and out of sheer necessity, the colony's government quickly passed an ordinance recognizing customary law and procedure that were "not repugnant to natural justice nor incompatible with any ordinance of the Colony." New courts headed by the chief administered such laws as they pertained to petty civil and criminal cases. Families arguing over rights of land use, persons wanting to obtain damages from an offending party, or individuals accused of arson or theft were likely to wind up before respected elders of the "Native Court," much as would have happened before.[16]

Social change that accompanied the onset of colonial rule was more subtle. H. Lloyd Price, the commissioner who replaced Ozanne, reported in 1906 on how society in Niumi and neighboring Baddibu was changing: "The family system among the Mandingos is still very strong, but there are signs of its eventually breaking down. The young men are moving about

Box 10. **Forced Labor**

One aspect of colonial rule for which the English have a more favorable reputation than the French involves forced labor. French colonialists made no bones about having the *indigenat,* the law that required every able-bodied colonial subject to work a certain number of days each year for the state. It was a nasty policy, and the French probably deserve the derision they receive because of it. But the English forced Africans to work for them too, though they were less up-front about doing so. With a 1905 ordinance, chiefs and village heads became responsible for maintaining such public facilities as roads, bridges, wells, and boundary markers, and for picking up rubbish and otherwise looking after the public good. Every annual report comments on how well chiefs performed these duties. There even was a competition with awards given to the chiefs whose districts had the best roads, and woe to the chief in whose district excessive rubbish heaps turned up or bridges washed away. But the reports never explain how the chiefs got the work done. Their basic way was by tapping the young men's age groups that traditionally performed services for the good of the community, the elderly, or the infirm. In the past these groups did such work, but they received something for their collective pursuits, payment that went toward helping one of their number accumulate wealth for a first marriage or the slaughter of a cow and a subsequent feast. With the new regime there was no such payment.

British officials required considerable labor in the early years of their rule too, for they traveled considerably without automobiles and they needed all of their gear toted. In North Bank Commissioner Dr. Emilius Hopkinson's diary for 1923 one finds: "Sent the loads with a change of carriers to Jurunku and went myself in a big canoe with ten paddlers to go by water to the same place." The porters and paddlers were local "recruits." And five years later, when the West African Frontier Force was planning a two-week exercise in Niumi, their commanding officer noted that if they had to land at Albreda, they would need "60–70 carriers per day" to accompany them on their exercise. Commissioners, chiefs, and village heads tabbed individuals to serve as carriers.*

Residents of Niumi disliked forced labor (they refer to it as "carrying heavy loads") as much as any other aspect of British rule. Indicative of this was the situation with badge messengers, the Africans who served at the lowest level of colonial authority with duties ranging from carrying messages to arresting petty thieves. Badge messengers received no salary for their service; instead, they received certain privileges, the primary one being "exemption from porterage." "The privilege of being exempt from carrying loads is much appreci-

Box 10 *(continued)*

ated," noted Niumi's commissioner in 1913. Long after colonial rule was over Niumi resident Lamin Sowe, a fair-minded man who gave the British credit for bringing peace to the territory, reflected on the down side of British rule: "They were rude and they made us work for them a lot," he recalled. "They came to the village and just rounded us up and made us go off and clear the road or carry loads on our heads." When asked if he ever was paid for such work, Sowe let out a mighty, snorting laugh.[†]

*Monthly Diary, North Bank Province, 1923, CSO 2/587; Captain C.S. Burt to Colonial Secretary, Cape St. Mary's, January 19, 1928, CSO 4/27.

†Annual Report, North Bank Province, 1913, CO 87/194; Lamin Sowe, interview in Berending, Lower Niumi District, The Gambia, March 16, 1996.

more, going from place to place instead of hardly ever leaving their own towns and villages as formerly. They visit Bathurst and ports in French territory and get wider ideas thus becoming inclined to resist parental authority, and to forego that blind obedience the young rendered to the aged for years in the Gambia."[17]

Still, the form of social change that some of Niumi's residents feared most from the coming of British rule was the ending of slavery. Niumi's population might have known nothing about the Berlin Conference and the broad European pledge, as partial justification for imposing their authority on Africans, to stamp out slavery and the slave trade, but they had no doubt about British intentions in that regard. For the most influential element in Niumi, this was especially serious business. Slavery, or conditions of dependency that approximated slavery, were important to Niumi's economy and society. Ozanne noticed that virtually every lineage head had one or more slaves, whom he fed, but did not clothe. The slaves had to work for the lineage between sunup and mid-afternoon, five days a week. They had the remainder of the time to tend their own plots and thus they could grow their own crops and acquire some wealth. Ozanne found some living with their masters "more as a friend than as a slave," but such was rarely the case for women, who simply worked hard. Seldom did masters free slaves, and their chances of running away were almost nil. Niumi's Muslim clerical families held large numbers of slaves, who worked their ground as their masters went about their "Muslim business." Some of the Muslim teachers kept students in a position of dependency that was close to slavery. Slaves were so prevalent and so important to production in Niumi that, according to Ozanne, "proclaiming freedom would paralyze all trade and cultivation," and he predicted that slavery would not end without a struggle because, as one slave owner admitted, "they are our hands and feet."[18]

As it turned out, the headmen's fears were unfounded, at least for the short run. Not wanting to render the already difficult situation chaotic (and, of course, fearing the blow that paralysis of all trade and cultivation would level on the colonial treasury), Gambia's Administrator R.B. Llewelyn, while outlawing slave *trading* in 1894, allowed slavery to continue on condition that masters not mistreat their slaves and that the slaves be freed on the master's death.[19] Slavery in Niumi thus died a slow death, and the effects such change would bring to society were gradual. By the end of the second decade of the twentieth century there were no longer many individuals who, in any legal sense, were bound to others in conditions of servitude. Memories of slavery, and of who were slaves in previous generations, lingered much longer.

One important change that occurred in relation to the ending of slavery was in how people accumulated wealth. For hundreds of years the wealthiest people in Niumi—the ruling families and other prominent lineages of farmers, clerics, artisans, and traders—invested a portion of their wealth in horses or slaves. But by the last years of the 1890s, conditions had so changed that it was no longer necessary for ruling lineages to buy horses and it was not possible to buy slaves. "Now there are no slaves and they keep no more 'war boys,' " wrote Ozanne in 1896, "so they don't need horses." In five years the price of "native ponies" dropped by 75 percent. Men who had wealth began investing it in cattle, and to a lesser extent sheep and goats, the price of which rose accordingly. Moreover, because Mandinka were agriculturalists, those who owned cattle welcomed into the region increasing numbers of Fulbe pastoralists, who tended the burgeoning herds for a portion of the produce. As the herds grew, more milk and milk products entered the diets of Niumi's farmers, and the manure from cows tethered in fallow fields improved fertility and made the necessity of moving villages to find fertile farmlands less necessary than before. By 1907 there were "practically no horses" in Lower Niumi District and "very few horses" in Upper Niumi—a telling commentary on the end of a way of life. Colonial agents believed all of this to be an improvement, and in some ways it was. But the fact that wealth tied up in great herds of cattle could be wiped out by disease and that the great coming together of people and animals of the world was introducing new diseases to mammals living in West Africa meant that regularly through the first half of the twentieth century wealthy lineages in Niumi would see a good portion of their wealth disappear with the onset of a "cow killing." As with most elements of change, for the people going through it, this was a mixed bag.[20]

Box 11. **Sexism: A Prejudice Across Cultures**

Niumi's colonial governors, mostly upper-class Englishmen, had next to nothing in common with Africans living in the Gambia Protectorate. Seldom did persons from two such different worlds have a chance to interact. When they did, they had few bases from which to understand one another. Only once in a while did something turn up. One involved their outlook on women.

During their service in Gambia, governors were expected to make tours of the protectorate, partly to oversee the commissioners' work, but also to keep in touch with "the natives," to learn what was going on in the portion of the territory that supported the colony, to look at crops, listen to complaints, make speeches, and show authority. George C. Denton, Gambia's governor from 1901 to 1911, made a number of such "tours of the provinces," and toward the end he became more familiar, and more relaxed, with the African men he encountered.

In April 1910, on a tour of Upper Niumi, he met in Sika with the chief and headmen of eighteen villages. They sat in a circle; the African men listened to the governor's pronouncements and then had an opportunity to make statements and ask questions. At the end of the session, one of the chief's questions elicited a cross-cultural male bonding. Denton's report reads: "Again the Head Chief prompted by some old Kebas [respected elders] asked me if I would give them a Prison in which to shut up their wives who were very 'puzzling.' I told him that it was not only in Niumi that the ladies were 'puzzling'; it was the same all the world over and was one of their many charms and I certainly could not give him a prison in which to shut them up for such a reason. After a little thought and consideration they grasped the point of what I had said and went off into fits of laughter, a thing they very rarely do at a meeting."*

---

*Denton to Secretary of State, Bathurst, May 1, 1910, CO 87/183.

The World of Peanuts

For all the years of the twentieth century, the typical resident of Niumi, male or female, old or young, directly and indirectly, has teetered along a delicate, annual life balance, set in course each May or June by a decision about how much land to plant in the lone cash crop, peanuts, and how much to plant in food crops. After a little experience the decision is a rational one, and families are able to get by with the results of the choice—in some years. The problem that arises comes from the variables: weather and pests on the one hand, and fluctuations of world market prices for peanuts and imported commodities on the other. People in Niumi are dependent on each; every year, the difference between general well-being and starvation and misery rests on these factors.

Like farmers everywhere, men and women in Niumi had always been at the mercy of the rains, wild animals, insects, and crop diseases. When too little or too much rain fell, when warthogs and baboons rampaged, or when swarms of locusts descended, people knew they would be in for a long, hungry season. But by the twentieth century the less-obvious force of the world market became a factor as important as rainfall and crop-devouring animals. Governor Denton took note of the situation in 1903:

> With regard to the general condition of affairs in the Protectorate the Ground nut crop is a very large one and I hope that the export will reach 40,000 Tons. Unfortunately the crops in other countries are also large and in consequence the price has fallen very low. . . . If the price in the European Markets goes up there will, perhaps, be a rush later on in the season but this is very doubtful. Several Natives have said to me, "What is the good of our growing more nuts than the merchants can buy?" It is very difficult to answer this question satisfactorily as, except in a very few instances, it is almost impossible to make them grasp that the Gambia Crop has very little effect on the European Nut Market.[21]

And the European nut market was a fickle one indeed. People in Niumi faced that reality soon after they began exporting peanuts. In 1852 Gambian farmers sold 9,295 tons of peanuts worth £153,098. The next year they increased peanut production by nearly 20 percent, to 11,226 tons, but the crop was worth 12 percent less, £135,404. In 1854 the size of the export crop fell back to the 1852 level, 9,162 tons, but it was worth one-third less than the 1852 crop, £109,846. Later years hammered home the theme more dramatically: peanut prices bobbed up and down like a canoe on the Atlantic, with various world events causing major waves. Rises in the 1880s brought about by the growing popularity of margarine and entry of Germany and the Low Countries in the trade were offset by drops related to global economic retrenchment in the first half of the 1890s. Invention of the hydrogenization process that made it easier to convert peanut oil into soaps and fats boosted European demand and resulted in a run of good prices after 1910.[22] In response, in 1914 Gambians exported 66,885 tons of peanuts worth £650,461. Then World War I turned the global market upside down. Buoyed by the previous year's success and blessed by steady rainfall, Gambian farmers in 1915 turned out their biggest crop yet, half again as large as in 1914. But France, which had been purchasing three-quarters of Gambia's peanut exports, stopped buying. Germany had invaded northeastern France, where much of the oil rendering was done; the war siphoned off

French industrial laborers; and oil extraction was a low priority in the war economy. The result was that the price of peanuts dropped by £2 to £4 a ton. The Gambian crop eventually sold, but for only £400,435, two-thirds the value of 1914's much smaller crop.[23] Something besides rain, wild animals, and insects was affecting how much Niumi's farmers were gaining from their hard work. Of course, trading people living along the Gambia River were no greenhorns in international commerce; they were used to price fluctuations for slaves, hides, beeswax, gold, and the host of commodities that they demanded from foreign importers. But now, reasons for the rising and falling prices of peanuts were less obvious. What was clear was that a bountiful peanut crop did not always bring bountiful income.

The colonial government was mindful of the consequences of the planting decision and had no desire to see people in Niumi experience hunger through the growing season. Yet in most years the government lent its heavy weight to the peanut side of the balance, simply because Gambians had to grow peanuts for the fiscal health of the colony. Taxes (paid with cash from peanut exports), export duties (on peanuts), and import duties (on items farmers purchased with cash from selling their peanuts) paid for colonial administration and, in theory, anyway, were eventually going to support projects that would improve the lives of the colonial subjects. Thus, commissioners made sure chiefs and village heads recognized the importance of planting peanuts, even if it meant growing less food. Rice imports could make up the difference.

For this reason, it was important to colonial officials, early in the twentieth century, to regularize and gain control of the importing of rice and the extension of credit. Too often farmers were adhering to locally proclaimed *tongs* (peanut holdups) and merchants, stung by such action and resulting unpaid loans, were denying credit. So when, early in the twentieth century, such a holdup and refusal took place, the government stepped in and distributed 4,000 bags of rice on credit. By 1906 the number of government-distributed bags more than doubled, and it gave out on credit 500 tons of seednuts as well. It became normal procedure for village headmen to sign, in the presence of the commissioner, to be responsible for collection of villagers' "rice debt." From then on, government and traders would be in the same position, depending on the year, of being the peanut farmers' creditors. Even when merchants made the loans, the government helped press for repayment.

Not all government officials were fond of the growing dependence and indebtedness, and especially of the enhanced government role in it all, but they did not have workable ideas about how to change the situation. Governors seemed forever lamenting the situation and railing at commissioners, who lectured chiefs, who spoke to village heads, who passed the word

Box 12. **Debt Peonage on Both Sides of the Atlantic**

It is instructive to recognize how closely the lives of persons in Niumi paralleled those of several million persons of African descent—some probably related to them through common ancestors—living in the American South in the first half of the twentieth century. A situation of dependence was key to both situations. The poor, southern, rural, African American family, not long out of slavery in the latter nineteenth century, had no money and no land. To make a crop the farmer had to strike a deal with a landowner, allowing the family to live on and work a plot through the growing season and then, once the crop was harvested, providing for the landowner's payment: a share of the crop. But this did not feed and clothe the farming family. To subsist before the crop's sale, the farmer also had to negotiate with a merchant to "furnish" him—to provide food, and perhaps other items, on credit, to be paid for, with interest, after the harvest's sale. As it turned out, once the landowner took about half the crop and then the farmer sold his portion, he often did not have enough cash to pay off his "furnish," and almost never did he have enough to be able to provide for his family through the next growing season without having to borrow again. He had to stay put, agree to grow cotton again, and hope in vain for better times. It was a life in perpetual debt, at the mercy of the elements and such human and economic-related matters (which were just as far outside his control as weather and the boll weevil) as the honesty and goodwill of southern whites or the price of cotton on the world market.

At about the same time, farmers in Niumi were in a similar situation. Niumi villagers were not dependent on someone else for land, but as farmers there began growing more peanuts to sell, in place of millet or rice to eat, they began to have to purchase grain, normally rice, from traders. If harvests were not good or peanut prices not sufficient, the farmers would not have sufficient cash to buy enough rice in May or June to last until the fall harvest. In such situations, traders initially, and then the colonial government, advanced them rice, and later seed nuts and fertilizer for the next season's crop, on credit, to be paid when they sold their peanuts the next year. Thus, they found themselves bound by debt to grow peanuts, and they sometimes found themselves in debt to the extent that they could not obtain enough money from the next year's sale of peanuts to repay what they had borrowed the previous year. This was especially true if, in hopes of a bountiful harvest and good prices, they borrowed—often at usurious rates—to obtain clothing, tools, or (perhaps with reckless anticipation) a bicycle. As with their counterparts in the American South, debt became a way of life for farmers in Niumi.

Unlike American sharecroppers, whose exploitative system withered away with the mechanization of cotton production after World War II, the situation of continuing debt did not end for Niumi's villagers. In March 1996 Niumi farmers already were beginning to run short on food. This was half a year before the harvest, and some were heading out to "find some rice," seeking an advance so they could make it through until the next "trade season" and hopes of better times.

along to farmers about ensuring a sufficient planting of food crops.[24] But most of them knew that family work units were planting close to capacity, so growing more millet would mean producing fewer peanuts, which no one seemed to want. "For over twenty years the natives have been urged to grow groundnuts for export to the exclusion of foodstuffs," wrote a feisty new director of agriculture for the Gambia in 1930, "and this policy has placed them entirely in the hands of merchants who pay them what they like for the local produce raised and charge them what they like for the necessary food."[25] Almost everyone involved recognized that it was a bad deal.

But the ones who suffered from the bad deal were the farming families, who regularly experienced hunger, or lived in poverty, or both. As years of the twentieth century turned into decades, the situation worsened. Fairly good peanut prices after 1915, topped by record-high prices in 1920, prompted people in Niumi to borrow more heavily than ever from traders at the beginning of the 1921 growing season. For their part, the merchants eyed the bonanza and extended credit to all comers. Then came drought and locusts, followed by a dramatic drop in peanut prices related to a worldwide postwar depression. Niumi's farmers simply could not pay their debts following the sale of their peanuts. Commissioners had to intercede between farmers and traders and work out a schedule for debt repayment. Many would pay small amounts at the end of every year through the rest of the 1920s.[26]

Making these bad matters worse was a Gambian economic crisis in 1921 caused by a government decision to demonetize the long-used French five-franc piece. Back in 1843, when the peanut trade was getting under way on a large scale, British authorities recognized the silver five-franc piece as legal tender in the Gambia, fixing the exchange rate at the awkward amount of three shillings and tenpence halfpenny. Gambians liked the coin: it had heft, could be made into attractive jewelry, and held up well when buried for saving. It eventually made up much of the colony's circulating money supply. But World War I upset exchange rates and brought about a much lower rate for the five-franc piece worldwide than the Gambia was offering. The British Treasury had its hands full with wartime matters and was slow to react to this discrepancy in the small colony, so banks in Bathurst spent a long time paying 1.75 times the world rate for the piece. From all over, the coins flowed into Gambia at an alarming rate. In the face of a monetary crisis, British officials decided in January 1922 to buy all the outstanding five-franc pieces and take them out of circulation. The effort cost over £400,000 and melting the silver coins gained back only half the sum. Although British decisions alone had been at the root of the problem, it was the Gambian Treasury that had to pay for demonetization; it did so by borrowing £178,000 from the West African Currency Board.[27]

How would the colony repay the loan? As in all other Gambian fiscal matters, with money from peanuts. In November 1921, six weeks before the franc buy-up began, the Gambia's government more than doubled the export duty on peanuts, from 6/8d. per ton to £1.5 per ton. Although the governor announced that additional revenues from the increased duty would be "earmarked for development works," government officials knew that for the next nine years extra revenues would end up going to the Currency Board.[28] Most people in Niumi knew nothing of the monetary crisis, the loan, or the repayment. What they realized through the 1920s was that they were raising more peanuts and receiving less for their efforts.

In fact, neither nature nor man seemed to be smiling on Niumi between the wars. Insufficient rains, locust attacks, and visits of a "cow-killer," contagious peripneumonia, in 1923 and 1925 made life generally difficult for Niumi's villagers. So did the ungoverned hand of shippers and traders. By the 1920s the buying and shipping of peanuts from West Africa to European ports involved the worst sort of collusion, monopoly, and price fixing. The largest shipping lines doing business with West Africa— England's Elder Dempster, Germany's Woermann Line, and Holland's West African Line—formed a Shipping Conference in which, rather than compete with one another, they divided the market among themselves and set inordinately high rates for hauling produce to markets in France, England, or the Netherlands and bringing European goods back to West African ports. Merchants in West Africa subtracted the high shipping charges from the price they paid growers for their crop and added them to prices they charged for imports. Moreover, the largest trading company in British West Africa, the African and Eastern Trading Corporation, merged in May 1929 with the second largest, the Niger Company, to form the United African Company, a firm doing eight times more business than its nearest competitor. The UAC undercut independent buyers and sellers and drove them out of business; then, once enough competition was eliminated, it raised prices on the goods it imported and lowered prices it paid for exports.[29] During World War II, a disinterested commentator included among a listing of Gambia's shortcomings, "A commercial life which was dominated by one firm, the U.A.C.; a firm which . . . has, I think, no obligations to the Colony bar the payment of a lowish rate of Income Tax [and shows a] high-handed disregard . . . for the interests of the natives. . . . In theory there is competition in the Gambia, but in practice I always felt that the U.A.C. could make on its retail sales of imported goods, pretty-well what profit it wished."[30]

In spite of the ill effects of monopoly and collusion, it appeared to some that Gambian economic skies might be brightening by the end of the 1920s, when personal and government debts were repaid. But the onset of the Great Depression proved otherwise. World commodity prices fell in 1930, rallied slightly in the middle of the decade, and then fell again. The price for peanuts dropped so low in 1930 that the governor advised Niumi's farmers to eat their peanuts rather than sell them. Gambia's government quickly scaled down spending, putting to rest plans for temporary increases for education, among other things, and raised existing import duties and levied new ones, meaning Niumi's population had to pay more for what they purchased. Rapidly developed austerity programs meant that the government stopped advancing peanut farmers seed nuts to plant at the start of the rains or food to eat toward the end. Then, as peanut prices remained low, Great Britain felt it necessary to take action to support British industry. With depression-fueled unemployment in England at unprecedented levels, the Colonial Office in 1932 instituted "Imperial Preferences" throughout the empire, enabling colonial governments to place tariffs on foreign imports, to the advantage of more expensive goods made in England, and thus raising prices again for Gambian consumers.[31]

What hurt people in Niumi most was a 1934 Importation of Textiles (Quotas) Bill, which limited the amount of non-British textiles British colonies could import. Recent flooding of the world textile market by manufacturers in Japan, where labor was cheap and the currency recently devalued, prompted the action. In rationalizing the Textiles Bill, Gambia's governor, H.R. Palmer, showed that he recognized the disastrous effects the resulting rising cloth prices would have on the likes of Niumi's farmers:

> We cannot stand by and watch the British connection with markets made by British enterprise being destroyed. The benefits of the British connection are many and immediate. Great Britain has always held her Colonies as the trustee of Civilization. In the past she has offered in those markets the same open field to foreigners and British subjects alike. But since the War the principle and practice of economic nationalism has in every direction closed foreign markets against British goods. Great Britain has found herself with increased costs, a load of debt and contracting trade in a world where fresh barriers are daily erected. Increased protection is more than ever necessary today to enable her to meet the debts which she incurred in preserving the liberties of the world. The Colonies owe it to their inclusion in the Empire that they escaped. Is then the native of the tropics to bear no share of the economic burden which the War has left? It is unlikely that any African who understands the issue would make this claim. We aim at a return to the happy condition of former days, but until exchanges have been stabilized, until the barriers which other nations have erected can be lowered by negotiation, until prosperity and rising prices return to an impoverished world, until trade revives, some measures must be taken to preserve for the Empire the markets which her enterprise has created and defended. If those measures involve

some hardship to Africans, as indeed they do, that hardship is nothing compared with the burdens borne by British citizens in the British Isles.[32]

If they remained unaware of the fact before, the depression years of the
1930s showed Niumi's farmers once again that the size of the local peanut
crop did not necessarily relate to the amount of cash in their pockets at the
end of the season or the amount of food they would have to eat through the
"hungry season." It convinced them, too, how much they were at the mercy
of unseen forces, visualized in the figure of the local trader. "The beginning
of the wet season is already bringing the customary purchase of foodstuffs
on credit at excessive rates of interest and the pledging of next year's
groundnut crop,"[33] reads a quarterly report from the North Bank Province
in 1937. The report from the previous year was more specific: "There
seems to be flourishing a credit trade in rice which is sold at enormous rates
of interest against the security of the coming groundnut crop: the usual
profit is 100% and this is so generally recognized that even constant warning that such a rate of interest would be unenforceable in a Court of law, if
made the subject of a civil action, will not, it is feared, produce the proper
number of refusals to meet the creditors' demands."[34]

As we later see, economic prospects brightened for many during the
years of World War II, but the basic situation of dependence on a world
market for peanut prices and imported goods did not go away in the waning
years of colonial rule. Notes from Niumi in the 1950s read, "short on food
during the rains . . . 821 bags of rice issued on credit . . . traders are confi-
dent enough to give out a considerable amount of goods on credit during the
growing season."[35] By then, it was an old story.

Development

Deepening dependence on the fickle world market was a down side of
colonial rule, but there was supposed to be a corresponding up side: development. When European colonial powers took over African colonies in the
last decades of the nineteenth century, development was not high on their
agendas. They spoke more about ending slave trading, opening Africa to
commercial opportunity, and bringing the light of civilization to backward
peoples. Perhaps this latter included something akin to development, but
that was not clear. No European nation had sketched out plainly how it
proposed to go about improving the lives of the residents of their colonies
over the coming generations. Roland Oliver states it well: "The European
powers had not partitioned the continent with a view to securing early gains
through its rapid development. They had done so as an insurance against the

future of growing protectionism, and their main concern was that the annual premiums should be kept low."[36]

One way to keep the annual premiums low was to stand firm on the policy that colonies be self-sufficient, each paying for its own administration and improvement projects with its own revenues. But this policy did not preclude development and social welfare in Great Britain's Gambia colony. Contrary to a commonly held notion that such colonies were forever economic liabilities, Gambia in most years had revenues sufficient for reasonable levels of administration *and* development. Harry A. Gailey points out that the Gambia colony had always been self-supporting, that it was more prosperous than Sierra Leone when the two were attached administratively, and that over the years immediately following World War I it was second only to the Gold Coast in total imports and exports per capita among Britain's West African colonies.[37] So why was there not more improvement in living conditions for Gambians? The answer is different for different periods, up to about the middle of the twentieth century.

Special circumstances involving Great Britain, France, and the Gambia rendered the small colony far less likely than others to be the site of efforts at improvement through the first three decades of British control, or even longer. Colonial Gambia was surrounded by French territory—it was almost literally a knife in the side of French Senegal—and it was in a larger region where French commercial interests were overwhelmingly predominant. Since 1866 there had been French initiatives to work out a trade of spheres of influence, with the possibility of Britain exchanging Gambia for some areas of the West African coast farther south where British traders were more active. Such an exchange might have taken place had not British commercial interests in the Gambia pressed Parliament to oppose it. Ideas of exchange were alive in the minds of officials in both countries into the 1890s, and the notion did not die when Britain and France demarcated the colonial boundaries for a final time in 1904. Through the first two decades of the twentieth century, the British Colonial Office was never entirely certain that over the long haul the Gambia would remain in British hands. Thus, it was reluctant to spend money on improvements for the colony or its population that might one day end up benefiting France or French subjects.[38]

Not long after British officials began to accept that Gambia was not going to be traded—a fact that never sunk in completely, but was recognized generally by the time of World War I—notions of colonial development were blowing in the wind. The 1922 publication of Lord Lugard's famous tract on colonial design, *The Dual Mandate in British Tropical Africa,* set protecting and advancing colonial peoples, along with developing Africa economically for the benefit of the world, as essential duties of colonial rulers. Thus, residents of Niumi might rightfully have expected steady, significant improvement in their lives, in health and education, for instance, through the 1920s and 1930s. That such improvements barely occurred was due largely to British fiscal policies as they applied to Gambia.

One conservative policy that continually applied the brake to development had to do with the size of reserves in the Gambia's treasury. In only eleven years between 1899 and 1940, through grand fluctuations in world prices, too much and too little rainfall, plagues of locusts and plant diseases, and spending related to world wars, did the colony's expenditures exceed its revenues. On this basis, the colonial treasury gradually built up a sizable reserve—£107,000 by 1912 and a whopping £328,657 by 1920, the latter figure being twice as much as the colony spent that year.[39] Gambia's governors followed guidelines from the conservative Colonial Office and made sure there was plenty for budgetary emergencies. When an emergency did arrive—as in the demonetization crisis of the 1920s—the government borrowed, tightened the budget, and used current revenues. Funds held in reserve remained to accumulate. Perhaps it was a factor that they were invested in British government securities.

With such policies, government efforts to make life better for Niumi villagers remained few and of little significance. Records from the 1910s and 1920s show yeoman-like work on the part of commissioners to vaccinate people against smallpox and cattle against rinderpest. But most of what the British regarded as "development works" consisted of constructing and maintaining roads, bridges, causeways, and the like that would tie Niumi's farmers more directly to the Gambia River, which was their access to the world market. Priorities were clear from the beginning: when the French in 1904 began charging duty on peanuts that Niumi's farmers were conveying to Bathurst via streams that ran through Senegal, the governor offered Lower Niumi's chief £100 if he would organize the digging of a long channel to give the boatmen access to the sea in Gambia territory. That same year the government spent nothing on medical care or education in Niumi.[40]

Outside of the vaccinations performed by the commissioners and an occasional visit of a medical officer on tour, people in Niumi received no formal medical treatment through the first three decades of the twentieth century (though one cannot help noticing such government expenditures as the £1,100 in 1921 for construction of new tennis courts at the Bathurst Sports Club, where European agents of mercantile firms got exercise[41]). In 1931 the untrained wife of North Bank Commissioner R.W. Macklin, with the assistance of a former Boy Scout who had a first-aid merit badge and training in first aid from the Protectorate Medical Officer, traveled with her husband throughout the province and did her best to minister to those with wounds and infections. Not until 1951 would the government open a Health Center for Niumi residents in Essau, and even then the center received only weekly visits of a "health sister," a dispenser, and two community attendants.[42]

Of course, the vaccinations were welcome and new roads and bridges beneficial—people did their dry-season traveling among villages more easily than ever—but within a generation most adults in Niumi recognized that the most important development matter was education, the key to advancement in the new colonial world. Thus, nothing frustrated them more than their inability to get even the basics of the English language taught to children on Niumi soil. The fact was that no one in the Gambia was getting much education—it was one of the colonial government's most glaring and, in the end, telling failures. Government records show education's low priority. Minutes from the Gambia Legislative Council for November 22, 1929 read, "The Honourable L.C. Ogden said that in past years it had always been contended that the Colony could not afford both the main things which it needed, *i.e.,* Education and Agriculture. It had previously been decided that Agriculture should take the first place."[43]

The cheap way to educate colonial subjects was to allow missionaries to do it, and the colonial government was all for that. Roman Catholics, Methodists, Anglicans, and Muslims had schools in Gambia, but, aside from the latter, which instructed most students only in the Qur'an and elementary Arabic, the Christian schools served a tiny number of select people, almost all of whom resided around the capital. The colony's first governor labeled the educational situation "a lamentable condition, and injurious at once to the best interests of the people and the government," but injurious it would remain. In 1900 the government granted £416 to the Christian and Muslim schools, and twenty-five years later, when the colonial budget was nearly £275,000, it designated only £3,460 to education.[44] In 1923 Gambia's Governor, Sir C.H. Armitage, opened a school intended for the sons of protectorate chiefs at Georgetown, halfway upriver. It was here that a number of influential Gambians of the post–World War II period received their primary education. But aside from a Wesleyan elementary school at Georgetown and a Catholic mission school at the far end of the colony, there was nothing outside of Bathurst.

Young boys and girls in Niumi had nowhere to turn. In the spring of 1932, St. Mary's Catholic Church opened a mission station and school in Essau, but it lasted barely a year.[45] It would be another seventeen years, in October 1950, when the government finally would see fit to open a school, again in Essau, and it would not be educating students effectively for another decade. A 1953 report of the school called it "the worst in the Protectorate," and included such damning remarks as "girls used as teachers' servants . . . children should not be allowed to use razor blades for handwork . . . discipline is appalling . . . useless teachers . . . all writing is poor." A 1961 review of the school that by then had 163 pupils, 50 of them girls, found improvement.[46]

Six miles up the road lay Berending, with Bunyadu a mile and a half away, and both of these former royal villages smarted over the privileges Essau received because its Sonko family provided Lower Niumi's chiefs. So when Essau got a school, the elders of Berending took action. With fifty Berending children needing schooling, they decided in 1955 to build their own school, and they did so and arranged for a teacher before requesting permission from the Board of Education. Government had little choice but to sanction the impressive initiative, especially since the Berending school was going to pay its own way, and in March 1956 the school opened with thirty-eight students. They met in a low, mud-brick building with a thatched roof; the main classroom was 40 feet long and 14 feet wide; half a dozen students sat around desks designed for two that villagers had constructed out of old packing cases; and the latrine consisted of three boreholes. The initial students, in only one grade, got instruction in the Qur'an as well as in arithmetic, English, and Mandinka. The quality was low. "The teacher talks far too loudly and children must not be struck," reads a 1957 inspection report; "the standard of writing is appalling and the books are disgracefully untidy." In 1959 the school met in a United Africa Company store while new buildings were constructed. After that, with a new teacher and advanced grades, the situation improved.[47]

But there still was no secondary school in Niumi. Those who qualified for the government-sponsored secondary school in Bathurst and who could afford the fees could seldom come up with the additional cost of room and board in the capital. Not until 1995 would a new government see fit to construct a secondary school in Essau, a handsome gray block building, where Niumi's youth could continue their education on their own soil.

As it was, education was something of a barometer for colonial development in Gambia. War, demonetization, depression, another war—all made colonial officials jumpy about spending money that would not lead in a short time to enhancing revenues. When empirewide initiatives for development came along, as they did in 1929 and 1940, Gambia gained little, and the largest postwar development efforts were pointed toward making Bathurst a cleaner and healthier place to live and grand economic initiatives. Between 1948 and 1952 Britain lost over £1 million on a failed scheme to raise chickens outside Bathurst and produce eggs for the English market—this before Niumi had an elementary school.[48]

A Quiet Broadening and Deepening of Islam

For West Africa as a whole, the colonial period was the time of Islam's greatest expansion. The number of West African Muslims doubled in the first half-century of colonial rule, gaining the religion more adherents in those fifty years than in the previous thousand.[49] But such was not the case in Niumi. By the time of the colonial takeover, most Niumi residents accepted Islam and considered themselves Muslims. The most important period for the religion's spread in the state had been the middle of the nineteenth century, when the wave of Islamic reform, abetted by the social and economic change that accompanied peanut production, swept through, slowed only by British interference. But by the century's end British officials were less antagonistic toward Islam; in fact, they recognized ways it could benefit colonial government and their subjects in the protectorate, and they established policies that had the effect of encouraging the religion. Thus, the colonial period stands more as a time of consolidating gains and increasing the depth of knowledge of Islam in Niumi.

If Gambian Administrator d'Arcy in the 1860s looked upon Niumi's Muslims as "crafty, ambitious, and sensual," his counterparts at the end of the century were much more favorably disposed toward the devout, austere men in long robes who conducted prayers in Niumi's villages. The reason for the change of attitude in the late nineteenth century was the widespread acceptance in Western intellectual circles of ideas about human progress set down initially by Auguste Comte. In league with some of the popular Social Darwinists of later years, Comte argued that monotheism was the highest stage of religious development, far above the "fetishism" of traditional Africans and others. "Muslim propaganda is a step towards civilisation in West Africa," reads a 1910 French account that summarized the opinions of many, "and it is universally recognised that the Muslim peoples of these regions are superior to those who had remained fetishist, in social organisation, intellectual culture, commerce, industry, well being, style of life, and education."[50] Certain practical considerations lent weight to the colonial governments' protection and encouragement of Islam. Throughout the Gambia protectorate, where the British had to establish and enforce the law despite being painfully understaffed, the existence of Maliki law and a body of Muslim legalists who studied and knew the law made administration easier. That Niumi's chiefs enforced Muslim law lent stature to the religion in general and to the learned men who knew the law in particular.

Continuing to be instrumental in popular acceptance of Islam in Niumi were old and new religious brotherhoods that had unique prayer rituals and emphasized different interpretations of Allah's will. The most important of these continued to be the Tijaniyya, which Maba had championed: most of Niumi's learned Muslims and most of its Qur'anic schools had identified with the Tijaniyya since the nineteenth century. Moreover, not far north of Niumi was the home ground of Ibrahim Niass (1900–1975), who started a reformed branch of the Tijaniyya that gained broad acceptance. The Niass family was a lineage of Tijaniyya scholars respected among Niumi's population at the beginning of the twentieth century. In the late 1920s Ibrahim broke from the family and established his own center of the Tijaniyya near Kaolack in Senegal, thirty miles north of Gambian Niumi. In his reformed doctrine he emphasized spirituality and mysticism, and wisely eschewed militant activities, instead focusing on personal purity—*jihad* of the heart. Niass named himself "Saviour of the Age" and following a successful pilgrimage to Mecca in 1937, perhaps with some sense of ordination by the Caliph of the Tijaniyya in Fez, he began sending representatives across West Africa to gain followers. Ardent Muslims in Niumi were among others who made the pilgrimage to Niass's mosque near Kaolack, where he could personally initiate them into the reformed brotherhood. Niass popularized Islam through use of such modern devices as radio to spread knowledge from the Qur'an and encouragement of active participation by women and children. The existence of other, altogether new brotherhoods—the Muridiyya, for example, which glorified hard work as a means of gaining spirituality—in the hotbed of Islamic reform in nearby Senegal added to interest in the faith through the colonial years.[51]

A change that occurred in the first half of the twentieth century that helped Muslim teachers and healers do their work and gain in popularity was the increasing ease of travel. No one ever moved too far from their homes in the rainy season, needing to remain close to crops and caring less to venture down puddled tracks amid the malaria-carrying mosquitoes that abounded. But in the dry season, between November and April, persons with things to sell—itinerant merchants, women with rice or vegetables, or Muslim diviners—looked to move from village to village in search of customers. Such travel had always been slow and dangerous—slow because it normally was on foot, perhaps leading a donkey or with human carriers, and dangerous if warfare was going on, brigands were lurking, or predatory animals stalked the wooded shoulders of paths. Colonial rule helped speed travel and make it safe. During the 1920s, motor lorries appeared in Niumi, first to carry peanuts to market and then to haul people and goods about. Through the 1930s Niumi's roads were widened to support the motor traffic. Moreover, the *pax colonia* was a reality. The ending of warfare and the seasonal raiding and marauding of precolonial times, the rounding up and bringing to justice of bandits and thieves, the ending of toll charges in individual villages and states, and the killing of dangerous animals—all of which occurred soon after colonial authority was established—made short- and long-distance travel cheaper and safer. This helped the itinerant Muslim diviner move about and do his work, but, more important, it allowed persons from a broader area to travel to villages where Muslim scholars conducted schools, healed, and sold various protections. By the 1930s Niumi was dotted by villages that were magnets for young men who wanted to learn to read Arabic and advance their knowledge of the Qur'an. Jinak, Aljamdu, Tubab Kolong, and Sika were villages that gained reputations for the learning, scholarship, and magical works that took place there in the hands of noteworthy clerics.[52]

Perhaps it was primarily Niumi's location near the leading Senegambian reformers, from Ma Ba to Niass, that made it something of a regional center of Islamic learning and magic. By the mid-twentieth century it was a place where widely noted Muslim lineages conducted schools; students came to reside from a broad hinterland to learn Arabic and know the Qur'an; and Muslim mystics divined, practiced healing, and made charms to bring good or ward off evil. Much of this activity is not evident in the records of colonial commissioners, who developed a *modus vivendi* with prominent Muslim scholars. Apparently government officials did not want to know too much about activities taking place in the major Muslim towns during the colonial period. This may have been because Muslims clung to forms of dependence not far removed from slavery, compounded by the fact that Muslim teachers took in students and made them work almost as if slaves in return for their board and spiritual guidance. But just below the more accessible veneer of chiefs, traders, and farmers, a greater Muslim subculture existed in Niumi through the years of the high tide of colonial rule.

The village of Aljamdu, several miles south of the old royal villages of Berending and Bunyadu, is an example of a center of Islamic scholarship and mysticism that thrived in the colonial period. Muslims settled Aljamdu late in the eighteenth century, at the request of the *mansa* residing in Berending, who wanted the best protective charms for the royal lineage and assistance for Niumi's forces at war. But as the Niumi state weakened through the middle of the nineteenth century, the marabouts of Aljamdu took the side of Ma Ba against their sometimes oppressive rulers. When British intervention thwarted their efforts and propped up the ruling lineages, Aljamdu's Muslim leaders stoically accepted the failure to create an Islamic state and went about their business in other ways. They opened schools and gained reputations as among the best scholars, teachers, and workers of magic in the lower Gambia. Families sent sons to Aljamdu to study the Qur'an; the Muslim leaders worked the young pupils hard through the farming season to produce peanuts. Aljamdu's mystics also made protective charms, and the village became a place to visit for healing and divining. Students from outside Niumi, who were especially gifted and promising young Muslims, stayed in Aljamdu or moved there, built families, and eventually participated in the business of schooling and mysticism that was the village's trademark. All was not absolute harmony among the various Muslim lineages that lived in Aljamdu; they sometimes competed for primacy in the workings of the schools and mystic practices. Disputes among competitors occasionally reached a level that brought attention: a commissioner's Quarterly Report of September 1939 notes, "Once again Upper Niumi District's numerous Mohammadan teachers have had a dispute over the appointment of an *Almami* [religious leader] at Aljamdu and unseemly brawling took place on two occasions in the mosque."[53] Such struggles suggest the importance of positions of authority among Aljamdu's Muslims and lead one to assume that with Islamic leadership went relative wealth and prestige.

One aspect of the broadening and deepening of Islam in Niumi was not entirely positive: the more devout persons became in their belief, the more conservative and accepting of their fate they tended to be. By the mid-twentieth century the intense desire for change and the militant approach to bringing about such change that were evident in the likes of nineteenth-century reformers were vague memories from the past. Niumi's widely respected Islamic scholars and teachers of the colonial era and after are quiet, austere, judicious in speech and action, and not inclined toward politics. These were qualities the colonial government appreciated—it all fit with the more positive attitude toward Islam as being appropriate for residents of the Gambian protectorate.

Naturally, the growing respect of the most scholarly of Muslim clerics and most devout of believers meant that their ways and attitudes spread among increasing numbers of Niumi's population. One who could not attain prestige through acquisition of wealth might be able to do so through strength of beliefs and the depth of devotion to Allah. The difficulty of this position is that when one becomes less able to recognize the human hand in one's misfortune, one becomes less inclined to take action to improve life on earth. This seems to be a problem in contemporary Niumi, where hardships relating to insufficient food, poor medical care, poor education, and lack of government concern for people's welfare are written off to "Allah's will." It is life after death that will be more rewarding.

Niumi in a World at War

As in most places around the world, the periods of the twentieth century when villagers in Niumi experienced the most sweeping and rapid changes were those when the world was at war. For about a decade following 1914, and for the same time or longer after 1939, people throughout Europe's African colonies came closer to realizing the extent to which they were involved in a world stretching far beyond their villages, their administrative districts, their colonies, or their regions of the continent than ever before. New experience opened wider the eyes of Niumi residents.

World War I

Official word of the outbreak of World War I came to Niumi at a district meeting in November 1914. In the shorthand of his diary, Commissioner Pryce notes, "Explained position of affairs in Europe, all much interested, and proclaimed their loyalty. Warned all to be careful over their food, no waste to be allowed anywhere." But people in Niumi did not need Pryce to let them know something was afoot overseas. France had begun drafting Senegalese men soon after the war's outbreak, and large numbers of them fled southward into British-ruled Niumi to avoid call-up. They brought word of the European war from the French perspective. Niumi's farmers put the Senegalese to work pulling groundnuts.[54]

War-related problems came to Niumi in a rush. By 1914 persons all about the protectorate were dependent on imported rice. In theory they bought rice only when one or another of their food crops failed, but in practice the crops failed frequently enough, or farmers (with considerable encouragement from traders and seemingly quieter nods from colonial officials) simply opted to plant more peanuts for export and less foodstuffs to eat, so that imported rice had become a staple of their diets and their preferred grain. Rice imports came to Gambia mainly in British ships, but British exporters got much of their rice from Germans in Hamburg, who had cornered a good portion of the East Asian market. German firms had been quietly making a concerted effort to capture more of the West African trade, acquiring some goods from abroad and manufacturing for export what one Gambian official called "cheap, attractive articles of fair quality." By 1914 Gambia was getting over half its rice from Germany, and also a good portion of other commodities people wanted: cotton goods, spirits, hardware, beads, shoes, hats, and perfume. With the outbreak of war Germany ceased being a source for Gambian imports, and soon German U-boats were doing their best to sink merchant ships leaving British and French ports for any destination. British firms were able to find rice from other sources, but not always enough, and prices for most imported commodities soared because of the war. "The behavior of the natives during a very trying and anxious time," writes Pryce in the middle of 1915, "has been all that could be desired. The low prices paid for the nuts after many excellent seasons, combined with the difficulty at times of obtaining essentials (these frequently at higher prices) from the traders, caused naturally a certain amount of discontent, but nowhere was there the least sign of disloyalty. . . . In all the Mohammedan mosques throughout the Province, prayers are offered daily for the success of the British forces, and for a speedy and successful termination of the War."[55]

There may have been no outward sign of disloyalty and daily prayers may have sounded for the Allied powers, but there was no enthusiasm among Niumi's young men to participate in the largely European affair. As the war turned to stalemate and consumed manpower and resources, Great Britain joined France and Germany in deciding to use colonial forces to assist in the war effort. For the Gambia, this meant recruiting for enlistees in the Gambia Company of the West African Frontier Force. The WAFF was an organization of troops from each of Great Britain's West African colonies; Gambia got its own company in 1902. Fitted out in khaki shorts and shirt, red vest, fez, and chocolate-brown tunic, the unit was to drill and stand ready to serve imperial needs.[56] Beefed up with fresh recruits, the Gambia Company trained outside Bathurst and on April 15, 1917, shipped off to German East Africa, where it would participate in the war, largely against Africans fighting for Germany.[57] As casualties mounted, authorities in London recognized the need "to replace wastage," so called for 250 new Gambian recruits. The colonial government was able to sign up fifty in Bathurst "from the large number of labourers and drifters, mostly from the Protectorate, who are numerous toward that period of the dry season," but getting the other 200 from such districts as Niumi was not so easy. "Under European leaders the Mandingos make good and reliable soldiers," reads a retrospective military report from 1923, "but they do not enlist very readily."[58]

Asked to round up twenty-five men in a month's time, Pryce went recruiting across Lower and Upper Niumi with a vengeance, only to be disappointed and frustrated in his failure. Meetings in the clerical villages, where people prayed noisily for British victory, turned up no eagerness for military service. "People here evidently require to be fetched," writes an angry Pryce. One reluctant Niumi man on whom Pryce was leaning to enlist told the commissioner, "Since you white men have come and taken us over we have come to look on ourselves as women. Now all of a sudden you ask us to be soldiers and we find we are supposed to be men after all." Another Gambian commissioner noted that by 1917 most Gambians just wanted the war "finished quickly before, as they put it, 'the whole world is spoilt.' "[59]

Price recognized the difficult spot chiefs would be in if made to force

Box 13. **Niumi Gets the Flu**

In global terms World War I involved a great coming together of the world's peoples. As they mingled, they spread diseases that previously had been confined to more isolated regions or spread more slowly. One of these diseases was a strain of influenza that passed among peoples of the world just after the war's end with great speed and devastating effects. Eighteen million Americans died from the postwar influenza epidemic, for example, and few on any populated continent were spared the disease.

Flu arrived in Gambia in August 1919 with an infected passenger on the SS *Prah* from Sierra Leone. It quickly swept through Bathurst, closing mercantile offices and bringing government operations to a standstill. Within a month 322 of Bathurst's 8,000 people had died. The acting governor reported that for three weeks "funerals were passing the bungalows at a rate of fifteen a day."* A posting of guards at docks and the only bridge leading out of Bathurst to enforce a quarantine apparently did not work. The flu crossed over to Niumi and, according to the commissioner, "raged in the district."

If there were good and bad times in Niumi for people to get sick, late summer was a bad one. Because of the shortage of food and the prevalence of malaria-carrying mosquitoes toward the end of the rainy season, it was an unhealthy time under any circumstances, and it was a period when all hands were needed to keep farms free of weeds and predators. The flu nearly brought farming in Niumi to a halt. "Weeding and clearing came to a complete stand-still for a considerable time in August and September," reads the district's 1920 annual report; "people who were not suffering themselves from the epidemic, and there were but few, having to look after and attend as best they could to those who were ill, farms were neglected and had to take their chances, the result being that all crops suffered considerably."† Weeds took over farms, forcing their owners simply to abandon them. This was particularly harmful since postwar prices for peanuts were high and a bumper crop would have meant relative prosperity. Across the North Bank Province, 1,600 persons died in one year from the influenza epidemic. The greatest mortality was among children, for whom it was a struggle to reach the age of puberty under normal conditions.

---

*H. Heaton to Secretary of State for the Colonies, Bathurst, November 8, 1918, CO 87/208.

†Annual Report, North Bank Province, 1919, CSO 1/162.

people to enlist. Still, he thought the forceful approach the only way to get recruits, especially at the start of the planting season when men wanted to remain and get their crops in the ground. In the end, his "constant hammering" on Niumi's chiefs and village heads turned up twenty recruits, but they came from among the lame and the halt; many were rejected for medical reasons.[60]

On top of local problems related to the wartime restrictions on world markets and fighting the war, people in Niumi faced other issues of more pressing concern. Smallpox broke out in three riverside villages before the end of 1914 and the colonial government could not get serum for vaccination. It isolated the villages and hoped for the best. Then, in the rainy season of 1917, one of the "cow-killers," this one probably rinderpest, swept into Niumi from Senegal, its first appearance since the 1870s, and decimated the large herds of the wealthiest families. Pryce estimated that between 75 and 95 percent of the cattle in Niumi died before the year was out. Because lineages kept a good part of their wealth in cattle, the disease wiped out family fortunes. One of the many long-term results of the epidemic was its effect on agriculture, for cow manure was the only fertilizer farmers had for their food crops and peanuts. Pryce notes that the people accepted the loss "with their usual equanimity."[61]

Nondomesticated animals, on the other hand, had a field day. To forestall smuggling of guns and gunpowder following the outbreak of war, the colonial government prohibited their importation and sale. Before long, hunting and animal control came to a standstill. There had not been an elephant in Gambia since 1906, but the number of lions increased and packs of hyenas grew in size, and the animals grew bolder. Through the war years, Niumi villagers had serenades of roaring and cackling through many nights, and it was common knowledge that one had to keep a lamp burning atop a grave for a full week after burial to keep hyenas from digging it up.[62]

World War II

World War II had still greater effect on Africans than its predecessor, and residents of Niumi felt the war earlier and more strongly than many others in the colony. From the moment the commissioner called in Niumi's chiefs and told them of the war's outbreak, the colonial government applied itself to controlling the dispositions and sentiments of Niumi's people. "The intricacies of European politics are, of course, beyond the comprehension of the majority of Protectorate natives," reads a North Bank Province Intelligence Report of September 9, 1939, "but steps have been and are being taken to ensure the correct direction of their sympathies."[63] Niumi's residents were soon treated to the riverside arrival of a "show boat" with catchy music and films with anti-German messages, and bards from Niumi attended a "griot competition" in Bathurst where, according to a London-based propaganda agent, competitors were primed "with rude things to sing about Vichy and the Germans, and the opposite about the British Empire."[64]

Niumi's location, across from Bathurst and astride the major road leading north into Senegal, was a major reason why its people felt the effects of the war so strongly. The commencement of war turned the once sleepy colonial capital into a bustling entrepot for Allied efforts. In the late 1930s the British ran residents out of the lower end of the Bathurst sandspit, converted it into a seaplane base, and constructed storage facilities for fuel and supplies. From then on, it seemed that construction projects were everywhere in the capital: Bathurst and settlements between there and the Atlantic grew into an important communications and storage point for the Royal Air Force and Royal Navy, a major BOAC staging base, and after the United States entered the war a passage point for American flyers on their way to campaigns in the Middle East and Mediterranean. The pull of laborers to the capital to construct the new facilities drew Niumi's young men. A 1941 intelligence report notes "a steady flow in the direction of Bathurst of anyone with anything to sell or with spare time after farming and hopes for a job," and as the war progressed the movement became steadier. "How frequently the younger men in this Province go to and from Bathurst," the North Bank Commissioner commented. "After returning for planting and weeding, many went to find work—and buy food. Now they are coming back to dig nuts, and shortly will be wending their way again to Bathurst."[65]

Finding work to buy food became critical for Niumi residents as Bathurst pulled in foodstuffs from the lower third of the colony to feed its workmen, foreign servicemen, and expatriate civilians. A colonywide "Dig for Victory" campaign to get men and women to grow more food crops, so they would have to import less, met only mild success. For some, the Bathurst market provided a grand opportunity. A 1941 Intelligence Report notes, "Ready employment and good wages, as well as the market for fruit and garden produce, has to some extent offset in the people's economy the rise of all prices." Yet, for others without sufficient foresight, effects of the war could hasten starvation. Elimination of a number of markets around the world where importing firms had long obtained products for Gambian consumption compounded colonywide food and commodity shortages. Gambians had grown dependent on rice from Burma, for example. In December 1941, when Japan entered the war and effectively cut Europe off from many Asian markets, the Gambia had outstanding orders for 1,400 tons of Burmese rice. As early as 1940 Niumi's chiefs forbade removal of food from their districts without permission, but the decree was largely unenforceable because of the high prices paid in Bathurst. The colonial government had to find ways to provision Bathurst and importing food from Niumi was one of the easiest. To compensate for the drain on Niumi's food, the government brought in and sold cracked wheat from the United States, but people did not take quickly to wheat and there never was enough. A Provincial Bulletin of August 15, 1944, reports people buying leftover seed nuts to eat in place of missing grain and laments, "there has certainly been hunger in the bigger Mandinka towns." Rationing of foodstuffs and other items went into effect in 1942.[66]

Niumi felt the war's effects too, because of its border with Vichy-controlled Senegal. Senegal's government regarded British Gambia as actively hostile (and vice versa), and Niumi lay astride the logical invasion route of soldiers coming south from Dakar. As early as 1940 a battalion of the West African Frontier Force crossed the river to patrol Niumi's roads and paths, and the British began mounting espionage and counterespionage activities along Niumi's border.[67] As 1941 progressed and Allied fortunes in the war looked bleak, war-related activities picked up considerably in Niumi. By June the government had erected a coastal battery on Barra Point, inside the remains of Fort Bullen, to ward off Axis planes.[68]

Recruitment for the Frontier Force reached Niumi at the same time the gun battery was being set in place. The colonial government put together recruiting parties, accompanied by a noisy band, that marched from village to village and offered rousing speeches.[69] Chiefs put the conscriptive bite on young men and, perhaps with exaggeration, Commissioner George W. Lorimer notes, "it was every where good naturedly accepted." (Colonial authorities never doubted the loyalty of their Gambian subjects—at least as manifested by the appointed colonial chiefs. When told of the collapse of France and the pending threat to Great Britain from German attack, chiefs in Niumi collected over £200 from residents for the War Charities Fund and the Spitfire Fund.)[70] Good naturedly or not, by April 700 men had stepped, or had been pushed, forward from the larger North Bank Province, and Lorimer reckoned that "after the farming season a further 250 recruits could be similarly obtained." By Lorimer's estimate, 5 percent of Niumi's male population had enlisted by the middle of 1941.[71]

With local troops shipping out, Niumi's border with Senegal still needed protection. The government met this need in two ways. In mid-1941 it authorized formation of two platoons, sixty men, of a "Home Guard," officially named the Gambia Local Defence Volunteers. These were men who knew the region well and thus would be able to act as guides, guards, gatherers of intelligence, and if necessary, saboteurs. If Gambia faced an assault from Senegal, they would then become guerrillas, harassing the enemy and delaying their advance. Commissioner Lorimer joined the force himself, and through two years in the middle of the war men of the Home Guard met, drilled, and passed along what information they had of French activities across the border.[72]

But the Home Guard was something of a ragtag band of quasi soldiers. There was forever difficulty finding boots for them to wear, let alone the puttees that their dress requirements called for, and finally the government purchased locally made sandals to outfit them. It was hardly a force to stop an advancing line of trained soldiers as might come south from Senegal. So before the end of 1941 the government decided to station permanently, on the edge of Essau in a new camp (appropriately camouflaged to look from the air like an African village), an organized battalion of the Frontier Force. This necessitated construction of the camp site as well as a supply depot at nearby Barra Point. Laborers for this work were Niumi males. Such activity brought more vehicle traffic than Niumi's meager roads had ever carried. Following the rainy season of 1941 Lorimer found the roads "well-nigh impassable," so the British brought in and stationed near Berending a company of Nigeria Pioneers, whose members could supervise road rebuilding and repairing beyond what chiefs could accomplish.[73]

Allied victories in North Africa in 1942 had the effect of removing the threat from Vichy-controlled Senegal, but did not lessen the unpredictable effects of the war on Niumi. Problems related to food shortages in Bathurst would not go away. When meat grew scarce in the capital in 1941, the Gambian government allowed herdsmen from Senegal to bring their cattle down a "free lane" through Niumi to Barra Point so that the animals could be transported across the river for slaughter. This seemingly benign act brought hardship because the herdsmen carried smallpox and caused an epidemic in one Niumi village. Also, the foreign cattle brought in once more the dreaded rinderpest and more local cattle died. Government efforts to rid Gambia of these killers of humans and animals had nearly succeeded before the war.[74]

In addition, there were typical wartime clashes between soldiers and civilians around Essau and Berending. Through 1942 a normal amount of testiness existed: young Berending men did not like soldiers congregating near the Berending pool where girls and young women did laundry. There had been minor incidents and one serious one, a rape. Most men were uneasy too, because of the colonial governor's decree of October 1942, making "every British subject and British protected person . . . age 18–55, and ordinarily a resident of Gambia . . . liable to combatant service for defence of Gambia either in or beyond Gambia." Even if not tabbed for combat duty, Gambians could be called to perform any work or personal service the governor deemed necessary in connection with the colony's defense.[75] The simmering pot boiled over in January 1943 when a group of soldiers decided to attend a Berending dance. A procession of drummers was advancing through the crowd and the soldiers were asked to make way.

Apparently, the way they made was not sufficient for a "juju drummer," one Demba Sonko, for the latter shoved a batallion sergeant, swore at him loudly, and, ripping off his shirt, challenged the soldier to a fight. Before the incident was quieted, villagers had brandished machetes, soldiers showed up with rifles, and although ordered back to their base, the soldiers made loud threats to burn Berending to the ground. Sonko's harsh sentence of six months in jail and then banishment from Niumi was not enough to satisfy the soldiers, while it further angered villagers.[76]

Yet the significance of most of this paled in relation to effects Niumi villagers felt indirectly because of the damage the war did to international trade. As the middle of the twentieth century approached, Gambians were more than ever dependent on an exchange relationship with the larger world. They exported peanuts at world market prices and purchased imported foodstuffs and various manufactured goods. The war-related threat to merchant shipping and emphasis on production of war materiel over consumer goods cut international trade. People felt the effects in every Niumi village. With 5 percent of its most robust young men off fighting for the Allies, crop production was considerably reduced and the Bathurst market pulled in locally grown fruits and vegetables so that villagers had to purchase food from somewhere else. What made this all especially frustrating was that, because of the construction work, soldiers' pay, and increased demand for the foodstuffs they were selling in Bathurst, Niumi villagers had far more cash in their hands than ever before. But now there was nothing to buy. Lorimer labeled 1941–42 "the worst trade season for years," noting that "cloth is almost unobtainable and food very scarce in the towns." The absence of sugar, cigarettes, and cloth were, in Lorimer's estimation, "bad for morale." Gambia's governor expressed his "great concern . . . that, at a time when financial opportunity is provided for a general raising of the standard of life for the African, the imports necessary to achieve this aim should be in such short supply."[77] Colonial officials would lament the shortage of trade goods long after the war's end.

Lorimer may or may not have been one of the more perceptive colonial agents, but he seemed to have an immediate sense of the range and depth of effects the war was having on Africans in his district. Applying what he knew about Niumi's residents to all Gambians, Lorimer writes in 1943:

> The Gambian realises that relations between the two races [here he is referring to the French and English] are still not normal: the threat of war has vanished, but he is mystified by the present situation, as are indeed some others. Internally, however, the events of the past year have provided an immense "opening of the eyes" to European methods and "civilisation." The Gambian has received much enlightenment and some rude shocks. But he is

an intelligent citizen with a good deal of hard common-sense and I think that the events of the period have done incomparably more good than harm. They have, especially, made him conscious of the advantages of proper education and a higher standard of nutrition and housing—all this due to contact with the Army—and this consciousness should provide the spur to the successful carrying out of the various development schemes now planned, to the lasting benefit of the people.[78]

Lorimer was at least partly right. Soldiers from Niumi had their eyes opened to other ways of life; were more conscious of the benefits education, better nutrition, and better housing could provide themselves and their families; and expected rapid improvement in their lives that development would bring. What Lorimer failed to mention in his optimistic assessment was what might be the result if such improvement did not arrive with anticipated speed.

Postwar Malaise

For a while, Niumi's men fighting for the Allies overseas kept things astir back home. The North Bank Province (it was renamed a Division in December 1944) provided more soldiers than any of the other Gambian provinces, and nearly all of those posted outside Gambia sent a good part of their paychecks home. Whenever Lorimer distributed drafts from the troops to their families, he noted a run on such cloth that existed in local shops. "Soldiers on leave and discharged heroes return to very well dressed wives," he commented wryly.[79]

But all was not good news coming from the Gambia Battalion. By the rainy season of 1944 the reality of the worst that war could bring began to filter in. Lorimer refused to allow the announcer on the colony's river steamer to read publicly a two-page list of those from the province who had been killed or wounded in Burma, but on October 12 some of the partially disabled members of the battalion came home. Thereafter, there would be a steady stream of men, most wounded or otherwise traumatized by the war, returning to Niumi's villages. The stories they told of fighting the Japanese halfway around the world may have enchanted some, but they frightened and angered others. The largest group of survivors returned from Burma in January 1946. Some, of course, did not come back. All together, 288 Gambians who saw action in Burma died there.[80]

Of course, those coming home to Niumi after the war were different men, returning to altered circumstances. Gambia's governor received "an interim warning of a confidential nature" from his counterpart in the Gold Coast: Such men, it read, "have had much time on their hands and have devoted it to improving their educational and technical qualifications and to discussing their future civil lives. In the opinion of their officers these men will expect on their return to find opportunities and facilities for employing with profit in civil life such skill and knowledge as they have acquired."[81]

Moreover, although they complained of their treatment in service to the British Empire, Niumi's men in the Frontier Force were paid as common soldiers and had managed to accumulate savings, most through Post Office Savings Bank accounts. Once home, they had money to spend. Many used part of what they accumulated to marry—certainly, for some, into families they never would have had the means to enter before. Others used their money to buy traders' licenses in hopes of entering into the world of buying and selling and thus competing with foreign merchants on their soil, but they were frustrated. Since early in the war, Gambia had been having trouble obtaining cloth, the commodity villagers wanted most. Such phrases as "extremely bad news about cotton goods" pepper reports of Gambia's colonial secretary throughout the war years and beyond.[82] Then a localized economic depression hit Niumi and the lower Gambia when war activities around Bathurst fell off with the conflict's end. By early 1946 the British had shut down the military bases in Niumi and the electric lighting plant on Barra Point that provided them with power. Suddenly, nights in Essau and Berending were pitch black again. At about the same time, American and British military personnel returned home, and military and civilian operations in Bathurst's vicinity closed or were cut back dramatically. There was an exodus from the capital on an unheard-of scale. Women in Niumi, who had developed a profitable tomato-growing business during the war, suddenly lost their market. Prices for vegetables spiraled downward; the artificial, war-related economy was over; and Niumi's men and women quickly faced an economy similar to the one they had lived with in 1938—growing peanuts for export and food crops for local consumption; importing rice, kola nuts, cotton cloth, and such small items as soap, matches, and cigarettes; and not much else.[83]

And things got steadily worse. By 1947 officials in and out of British government were facing the reality of a markedly different world for the United Kingdom and the British Empire than existed before the war. Great Britain had huge war debts, was facing the loss of American assistance, and, perhaps most devastating of all, no longer was making money from overseas investments. "Any inability to hold our own in world markets," warned the colonial secretary in a July 9, 1949, telegram to Gambia's governor, "must deprive us of essential supplies and our standards of life will suffer."[84] "Our," in this case, referred to British citizens.

Of immediate importance was Britain's lack of dollars to pay for goods it needed to import, brought about by its lack of exports. In August 1947 the home government asked the colonies to bite the economic bullet by reducing imports—especially of petroleum products, automobiles, textiles, and appliances—and to increase colonial production of exports that could be sold for hard currency. For Gambians, that meant growing still more peanuts, but at the same time they were not to import most of the items they wanted to buy with the cash they would receive.[85] Naturally, the returned servicemen were angry, and so were a number of others who had accumulated money in the war economy and now wanted to consume items they never before could purchase. The educated and politically aware among them recognized that Marshall Plan dollars to rebuild war-torn Europe helped those economies, but did not alter the larger British economic position. The money seldom trickled down to the colonial level.

The servicemen were demoralized as they demobilized. Of the 4,000 Gambians released from duty by March 1947, 2,500 returned to homes in the protectorate. Several hundred of these returned to Niumi. Although the Gambia had an Employment of Ex-Servicemen Ordinance, it applied in reality only to those resettling around Bathurst, and without jobs the government's good intentions came to naught even there. Between December and April, veterans could gain low-level employment loading peanuts—just the kind of work few of them wanted.[86] Those with skills might find work in the civil service. But most of Niumi's veterans returned home, some missing a limb or limping from wounds, and planted a peanut crop when the next season's rains fell. The war was over and the narrowness of life's options settled once again onto those residing in Niumi's agricultural villages.

Toward Independence

Because educated Africans living in and around the colonial capital dominated Gambian politics, and because almost everyone in mid-twentieth-century Niumi was poor and uneducated, its villagers did not get involved in political activity and the movement for independence from British rule until the very end of the colonial period. Over the objections of their conservative chiefs, they were dragged into political participation only after independence was in the wind.

As with many others in colonial Gambia, people in Niumi got an introduction to modern politics through the activities of one Edward Francis Small. Small was the leading edge in Gambia of a political movement that had been more active in Britain's other West African colonies for a slightly longer time.[87] He was Bathurst born in 1890, but educated in Sierra Leone on a government scholarship through two years at Freetown's Wesleyan

High School. A succession of civil service jobs, teaching posts with Gambia's Wesleyan Mission, and a position with the Maurel and Prom mercantile firm either did not satisfy him or his employers. In 1918 he became connected with the National Congress for British West Africa (NCBWA), an organization consisting of educated Africans in Nigeria, the Gold Coast, Sierra Leone, and Gambia, who were working to gain greater influence for themselves and their more educated peers in the governance of their colonies. Small was placed in charge of Gambia's Local Committee, and as such he was the Gambia's delegate to the 1920 NCBWA Meeting in Accra on the Gold Coast and one the next year in London. A 1921 NCBWA mass meeting in Bathurst, attended by several hundred, got the attention of Gambia's colonial government and prompted commissioners to agree in their 1922 conference not to allow any NCBWA member to "tamper with chiefs."[88]

Small had apparently made earlier, abortive efforts at starting a newspaper, the *Gambian Outlook and Senegambian Reporter,* but following his 1920 trip to England he recommenced publication of the journal that would occupy part of his time for a number of years. The remainder of the 1920s saw him passing to and fro between London and Bathurst, organizing an NCBWA meeting in Bathurst in 1925–26, seeking money for a Gambian railroad scheme, and keeping barely a step ahead of creditors. He did not endear himself to Gambian authorities when he organized a Bathurst laborers' strike in 1929, nor did he calm any fears by reprinting in the *Gambian Outlook* anti-imperialism articles by the likes of John Reed and George Padmore or by attending the European Congress of Working Peasants in Berlin. Colonial authorities occupied themselves by speculating on Small's membership in the Communist Party.

Back in Gambia in June 1930, Small focused his energies on a cooperative marketing scheme, the Gambia Farmers' Union. His new focus was prompted by his awareness that Gambian peanut growers received only a fraction of the price European firms paid for the peanuts and by the depression-related, 40 percent fall in peanut prices between December 1929 and February 1930.[89] Small's idea was to have Gambia's peanut growers market their own peanuts and thereby cut out the expatriate middlemen and shipping lines that overcharged. By so doing, he believed, the union could "give Gambian farmers the full benefit of European nut prices, and by bettering the farmers financially to stimulate them to greater output, which should tend to benefit the whole country."[90] A tireless worker, Small wrote to a long list of bankers, shippers, and buyers to arrange credit and transport of the union's guaranteed output of peanuts.

Later in 1930, two agents of Small's Gambia Farmers' Union crossed the river from Bathurst and went among Niumi's villages, asking farmers to join the union at the cost of a shilling, and sought out both Niumi chiefs to see if they would call a district meeting so that people could be informed about the union's activities. Under the influence of buyers and shippers in Bathurst, who saw Small as a "self-appointed champion of non-existing grievances felt by an imaginary body of citizens,"[91] the colonial government had forewarned each chief, so neither joined or called a meeting. Only the headman of Berending, a village with a reputation for doing things its own way, paid his shilling and signed up.[92] Two years later Small was still at it, informing the North Bank commissioner of his intention to travel about Niumi "to organize delivery of a cargo of nuts by the Gambia Farmer's Co-operative Marketing Board, for which credit of £10,000 has been opened in the Bank of British West Africa in Bathurst."[93] The commissioner did all he could to prevent Small and his message from reaching Niumi's farmers.

None of these schemes benefited anyone in Niumi in the short run, but they eventually played a role in improving peanut-buying practices and establishing farmers' cooperatives. Small himself was a harbinger of the more active and better-organized Gambia politicians in the post–World War II era. The organized and effective nationalist movements in the Gold Coast and Nigeria after 1945 moved Great Britain to grant those colonies more liberal constitutions as steps toward becoming independent, and this in turn brought new constitutions and political parties to the less politically developed colonies of Sierra Leone and Gambia. Throughout the 1950s Gambian political parties were personalist in nature and reflected the interests of Africans living in and near the capital. This meant that all those residing in such protectorate areas as Niumi—all together amounting to nearly 85 percent of Gambia's population—were ignored. Thus, when the protectorate-born, Wesleyan-educated, Glasgow-trained veterinary doctor David Jawara formed the Protectorate People's Party (PPP) for the 1960 elections and made one of the party's major themes overcoming the long neglect of the protectorate in favor of the colony, he garnered nearly 40 percent of Niumi's vote. Two years later, when Great Britain authorized full internal self-government with a constitution that allowed the protectorate twenty-five of thirty-six seats in the House of Representatives, 81 percent of Niumi's votes went to the PPP. Residents of Niumi believed they had a government in power that would champion their interests; they looked ahead to independence three years later with considerable optimism.[94]

The optimism was unwarranted largely because political independence would not alter Niumi's position on the periphery of the world economy. Not that Niumi residents would have disagreed with Gailey's assessment on the eve of Gambian independence: "that the new state will enter this world with only minimal facilities provided by the seventy year colonial administration of Great Britain."[95] They recognized that within the boundaries of old Niumi, at the beginning of 1965, there were two elementary schools, one dispensary, one paved road, and no trained physicians. They realized, too, that none of this mattered much, for any services or amenities that cost money were practically out of everyone's reach. But it was not simply the authority of commissioners, ordinances, and courts that kept people in Niumi in poverty. Regardless of the source of the authority—and of the authority itself—Niumi's residents remained producers of a primary product wanted by the industrialized core nations and consumers of manufactured goods that industries in the core produced. There was no visible alternative to continuing in this position.

Through the postwar years the same efforts in search of revenue to run the government and provide for development continued without success. Following the failed poultry project, attempts to find exploitable minerals or petroleum proved futile. Still, there was optimism. After the Korean War, the world economy jumped ahead and there was a decade of prosperity. Prices for primary products held firm or advanced, the world's industrial core produced goods cheaply, and Gambians joined others in believing that prosperity was just around the corner at independence. As almost everywhere else in Africa, The Gambia entered the world as a sovereign state with its citizens mindful of what had come before, but hopeful nonetheless.

Notes

1. Monthly Diary, Traveling Commissioner, North Bank Province, Jan. 31, 1921, CSO 2/460.

2. Annual Report, North Bank Province, 1929, CSO 1/168.

3. "Agreement Entered into Between Administrator R.B. Llewelyn and Maranta Sonko, King of Niumi," April 7, 1893, CSO 9/824; Treaty of Protection, Jan. 2, 1897, CSO 9/824.

4. Denton to Secretary of State, Nov, 6, 1903, CO 87/170; Annual Report, North Bank Province, 1905 (CO 87/74), 1908 (CSO 2/123), 1911 (CSO 60/2), and 1912 (CSO 60/2).

5. A good treatment of effects of the war and its aftermath on the world economy, with focus on Africa, is J. Forbes Munro, *Africa and the International Economy: An Introduction to the Modern Economic History of Africa South of the Sahara* (Totowa, N.J.: Rowman and Littlefield, 1976), ch. 5.

6. Michael Crowder, "The First World War and Its Consequences," in *General History of Africa, vol. 7, Africa under Colonial Domination, 1880–1935,* ed. A. Adu Boahen (Paris: UNESCO, 1985), 283.

7. S.M. Martin, "The Long Depression: West African Export Producers and the World Economy, 1914–1945," in *The Economies of Africa and Asia in the Inter-war Depression,* ed. Ian Brown (New York: Routledge, 1989), 74–94.

8. Churchill made this statement on November 10, 1942. Quoted in William Roger Louis, *Imperialism at Bay: The United States and the Decolonization of the British Empire, 1941–1945* (New York: Oxford University Press, 1978), 200.

9. After 1893, Niumi's Ceded Mile, though technically still part of the colony, was administered with the rest of Niumi as part of the protectorate. Once Niumi joined the protectorate, the Ceded Mile's special status was all but forgotten.

10. Lord Lugard, *The Dual Mandate in British Tropical Africa* (London: Blackwood and Sons, 1922).

11. Jan Hogendorn explains the theory behind such taxes in "Economic Initiative and African Cash Farming: Pre-colonial Origins of Early Colonial Developments," in *Colonialism in Africa, 1870–1914,* vol. 4, *The Economics of Colonialism,* ed. Peter Duignan and L.H. Gann (Cambridge: Cambridge University Press, 1975), 302.

12. Annual Report, North Bank Province, 1899, CO 87/159.

13. Annual Report, North Bank Province, 1919, CSO 60/2.

14. Extracts from Annual Reports, 1901, CSO 9/134; Lieutenant-Colonel H. Moyse-Bartlett, *The King's African Rifles: A Study in the Military History of East and Central Africa, 1890–1945* (Aldershot: Gale & Polden, 1956), 41–48.

15. Interview with Lamin Sowe, Berending, Lower Niumi District, The Gambia, March 16, 1996.

16. Harry A. Gailey, *A History of the Gambia* (New York: Praeger, 1965), 115–17.

17. H. Lloyd Pryce, "The Laws and Customs of the Mandingos of the North Bank Province of the Gambia Protectorate," unpublished report, 1906, CSO 1/151.

18. Traveling Commissioner's Report, North Bank Province, 1893, CSO 60/1.

19. Traveling Commissioner's Report, North Bank Province, 1894, CSO 60/1.

20. Traveling Commissioner's Report, North Bank Province, 1896, CSO 60/1.

21. Denton to Secretary of State, Bathurst, March 30, 1903, CO 87/168.

22. Ken Swindell, "African Food Imports and Agricultural Development: Peanut Basins and Rice Bowls in The Gambia, 1843–1933," in *Agricultural Change, Environment and Economy: Essays in Honour of W.B. Morgan,* ed. Keith Hoggart (London: Mansell, 1992), 161.

23. P.H.S. Hatton, "The Gambia, the Colonial Office, and the Opening Months of the First World War," *Journal of African History* 7 (1966): 123–24; Gambia Ground-Nut Trade Statistics, CSO 54/157.

24. See, for example, G.C.B. Parish to Commissioner, North Bank Province, Feb. 19, 1932; and R.W. Macklin to Colonial Secretary, Jan. 22, 1932, CSO 2/1167.

25. Archibald J. Brooks, Report by the Director of Agriculture, Oct. 22, 1930, CSO 75/11.

26. At one point in 1921 commissioners discussed taking silver ornaments people were wearing in repayment of the debt. Information on the debt problem is in Commissioners' Conferences, CSO 56/1; Annual Report, North Bank Province, 1921, CSO 1/163; "Increased Export Duty on Groundnuts," 1922, CSO 3/49; and "Rice and Seed-Nut Debt," March 26, 1924, CSO 1/166.

27. Gailey, *History of the Gambia,* 167–69; Annual Report, North Bank Province, 1922, CSO 1/163.

28. "Increased Export Duty on Groundnuts," 1922, CSO 3/49.

29. R.W. Cohen to Undersecretary of State for Colonies, London, Jan. 3, 1930, CSO 4/33.

30. Maj. John Bingham to Mr. Stanley, Edinburgh, Aug. 29, 1943, CO 87/255/7.

31. H.R. Palmer to Legislative Council, Bathurst, Dec. 14, 1932, CO 89/23.

32. Palmer, Address to Legislative Council, June 27, 1934, CO 63/10.

33. Quarterly Report, North Bank Province, June 30, 1937, CSO 2/1632.

34. Quarterly Report, North Bank Province, Sept. 30, 1936, CSO 2/1589.

35. Annual Report, Western Division, 1951 (CSO 63/9) and 1952 (CSO 63/10).

36. Roland Oliver, *The African Experience: Major Themes in African History from Earliest Times to the Present* (London: Weidenfeld and Nicholson, 1991), 187.

37. Gailey, *History of the Gambia,* 166.

38. Ibid., ch. 5.

39. Ibid., 166.

40. Denton to Secretary of State, April 19, 1904, Bathurst, CO 87/171.

41. C.H. Armitage to Secretary of State for Colonies, May 26, 1921, CO 87/213.

42. Annual Report, North Bank Province, 1931, CO 87/236/11; "Lower Niumi District—Medical and Health Matters," CSO 9/421.

43. Minutes of Gambia Legislative Council, Nov. 22, 1929, CO 87/213.

44. Gailey, *History of the Gambia,* 177.

45. "Establishment of Mission Station and School at Essau by St. Mary's Church Body," 1931, CSO 2/1142.

46. "Essau School, " CSO 6/43.

47. "Berending School, " CSO 6/59.

48. Gailey, *History of the Gambia,* 152–57.

49. J.C. Froelich, "Essai sur les causes et méthods de l'Islamisation de l'Afrique de l'Ouest du xie au xxe siècle," in *Islam in Tropical Africa,* ed. I.M. Lewis (London: Oxford University Press, 1966), 166.

50. A. Quellien, *La politique Musulmane dans l'Afrique occidentale française* (Paris: Larose, 1910), 100, cited in Donal Cruise O'Brien, "Toward an 'Islamic Policy' in French West Africa, 1854–1914," *Journal of African History* 8 (1967): 305. Discussion of the influence of Comte on colonial Islamic policy is in Peter B. Clarke, *West Africa and Islam: A Study of Religious Development from the 8th to the 20th Century* (London: Edward Arnold, 1982), 189–90.

51. Clarke, *West Africa and Islam,* 202–12; Donal Cruise O'Brien, *The Mourides of Senegal* (Oxford: Oxford University Press, 1971).

52. Information in this paragraph and subsequent discussion of the village of Aljamdu is based on information from interviews in Aljamdu, Tubab Kolong, and Sika in 1974–75.

53. Quarterly Report, North Bank Province, Sept. 30, 1939, CSO 2/1777.

54. Myron Echenberg, *Colonial Conscripts: The Tirailleurs Sénégalais in French West Africa, 1857–1960* (Portsmouth, N.H.: Heinemann, 1991), 29–31; Quarterly Commissioner's Diary, North Bank Province, Nov.–Dec., 1914, CSO 2/167.

55. Hatton, "Opening Months," 123–31; "Trade of the Gambia," Sept. 14, 1914, CSO 1/156; Annual Report, North Bank Province, 1915, CSO 1/157.

56. "Military Report on the Gambia," Dec. 12, 1923, CSO 1/164.

57. "The Gambia Company in East Africa," May 31, 1918, CSO 1/159.

58. "Military Report on the Gambia," Dec. 12, 1923, CSO 1/164.

59. Governor of Gambia to Secretary of State for Colonies, June 10, 1917, CSO 1/159; Annual Report, South Bank Province, 1917, CO 87/205.

60. Annual Report, North Bank Province, 1917, CSO 60/2; Commissioner's Diary, North Bank Province, June 30, 1917, CSO 2/167.

61. Extracts from Previous Annual Reports, North Bank Province, 1917, CSO 9/134.

62. "Military Report on the Gambia," Dec. 12, 1923, CSO 1/164; Annual Report, North Bank Province, June 1921, CSO 1/163.

63. Intelligence Report, North Bank Province, Aug. 31, 1939, CSO 75/4. Part of British propaganda involved showing Ministry of Information photos of successful Al-

lied activities. Such photos impressed people in Niumi, though not always as intended. Lorimer showed photos in one Niumi village and overheard people saying, "The British are fighting with guns and beating the enemy, and all the time they are taking photos!" But the overall effect of the propaganda was as intended. After hearing Hitler speak on radio, a Niumi villager described the Führer as "a man whose head crack." Intelligence Report, North Bank Province, Jan. 31, 1941, CSO 75/4.

64. Bingham to Stanley, CO 87/255/7.

65. Intelligence Report No. 8, North Bank Province, Sept. 26, 1941, CSO 4/241; Provincial Bulletin, North Bank Province, April 30, 1944, CSO 9/224.

66. Intelligence Report, North Bank Province, Jan. 31, 1941, CSO 75/4; Provincial Bulletin, North Bank Province, Aug. 15, 1944, CSO 9/224; Governor, Gambia, to Wagon, Nigeria, March 28, 1942, CSO 4/302; H.R. Oke, Address to Legislative Council, Nov. 19, 1940, CSO 89/23.

67. Annual Confidential Report, North Bank Province, 1940, CSO 3/156.

68. "Local Effects of the War in the North Bank Province," 1941, CSO 3/246.

69. "Report from a District Commissioner in the Senegal," 2nd Qtr., 1941, CSO 75/20.

70. Quarterly Report, North Bank Province, 1940, CSO 2/1861.

71. Intelligence Report No. 2, North Bank Province, June 1941, CSO 4/241; "Report from a District Commissioner in the Senegal," 2nd Qtr., 1941, CSO 75/20.

72. "Future of the Home Guard," Oct. 8, 1943, CSO 4/250; "Gambia Local Defense Volunteers," 1942, CSO 4/254; "Local Defense Volunteers," 1943, CSO 2/1919.

73. "Local Effects of the War," CSO 3/246.

74. Intelligence Report No. 6, North Bank Province, July 1941, CSO 4/241.

75. Compulsory Service Ordinance, Oct. 31, 1942, CSO 4/131.

76. "Relations with the Military in North Bank Province," 1943, CSO 3/415.

77. Intelligence Report, North Bank Province, 1942, CSO 4/241; Hilary Blood, Address to Legislative Council, Oct. 15, 1942, CO 89/30.

78. "Relations with the French and Local Effects of the War," 1943, CSO 3/246.

79. Provincial Bulletin, North Bank Province, April 30, 1944, 9/224.

80. Provincial Bulletin, North Bank Province, July 31, 1944, CSO 9/224; Interview with Sowe, March 16, 1996.

81. Resident Minister, Gold Coast, to Sir Hilary Blood, Accra, March 19, 1945, CSO 4/480.

82. K.W. Blackburne to G.W. Lorimer, July 30, 1942, CSO 75/20.

83. North Bank Divisional Bulletin, Feb. 1946, CSO 9/224; Annual Report, North Bank Division, 1946, CSO 75/26.

84. Secretary of State for the Colonies to Governor, Gambia, July 9, 1949, CSO 116/37.

85. "Economic Crisis," 1947, CSO 85/54.

86. "Resettlement of African Soldiers after the War," 1947, CSO 2/2831.

87. Information on Small's early life is from "Extract from Confidential Despatch to the Secretary of State," May 7, 1921, CSO 2/165. A study that includes useful information on the National Congress of British West Africa and Small's activities in Gambia in the context of twentieth-century West African nationalism is J. Ayodele Langley, *Pan-Africanism and Nationalism in West Africa, 1900–1945: A Study in Ideology and Social Classes* (Oxford: Clarendon Press, 1973).

88. National Council For British West Africa, Gambia Committee, June 18, 1921, CSO 1/163; Commissioners' Conferences, CSO 56/1.

89. In 1924, for example, when peanuts were bringing 4/3 a bushel in Liverpool, Gambian farmers received only 2/6 per bushel. Annual General Report, 1924, CSO 1/166.

90. Small to ?, n.d. [first page of letter missing], CSO 54/231.

91. Colonial Secretary minute, May 19, 1937, CSO 3/291, quoted in Langley, *Pan-Africanism,* 137.

92. Commissioner's Diary, North Bank Province, March 1930, July 1930, CSO 3/147.

93. Small to R.W. Macklin, Bathurst, Feb. 5, 1932, CSO 54/231.

94. Gailey, *History of the Gambia,* ch. 10. The optimism was not limited to Africans. Respected journalist and historian Michael Crowder expresses such sentiments in "Rice Revolution in the Gambia," a piece he wrote for *The Times British Colonies Review,* 3rd Quarter 1956 and 4th Quarter 1957, reprinted in Crowder, *Colonial West Africa: Selected Essays* (London: Frank Cass, 1978), 263–68.

95. Gailey, *History of the Gambia,* 183.

7

NIUMI IN DEPENDENCE

THE REPUBLIC OF THE GAMBIA, 1965–1996

The global outlook is in general bright but masks wide differ-
ences across regions and countries—for many, global optimism
co-exists with local pessimism. Accelerating outward-oriented
growth in the poorest countries will be a challenge.
—World Bank, 1995

The more things change, the more they remain the same.
—Alphonse Karr, *Les Guêpes*, January 1849

Gambian independence, on February 18, 1965, was a time for countrywide celebration. At villages up and down the river, politicians made speeches, people slaughtered large animals and prepared feasts, and dancing went into the night. The grandest celebrations were in the capital. Bathurst was packed full. The Duke and Duchess of Kent were the most easily recognized of a group of visiting dignitaries. Since Niumi was just across the river, large numbers of its villagers put on their best clothes and boated over to the capital to see or participate in drama festivals, wrestling matches, or drumming and dancing contests. A Berending youth group was one of several organizations performing traditional dancing in Bathurst's Box Bar Stadium. Many from Niumi were in the crowd at MacCarthy Square on the night of February 17 when, as midnight approached, the Union Jack came down and Gambia's new, red, green, and blue flag inched up the flagpole. The fireworks that followed lighted faces full of contentment. It might be a rocky road ahead, but Gambians were driving their own vehicle.[1]

It took a few days for people to return to their villages across the river. When they did, they must have experienced the letdown one feels after the ending of such a long-awaited event. Three days after the independence hoopla, walking down one of Bathurst's empty streets, the few remaining decorations cluttering the sidewalk or flapping in the Sunday morning breeze, a Gambian told a friend, "You know? It's as if nothing had really happened. Everything's the same as it was."[2]

220

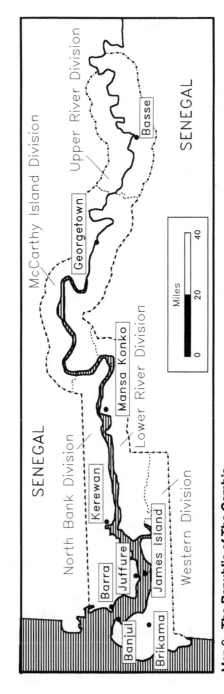

Map 9. The Republic of The Gambia

The speaker could have been any one of the several thousand Niumi residents. They had a new government, all their own, but most other aspects of their lives were about the same and not likely to change.

Global Realities of the Mid-Twentieth Century

The world that Niumi's residents were celebrating entering as part of an independent nation was one that neither their ancestors at the beginning of the century nor their colonial commissioners of a generation earlier could have dreamed of. And from 1965 the pace and scope of change have been so rapid and broad that few in any region of the world have been able to grasp the consequences and plan adequately for the future.

The major phenomenon of world history over the past thirty years has been what it is easiest to call "globalization"—the increased integration of peoples all about the world into a global network wherein changes in one place affect people in every place. At the root of this integration has been the desire of the world's strongest core nations to maintain or even broaden the openness of world trade, thus allowing them to take full advantage of their positions in the center of the world economy, coupled with advances in technology that have reached many aspects of human living, directly or indirectly, and built on themselves so that technological change has come faster, and affected more people, every year.[3]

The stage for increased globalization was set by the end of World War II. The Soviet Union and the United States emerged as the strongest nations in the world—politically, economically, and militarily. In its own way, each tried to institutionalize its position of power around the globe. The Soviet Union spent mightily on industrialization and military strength at the expense of social and environmental betterment for the future, and used that strength to support and control allies in selected spots around the globe. The United States, recognizing its need for markets for the goods it was producing (which amounted to 65 percent of the world's output in 1945), set about creating international economic institutions that would allow for management of the world economy to the long-term betterment of the country. To serve these ends, in the last years of the war, under the broad auspices of the United Nations, the International Bank for Reconstruction and Development (the World Bank) and the International Monetary Fund (IMF) came into existence. These institutions lent money, provided by member nations—over half from the United States at first, but more in recent years from western Europe, Japan, and oil-rich nations—to countries to assist in reconstruction and development "by facilitating the investment of capital for productive purposes [and] to promote private foreign investment by means of guarantees or participation in loans [and] to supplement private investment by providing, on suitable conditions, finance for productive purposes."[4] For a decade or more, most of these loans went to rebuild the economies of war-ravaged western Europe. Then more of the money went to developing nations. Loans and technical assistance from these institutions went to nations open to capitalist development, often went for projects (like improvement of port facilities) that would promote importing and exporting, and usually came with stipulations. These often tended toward such measures as abolition of import controls, wage freezes, limits on government expenditures, and removal of price controls that would turn out to be favorable over the long run for core nations that imported raw materials and exported manufactured goods.

Much of the technological change was the result of the prolonged period of hot and cold war. Western military-instigated advances in communications, transportation, and information management brought peoples of the world into closer and faster contact. The world economy became more integrated still, increasingly dependent on, and responsive to, world market conditions. The new technologies were most efficient when involved with large-scale production. Corporations expanded to increase the scope of their control. With worldwide operations, newly forming multinational corporations could take advantage of cheap labor, good access to raw materials, and expanding markets no matter where each existed.

The rapidly growing world economy did not immediately bode ill for the less-advantaged nations. For the third quarter of the twentieth century, as the rebuilding of the war-torn world and then military spending associated with the Cold War and conflicts in Korea and Vietnam created demand and stimulated production, world output tripled. The price of petroleum that fueled world transportation and some of its electrical production remained artificially low; most basic commodity prices held firm or rose; so even those on the periphery of the system found their economic lives improving (as measured by gross domestic product per capita), not as rapidly as in the core areas, but improving in real terms nonetheless.

Among the core nations of the world system, the catchword through the 1960s and 1970s was *growth*. As consumers of world resources and producers of goods to be sold about the globe, these core nations sought more and greater markets, especially those on the system's periphery, where improved and more widely disseminated medical technology was bringing about an unprecedented rise in population. Increased resource production in the peripheral nations, brought about in part by grants and loans from core nations and their associated banking system, would provide people more money with which to consume goods from the core nations—given a general openness of the market. And grants and loans were useful carrots to reward countries for political allegiance in the era of Cold War competition.

Some of this fit nicely with the philosophies of peripheral nations, where emphasis was on development. While a handful of nations allied themselves with the Soviet bloc and pursued socialist development policies that encouraged slow building from the bottom to improve somewhat equally the lives of most of the nations' peoples, more countries saw the practicality of accepting the inequalities in working with the capitalist world system that was in place. These countries recognized the need for money to develop; saw that their major way of getting money was through exporting the lone resource, or the small group of resources, they had been exporting; wanted access to the material goods the core nations could supply; and thus generally established policies that made for openness of trade and stimulated greater resource production. Early forms of development in these countries tended to focus on port construction, bridge building, and road improvements, rather than expansion of health facilities or schools, because the improved infrastructure would bring greater trade and more money, which could then be tapped for better medical care or improved education. In this fashion, through the 1960s and into the 1970s, with such notable exceptions as Cuba, Tanzania, and Guinea, most poor nations worked with a consortium of public and private institutions in and around the core nations to tie themselves more thoroughly to the world economy and build up their national wealth as the first step toward development. If foreign banks and multinational corporations were involved in a peripheral nation's economy more deeply than one might wish, well, so be it in this necessary stage toward general betterment.

Technology enhanced the fiscal position of many of these "developing countries" with advances in agriculture related to a "Green Revolution." With mechanization and new kinds of tools, agricultural-exporting nations could increase their acreage under cultivation, and with new seeds developed through hybridization and new chemicals for weed control and fertilizers they could improve crop yields. Perhaps the poorer peasant families could not afford the best seeds and fertilizers, but larger producers could, and export production shot up. Through the 1960s and beyond, the economic outlook on the periphery was brightening. Some thought the optimism of the independence period was not misplaced.

Naturally enough, those in charge of governments in the poor countries were impatient to experience the benefits of development. If better lives were to be led, they believed, if personal wealth was to grow, if the number and quality of material possessions were to increase, if more advanced schooling and access to health care were to be available, let it be now rather than later—at least for some. The *some* turned out generally to be themselves—government bureaucrats, loyal political allies, and wealthy private citizens, who often were involved in business that the government approved. This being the case, an important route toward social and material betterment was through the civil service. Government ranks swelled with educated and partially educated friends, allies, and kin of higher officials. Of course, so did the government payroll.

It would take just a few years of the middle-1970s to burst the bubble of satisfaction for core and periphery nations alike. In retrospect, one can see the unhealthiness of many relationships in the world economy of, say, 1970—of global dependence on petroleum, the price of which remained artificially low; of core dependence on exports to the world's growing numbers of poor people; of peripheral reliance on monocrop agriculture and dependence on imports for basic needs. But it took the drastic measures of the major oil-producing nations, acting together under the Organization of Petroleum Exporting Countries (OPEC), shocking the world with an oil embargo that ended up raising the price of crude oil by 380 percent between 1973 and 1975, to make many realize that dependence on the world economy had its pitfalls. The cost of oil was the trigger for rapid inflation of most of the world's currencies; as inflation rates soared, the volume and value of world trade spiraled downward. The Green Revolution was not beneficial in some world economic matters. While it resulted in much greater staple crop production and thus more food for growing populations, for many commodities it meant that supply outstripped demand, thus lowering world prices. From the late 1970s, nations that balanced their budgets with revenues from cocoa, cotton, coffee, peanuts, palm oil, or coconut oil found greater need for money (to purchase petroleum products and other imports, the prices of which rose because of the increased cost of petroleum-based transportation), yet had less of it because of their reduced revenues from exports. To fill the budget gap, such countries sought increased aid, and sometimes they got it: as long as Cold War powers were vying for allies, strategically important poor nations, at least, could obtain military and other aid to fill in budget deficits. Once the Cold War began winding down in the 1980s, however, neither Soviet supporters nor Western nations were as eager to prop up small countries with foreign aid. The countries thus turned to increased borrowing, something they had been doing to a lesser extent through the 1960s and 1970s. The amount of debt poorer countries owed to wealthier ones rose quickly. The proportions were staggering: from $50 billion in 1970 to $400 billion in 1980 to over $1 trillion in 1990.[5]

By the mid-1980s, conditions in the world economy were not improving for the poorer nations. The gap between rich and poor, core and periphery, seemed to be widening; the public debt of the poor nations continued growing; here and there governments toppled, replaced by military rulers or governments of questionable popularity and stability; and many countries tottered along the brink of default on their loans. With the global economic outlook dimming for the poorer nations, and with concerns over default in the world's wealthier nations, where economic well-being relied partly on interest from loans and profits from sales about the globe, the major international lending agencies of the capitalist world—primarily the World Bank, the International Monetary Fund, and cooperative private banks—took action. Before approving new loans that some poorer nations now needed desperately, sometimes simply to pay the interest on their existing debt, the institutions began insisting that such nations agree to alter certain aspects of the structure of their economies. Such "structural adjustment" programs often included curbs on government spending, reduction of the size of the civil service, devaluation of currencies, and ending price supports for imports (including foodstuffs). Into the 1990s, some poor countries that took these prescribed measures began recovering from the most immediate of their economic problems, at least in the short term, but it was often at the expense of their popular support. With fewer jobs, higher prices for most goods, fewer public services at greater expense, and a general deterioration of the quality of life, people questioned their governments and looked askance at the system that kept them hungry, unhealthy, and impoverished. It was not a situation that bred stability.

Around the developing world in the 1980s and 1990s, governments struggled, teetered, and toppled. Some, like Mexico, were important enough to their neighbors and the world economic system to be bailed out. Others, like Liberia, were economically and strategically insignificant, and so were allowed to collapse. Through it all, few thought much about The Gambia. It was full of "smiling, happy people," the tourist brochures read, and it had a reputation for being one of Africa's small number of working democracies.

New Rulers, Old Rules

As revelers returned from across the river, and as the hubbub of independence celebrations died down in Essau, Berending, Aljamdu, and Sika, Niumi's villagers took stock in those early months of 1965 and believed their lives to be on a better course. It was not just that their colonial rulers of sixty-eight years were gone and that fellow countrymen were now running the country: the party in power, the People's Progressive Party (PPP) of Prime Minister Jawara, had its origins in the plight of Gambia's long-neglected rural areas, where development paled in relation to the advances experienced in Bathurst. Essau's

Alhaji Mang Foday Sonko—Maranta Sonko's great-grandson—had won a
seat in Gambia's parliament. People in Niumi expected the government, the
party, the prime minister, and their new member of parliament to look after
them. They anticipated prosperity in good years and a fair shake even when
crops and prices might not be so good.

They did not get either. For a few years the optimism prevailed. The new
government was of the practical school that thought one must build on what
one did best. For The Gambia, that was growing peanuts, which still made
up 90 percent of the country's exports. "An amazingly simple answer to this
country's crushing economic problem is now being put forward here," reported an observer at independence. "It is just to grow more groundnuts. . . .
Instead of chasing difficult alternatives, why not make the most of what
nature favors? . . . If the annual crop was something like 100,000 instead of
70,000 tons this economy could look very different. It may be that the
country's main economic problem is not that its only export is groundnuts
but that there are not enough groundnuts to export."[6]

It seemed a reasonable argument. Only the world market stood as a
hurdle. "I can say with confidence," said Gambian Finance Minister Sherif
Sisay in 1966, "that this country could, in the foreseeable future, balance its
recurrent budget with a modest surplus available for development expenditure, if it could rely upon the world price of groundnuts remaining at the
levels prevailing during the past season."[7] These were arguments that
Niumi's farming families could understand and do something about. Crops
grew well through 1967—in fact, Gambia exported more peanuts that year
than ever before—and the government-set price of 140 dalasis per ton was
not too bad. Most Niumi farmers did not know that the government agency
that marketed the peanuts, the Gambia Produce Marketing Board, sold the
crop for 307 dalasis per ton, giving the farmers just 46 percent of the
export price.

But then the first of a series of drought years came along and cut production of peanuts and food crops. It was unfortunate that the drought arrived at
the time when Great Britain was reducing subsidies to the Gambian government, as scheduled with independence, prompting officials to seek ways to
enhance annual revenues. With such private buyers as the United Africa
Company and the Compagnie Française de l'Afrique Occidentale recently
excluded from peanut marketing, the government had an easier time still in
bringing in more revenue: it merely had to pay the peanut growers less of
the export price. Thus, in 1968, for the first drought-reduced crop, the
Marketing Board again paid 140 dalasis per ton, even though the price it
received had gone up to 372 dalasis per ton—rendering Niumi's farmers
just 38 percent of the export price. And over the next fifteen years they

---

Box 14. American Policies and Life in Niumi

The U.S. Government expresses an honest desire to improve the living conditions of the world's poor. Through national and international agencies, it provides money—loans and grants—to aid such people as those inhabiting villages in Niumi. But, sometimes, seemingly benign national policies that have at their root the support of influential American political interests have more of a negative effect on such people than the positive results of the grants and loans

The United States protects its peanut growers. Since the 1930s the U.S. Congress has enacted legislation to aid various groups of farmers, supporting prices, blocking foreign imports, paying to limit acreage planted, and more. Such support has helped peanut producers in the American South to the extent that peanuts are the country's fifth-largest commodity. In 1975, the year prior to the election of a Georgia peanut grower and processor as president, the United States provided $150 million in subsidies to its peanut farmers. At various times it has used tariffs and outright restrictions to keep foreign peanuts out of the country. "It is easier to import semi-automatic rifles or toxic chemicals into the U.S. than to import peanuts," wrote an American policy analyst in 1993. Such strong political action organizations as the Peanut Growers Association remain active in Washington to make sure efforts to reduce the federal supports and import quotas do not succeed. As late as February 1996 it was successful in blocking a vote in the House of Representatives to reduce the support level by about 10 percent.

How has this affected people in Niumi? Primarily by closing off one of the world's largest markets for peanuts and peanut products and thereby lowering the price Niumi's growers, and others around the world, get for peanuts. The United States consumes great quantities of peanuts. Of the 3.7 billion pounds of the product that were harvested in America in 1975, about one billion pounds went into peanut butter and another billion became salted peanuts, roasted peanuts, or peanut candy. Most of the rest was crushed and sold as oil or meal. The hulls become sound insulation, wallboard, or the lining of bottle caps. Opening such a market to foreign peanuts would raise world prices and mean the Niumi farmer would receive better prices for the nuts he produces.

There is growing national and international pressure to end preferential treatment for American peanut farmers and open American markets to foreign imports. The 1996 amendment in the House of Representatives to eliminate the peanut program failed by only three votes. But reduction or elimination of the program will not matter so much for Niumi these days. They have been getting so little for their peanuts that many have turned to other things. Strange farmers no longer come to Niumi to make a crop; young men in villages are heading off to urban areas in search of other opportunities. Maybe higher prices will return emphasis to peanut farming in Niumi. But maybe not.

Sources: A sampling of relevant materials on American peanut subsidies and related matters is "Peanuts: From Carver to Carter," *New York Times,* August 24, 1976, 37; "In Plains, Ga., Carter Is a Hero and Butz a Villain," *New York Times* March 31, 1976, 43; "House Vote Keeps Peanut and Sugar Price Supports, "*New York Times,* February 29, 1996, 15; and James Bovard, "Trade Nuttiness," *Wall Street Journal,* December 13, 1993, 14A.

received a steadily smaller proportion: 29 percent of the export price in 1974, 23 percent in 1984.[8] Retrospective criticisms of the Gambian government's first twenty years were sharp: "On the average, between 1964/65 and 1984/85, the peasants were robbed of 60 per cent of the international price of groundnuts!" wrote a commentator in *West Africa*. "For 20 years the Jawara government 'officially' took, free of charge, three of every five bags, leaving the peasant with a gross of two. With deductions for subsistence credit, fertiliser, seed, etc., the peasant would end up with a net one bag out of five."[9]

Adding to the difficulty was the growing need to import rice, and its cost. Gambians had not been able to produce enough food for its population for a long time, but as the population grew much more rapidly after the middle of the twentieth century (meaning a larger proportion of the population would be under a productive age), as agricultural production focused on peanuts, and as more people found alternatives to farming in urban areas, the need for food imports grew. Through the first half of the 1960s, The Gambia was importing between 9,000 and 10,000 tons of rice each year—at a time when the escalating warfare in rice-producing regions of Southeast Asia cut production and led to a rise in the world price. The Gambia's government controlled and subsidized the price of rice to keep it low—largely to mollify the city people, who did not grow any food for themselves and thus had to buy whatever they consumed—but by planting time in 1968, just when Niumi's villagers were running low on food and needing to buy rice, the rising world price forced the government to raise The Gambia's controlled price of rice. It was a bad year for peanuts and home-grown food because of the drought, and it turned out to be a bad year to be needing rice.[10]

Outwardly, the situation in The Gambia continued to look promising. Through the 1960s the country's economy experienced an annual growth rate of 4.5 percent, against a population increase of 2.6 percent. Annual per capita income for 1968 rose to $260, an all-time high. World peanut prices went up steadily through the mid-1970s, and so even with the persistent drought cutting into crop yields, the government could boast large exchange reserves and almost no foreign debt. Such was rare indeed for developing countries of the time.[11] Government planners must have been concerned by the rise in petroleum costs in 1974, the related rise in the costs of many other imports, and the dip in peanut prices that occurred in the mid-1970s, but not so much that it shelved its First Development Plan in 1975. The plan was an economic directive driven partly by government officials' political concerns and partly by their self-interest.[12] The PPP was comfortable with its support from the likes of Niumi folk; they were part of its traditional, rural political base that the party could count on. But party leaders worried about urban groups in and around Banjul (the new name for Bathurst, from the old name for the sandy island the city rested on, after 1973). They recognized that an economic plan to benefit urban dwellers that did not appear to ignore totally "the provinces" could enhance their grip on political control, adding urban support to complement their solid rural backing. Such a plan, too, would provide resources for their own personal, individual economic benefit, for they were now mostly urban dwellers, and policies that favored bureaucrats and businessmen living in Banjul or its nearby residential communities favored them. The new plan created several new, urban-based state agencies (that could be filled through patronage appointments); doubled the size of the civil service and increased public investment, largely in urban enterprises, over six years; and provided tax breaks and loan guarantees for urban-based businesses. What business were they fostering? It turned out that with import duties in The Gambia considerably lower than those in surrounding countries, Gambian businessmen could import foreign-produced goods and then re-export them to merchants in Senegal, Mauritania, Mali, Guinea-Bissau, even Upper Volta, where higher tariffs were in place to stimulate manufacturing. The re-export trade increasingly became an important element in Gambia's economy. From the mid-1970s, a major way to get ahead was to get involved in trade and transport: buying and selling goods and moving them, or moving the people seeking them, around the country and across borders.

As was typical, the plan was financed not by taxes on the trade, for such might slow the re-export business and would certainly irritate urban merchants, but by government profits from the marketing of peanuts that farmers grew in such rural areas as Niumi. Gambia's government was "taking from the poor rural areas to enrich a selected few in the urban areas," wrote a *West Africa* commentator.[13] Those few squeaky wheels in Niumi and other rural areas, who recognized that profits from their hard work were going to benefit businessmen and bureaucrats across the river, got a few squirts of government grease: a new road here, a grade added to a school there, and perhaps an opportunity to open a branch of a Banjul-based business enterprise in the local community.

Around 1980, The Gambia's peanut-based economy began to wither like the plants in the drought-plagued fields. In addition to the lack of rainfall, parasite infestation, and labor shortages in rural areas—the result of young men heading off for perceived opportunities in Banjul—cut peanut production. At the same time the world market price for peanuts plummeted. The Marketing Board kept a huge reserve so that it could cope with such fluctuations, but it was staffed largely by political patrons who were not particularly clairvoyant, and then the Gambian government drew off 40 million dalasies of the reserve to cover its own budget deficits. By 1984 the Marketing Board had no reserve and owed the Central Bank 110 million dalasies. A year later Gambian peanut production was 45 percent lower than in 1976.[14] With its usual source of revenue collapsing, but not wanting to alter its urban-friendly policies, the government sought grants from Western donors and loans from commercial banks. For either one, they trumpeted Gambia's "open" economy, its stable position as one of Africa's few working democracies, and its status—with peace existing all about and no standing army—as the "Switzerland of Africa." It was a package few lenders could turn down. In 1981 the World Bank declared The Gambia a worthy place for investment, noting that "the economic policies of the government, including producer prices, have been quite satisfactory . . . [and] the poor growth record of the 1970s was almost exclusively attributable to unfavorable weather conditions."[15] Even after an abortive coup in 1981 that left 1,000 dead and Senegal's army on hand to keep order, short-, medium-, and long-term loans were available. So between 1980 and 1985, as even core nations in the world system were fighting inflation and worrying about cash flows and balances of payments, The Gambia's government borrowed heavily so that many in the country could live beyond their means. By 1985 The Gambia owed the World Bank, the IMF, and private commercial banks in various core nations a sum equal to 114 percent of the little country's annual gross domestic product. It had fallen behind paying the interest on these loans, too; its debt-service arrears—simply the interest on its loans that was *overdue*—amounted to almost two-thirds of the 1985 gross domestic product. Yet, oddly, as more of the money for the civil service and urban development came from foreign borrowing, most Gambians seemed to notice less where it came from. Like some very slowly advancing disease, foreign debt came to be recognized as a problem only after its consequences threatened national death.[16]

Of course, under the circumstances such a threat was not long in coming. By 1985, as if smacked rudely in the face with Gambia's economic problems, foreign donors and lenders began refusing to provide further money. Food and fuel shortages began to appear, even around the capital, where at times electricity was off as much as it was on, and the government had only enough foreign exchange in reserve for two weeks of imports. In August 1985 a sobered government introduced an Economic Recovery Program that was generally in line with structural adjustment requirements normally set out by the IMF. There is no doubt that officials from the lending institutions had whispered in the government's ear.

In brief, the new program drastically cut spending by the Gambian government (forcing a layoff of 20 percent of the government workforce), allowed the national currency to depreciate 120 percent in six months (thereby raising prices of imports), and took measures to raise government revenues (raising utility and transportation prices, cracking down on customs fraud). This was mostly difficult news for poor villagers in Niumi, but it was at least partially offset by another portion of the policy on which the IMF insisted: raising the price paid to farmers for their peanuts 50 percent *above* the world price, which required a government subsidy equal to 8 percent of the country's gross domestic product. It was an effort to return peanut exports to the previously important role in the country's economy.[17]

The reform program worked rapidly: inflation fell to an annual rate below 10 percent, trade deficits fell, the government paid its debt arrears, foreign currency reserves grew, and over four years the annual per capita income in The Gambia grew by 4.9 percent. Foreign donors and lenders smiled and reopened their coffers. By 1990 The Gambia was again a developing country recommended for investment. But for people in Niumi the results of the program were mixed. The immediate rise in payments for peanuts, abetted by a return to normal rainfall for several years, meant that its farming families had more disposable income. Annual per capita incomes went up 12 percent in three years in The Gambia's rural areas. A temporary dip in the world price of rice even helped many get through the hungry season. The benefits for farmers were not long lasting, however. After three years of subsidies and higher prices for peanuts, the government began cutting such subsidies until they were gone altogether by 1990. In that year Gambians exported 130,000 tons of peanuts; then the falling prices and lingering drought brought a dramatic drop in peanut production—to 75 tons in 1991 and 65 tons in 1994. By the latter year, agricultural production made up only about one-quarter of The Gambia's gross domestic product, and peanut exports were just over 10 percent of export earnings.[18] By the 1990s, the peanut had lost its position in the center of the Gambian economy, a position it had held for 150 years. Older men in Niumi must have scratched their heads, patted their empty stomachs, and wondered what was happening to the life they had always known, tied into the cycle of the peanut.

A temporary alternative to peanut farming for some Niumi residents, which also was related to effects of the structural-adjustment program, had to do with the re-export trade that passed through the region. Measures intended to "liberalize" trade and enhance the "outward orientation" of The Gambia's economy kept import duties low. This meant that people in the country could import foreign goods at prices cheaper still than nearly all the neighboring countries. Thus, even more than before, Gambian merchants imported foreign products for rapid sale across the nearby international borders, to Senegal especially, but also to the several other regional countries. Following the 1990 breakup of the Senegambian Confederation, an attempted amalgam of the economies of Senegal and The Gambia in the wake of the 1981 abortive coup, Senegal took action to stop the cross-border trade, but official checks at formal customs stations merely brought about increased smuggling. It was almost impossible for Senegal to patrol its nearly 500-mile-long border with The Gambia. Between 1991 and 1994, re-exporting activity accounted for 85 percent of The Gambia's merchandise exports and made up 20 percent of government revenue. Because one of the major routes to Senegal was through Niumi, up the road that connected the Barra Ferry to the border at Fass, large quantities of goods moved across the river from Banjul and passed northward. Senegalese traders came to Barra to obtain merchandise too, so the market at Barra expanded considerably. Up and down the bustling road, wherever cars and trucks might stop, traders set up shop and serviced the traffic with food, drink, kola nuts, batteries, and matches.

Then, suddenly, the bottom dropped out of the re-export market. In 1993 a French franc crisis in the European Monetary System caused panic in European and related African currency markets. After further tightening control of the Gambian border, Senegal devalued its currency, the CFA franc, by 50 percent in January 1994, thus making Gambian exports more expensive in Senegal and neighboring countries. By the end of the year the harsh reality of these actions was apparent. Gambia's re-export trade had fallen by 66 percent from the year before. The Gambia's government would have to look for different sources of revenue to make up for the export losses, and some people in Niumi who had been enjoying economic activities ancillary to the re-export trade packed up their little shops and enamelware basins and went home.[19] Where to turn next? Quite a number of Niumi residents were not too sure.

A Chance Encounter with World History

Niumi never made it onto many world maps, nor African ones. Its name or any of the others it went by were almost never read or spoken by peoples outside the small area around the lower Gambia where people knew of its existence. But one village in Niumi, Juffure, the old commercial center on the southern riverbank where state officials long collected tolls from passing traffic, gained worldwide attention almost overnight in 1976, several years after an African American visited and interviewed one old village resident. The man interviewed was Keba Fofana, a member of one of Juffure's old maraboutic lineages. The interviewer was Alex Haley, a writer whose intention was to establish an African connection for a book on his family's history in America. Convinced that he had such a connection through Fofana, in Juffure, in The Gambia, Haley wrote *Roots: The Saga of an American Family,* which tied the Gambia River into the history of peoples of African descent across the Atlantic. The book was an instant success: Doubleday sold 1.5 million copies in just one year and the book went into translation in several dozen languages. A subsequent serialization of *Roots* for television played for more American viewers than any program that ever preceded it and eventually aired on televisions around the world. All of this focused world attention on the Gambia River's place in an important segment of global history and connected Juffure to popular intellectual currents in the larger world.[20]

Haley told the story behind his quest for his roots in a number of places.[21] The author said he remembered stories his elderly relatives told around the Tennessee home of his youth: of a family genealogy that went back to an African ancestor they called "Kin-tay," of certain words in an African language handed down over the generations, and more. With the help of a Gambian acquaintance in upstate New York and advice from academics, he identified his ancestors as speakers of Mandinka and likely residents of the Gambia River. In the mid-1960s Haley traveled to Bathurst, where he told his story to several Gambians, some of whom were government officials. These men promised to seek out an oral traditionist who could help Haley with his quest, and they found one—Fofana in Juffure—not a traditional bard, but an amiable old man who could tell an appropriate story. Haley returned to The Gambia and visited Juffure, where he conducted the interview and came away with a story about Kunta Kinte, the main protagonist of the first half of *Roots,* who was "kidnapped into slavery while not far from his village, chopping wood, to make himself a drum."[22] Haley had located a record of a ship that sailed from the Gambia River to Annapolis, Maryland, in 1767, so he came up with a way to date the episode to that year. This provided him with the makings of the story line for *Roots,* which he describes as "a novelized amalgam of what I *know* took place together with what my researching led me to plausibly *feel* took place."[23] The book won a Pulitzer Prize in an entirely new category of literature called "faction"—a story based on fact, but with fictionalized dialogue.

What *Roots* did for Juffure was to make it a tourist Mecca for Americans primarily, who wanted to visit an ancestral home of African Americans, but for others as well. In good years as many as 10,000 tourists traveled by boat, or by automobile following the ferry ride, to Juffure, a village of 500 people. Residents of the village eyed the bonanza. Haley returned several times; television crews, reporters from important Western newspapers, and sundry writers and students were frequent visitors to Juffure too. By the early 1980s, aware of the dilapidated state of some of the village's houses, residents had constructed a replica of the village as it might have looked in the eighteenth century, with round mud dwellings and thatched roofs (as opposed to the existing rectangular mud buildings with roofs of corrugated metal). Eventually they added a market catering to tourists, selling masks, statues, drums, and carvings. The Gambian government stationed a police-man in Juffure to keep order and limit tourist visits to three days per week, but such limitations were easy to get around.[24] In 1996, needing something to stimulate the country's economy and its waning tourist trade, Gambia's Ministry of Tourism and Culture sponsored the first annual Roots Festival, a several-week-long series of events focusing on Juffure and the country's history. The festival's effect on Niumi and Juffure remains to be seen.

Though it has not added Niumi or an accurate portrayal of the region's history to anyone's ken, the *Roots* phenomenon changed life in the village. Certain elements of the change are positive. The village has gotten an elementary school that it never had before and, unlike its neighbors, has its own diesel generator to provide electricity for night lighting. Tourists can buy cold drinks. The road that autos take south from Bunyadu down along Niumi's southern riverbank, connecting Juffure and a dozen other villages to the country's main east-west thoroughfare that leads from the Barra Ferry, is better than it was in 1976, but not remarkably so. More wealth exists in the village. Some tourists spend freely, and occasionally a visitor will "adopt" a young Juffure resident and send the family a regular check or agree to pay the child's school fees. Work associated with tourism is an outlet for a few young males who do not wish to farm. Some guide tourists around for a small fee; some carve and sculpt and weave and turn out masks and statues for the tourist market; some hawk sandwiches and drinks. Such work is seasonal; tourists do not venture to Juffure frequently in the rainy season.

But all of what *Roots* brought is not so clearly beneficial. Some Juffure residents are bitter because promises they understood Haley to make—one about building a new mosque for the village—were not fulfilled. Work on the mosque never got beyond the planning stage and the acquisition of 200 bricks for a foundation. With the author's death in 1992, it appears unlikely that whatever Haley had planned for Juffure will be realized. Still, some villagers have come to believe that the world owes them something for their residence in Haley's supposed ancestral home. They live off tourist money, so they get it where they can, pressuring, cajoling, or begging as appropri-ate.[25] One is tempted to consider that they are doing what persons in Juffure

Box 15. Alex Haley and Niumi's History

The late Alex Haley was a professional writer rather than a professional historian. Although he had a research staff and wrote of "years of intensive research in fifty-odd libraries, archives, and other repositories on three continents" (*Roots*, p. 584), he took liberties with historical fact in Roots. Respected historians have described the inaccuracies of many of his portrayals, and a professional historian and certified genealogist located documentation disproving Haley's pre–Civil War genealogy.*

Of interest for this study is Haley's portrayal of life in Niumi in the eighteenth century. His depiction of Kunta Kinte's village of Juffure has little basis in fact. The Juffure in *Roots* is a stereotypic African village in a bucolic setting, "four days from the nearest place on the Kambi Bolongo [Gambia River] where slaves were sold" (p. 47). Few residents of the Juffure Haley portrays in *Roots* have ever laid eyes on a white man, and when a band of whites and their accomplices overcome Kinte and spirit him off to waiting ships, everyone around Juffure is powerless to respond. The adolescent Kinte is portrayed as a proto warrior, who dreams of traveling to visit the Mali Empire on nights when he sits to guard peanut [*sic*] fields from predators.

In reality, Juffure was the very heart of commercial operations in the lower Gambia and the point of international contact where Africans, Euro-Africans, and Europeans representing different segments of an economic system spanning half the globe met to carry on the exchange of slaves, cloth, iron, and other commodities in agreed-upon and systematic fashion. The village was in sight of James Island, where for a century before the 1760s English traders had maintained a garrison, and immediately next to Albreda, where Frenchmen traded. And members of the Kinte lineage were not warriors, but traders. If a branch of the Kinte family lived in Juffure in the 1760s, it was likely there to participate in the exchange of slaves and other commodities with Europeans.

Furthermore, it was Europeans, rather than Africans, who were most vulnerable among those involved in the international trade of the lower Gambia. Had any European stepped onto Niumi soil and kidnapped an African, the *mansa* of Niumi would have exacted retribution that would have threatened the continuing existence of a European presence in the river. Nuno Tristão had learned this the hard way over three centuries earlier. But Niumi's *mansa* hardly appears in Roots. He is a shadowy figure some distance away whose "personal agents" supplied slaves to white traders in the river (p. 49).

---

*Philip Nobile, "Uncovering *Roots,*" *Village Voice,* February 17–23, 1993, 31–38; Gary B. Mills and Elizabeth Shown Mills, "Roots and the New 'Faction': A Legitimate Tool for Clio?" *Virginia Magazine of History and Biography* 89 (1981): 3–26.

Box 15 *(continued)*

Alex Haley was a warm, delightful raconteur, and *Roots* was an important phenomenon in raising interest in the history of African Americans and the African Diaspora. What remains difficult for historians teaching about African and African American history is that so much of the book and television series continue to be regarded as having a sound basis in fact. Their counterfactual portrayals enforce old stereotypes and generally distort much relating to this important segment of world, African, and African American history.

---

had done long into the past: taxing the trade for what it would bear. One of the consequences of such activity is that, just as Haley provided an inaccurate depiction of the Atlantic slave trade and life in a precolonial West African village, residents of Juffure are now offering Western tourists a distorted sense of life in a contemporary West African village. The *real* Africa they see in Juffure today is almost as different from the typical West African agricultural village as Haley's fictionalized portrayal of eighteenth-century Juffure is from the former center of Gambia River slave trading.

Modernization?

Since independence, a variety of environmental and ecological, demographic, social, political, technological, and economic changes—some local and regional, some global—have affected the way people live in the land that once was the old Niumi state. Most observers believe that, as in much of the rest of the world, change is coming to such places as Niumi faster than ever before.

Unfortunately, one of the things that has not changed much since independence is the general impoverishment in which nearly all of Niumi's residents live. Relevant figures are saddening: The mean annual income of persons living in Niumi in 1993 was just over the equivalent of $200; only 17 percent of the population had income of more than $300 that year and only 3 percent over $500. People spent more than these amounts—on average about $600 throughout the year—meaning their income was supplemented by something else, usually money sent home by relatives. But this is $600 for *everything:* housing, upkeep, clothing, food, transportation, medical care, school fees, taxes—everything. On average, Niumi residents in 1993 spent $1.60 on medical care (less than they spent on candles), $2 on rent and dwelling repairs, $7 on bus/taxi and ferry fares, $3 on school-related expenses, and $20 on clothing and shoes. They spent $90 on food, nearly one-quarter of which was for rice and other grains. There is still no doubt: a walk into rural Niumi is an opportunity to stare poverty directly in the face, and it is likely to remain that way.[26]

Because the great majority of Niumi residents have forever gained their subsistence and occupied themselves most fully by growing foods to eat and crops to sell, what happens with farming may be the most important factor in their lives.[27] For this reason, the regional drought that has afflicted West Africa's sahel and savannas since 1968 has been devastating for the existence and well-being of many in Niumi. The drought is by far the worst of the twentieth century and seemingly one of the worst for such a sustained period in centuries. Niumi's farmers believe that before 1968 the rainy season had more reliable rains that lasted a month or six weeks longer than now. Of course, the drought has reduced crop yields and rendered some swamplands unusable for rice production, meaning in a world of steady prices cash-crop farmers have had less cash and subsistence farmers have had less food. But it has not even been a world of steady prices: the government's Economic Recovery Program, based in part on devaluation of the dalasi, was supposed to help rural dwellers by bringing higher prices for their cash crops. This did not happen for long, however, because of a coincidental, dramatic drop in world commodity prices. Yet imported items cost more.[28]

If drought and prices were not enough, the absence of the most dynamic segment of its labor force adds to rural Niumi's woes. Many young adults are simply gone—off to one or another urban area. Their reasons for going are tied largely to the forces of "modernization." Many more young people in Niumi in recent years get some education. Over a quarter of the elementary-age children and 15 percent of secondary-age children are in school. This is good; one result is that nearly half of Niumi's population is literate.[29] But formal education is not conducive to rural development. After four or five years of schooling, or more, and acquaintance with other ways of life in other places, the small rural village, where one can barely scratch out an existence on the farm, is about the last place young men want to end up. So they leave. From all over Niumi, young people coming of age have been migrating to urban areas. The Gambia's annual rate of urbanization is 8 percent, and it is now one of the most urbanized countries in sub-Saharan Africa. Some from Niumi go off to Barra or Essau, nearer ferry access to Banjul, and where there is electricity for night lighting, better prospect for employment, and simply a lot more going on. Others take up with relatives across the river around greater Banjul, where one-third of the country's population lives and where nearly all of its economic opportunity lies. In 1993 10,000 persons living in Banjul and its nearby dormitory communities were migrants from Niumi. Most were young adults. All of this has changed the demographic nature of Niumi's villages, which are generally in decline. Populations of many are shrinking and nearly all the shrinkage is in the number of people of productive age, especially working males. (Virtually every village has fewer people of prime productive age, many more children, and more men and women beyond the prime working age than it had a decade ago.) This means that in spite of the rapidly growing population, there is a shortage of farm labor.[30] Thus, the drought, the Recovery Program, deteriorating terms of trade, and an absence of a workforce commensurate in size to the population have combined to deal Niumi's farming villages a near-mortal blow.

In altering farming practices to cope with the changing conditions, Niumi's farmers have exacerbated their problems. Their response to declining yields related to the drought has been to plant more fields more often. There is a growing tendency to plant the same fields year after year, even with their knowledge that the land needs a long fallow period for restoration of fertility. This practice is "leading to impoverishment of soils around villages," writes Kathleen M. Baker, and "is storing up trouble for the future."[31] Fertilizer could restore much of the soils' fertility, of course, but Niumi's farmers tend not to use it. It is expensive. So is renting cattle for nighttime tethering in fields to provide dung.

There are fewer viable responses to Niumi's chronic labor shortage. For nearly all of its existence Niumi had a small population. Since the peanut boom of the mid-nineteenth century, strange farmers filled in during the rainy season, migrating to Niumi to make a crop and return home. Now this is entirely a thing of the past. For the past decade, with only minimal exceptions, no strange farmer has ventured into a Niumi village to make a crop. The unprofitability of farming, coupled with the possibility of finding more lucrative work in urban areas, has put a complete halt to agricultural labor migration.[32] So who are the primary workers in Niumi's fields? The remaining village men of working age, men beyond the normal age for farming, boys younger than once considered appropriate for farm work, and, more than any others, women.

Women have had an especially rough go of it. Some men have acted in response to the decline of soil fertility by using ox plows to plant larger fields with less labor, switching their energies to growing drought- and animal-resistant cassava, or planting fruit trees. Mangos, which bear fruit after five years, have been especially popular. A small number of men, recognizing the importance of women's contribution to household food supplies from rice fields, look after children. None prepares food or, for that matter, helps with growing rice. Conversely, women in Niumi tend to shy away from machinery—looking upon such as in man's domain—and their rice farming, often on small plots of swamp, does not lend itself to mechanization. Niumi's women, who have become increasingly important providers for their families, do virtually all their farming by hand, bending at the waist to work in the rice. Development projects of recent years, financed by such diverse entities as the People's Republic of China, Taiwan, the World Bank, the United States, and Great Britain, have aimed specifically at improving rural women's lot, but for a variety of reasons not all have worked. ("It seems this project is just like the Chinese one when we suffered before," said one Gambian woman upon learning of another foreign-sponsored effort.)[33] Where women have made important changes is in expansion of vegetable gardening and, around larger towns, collectivization of vegetable plots with new wells providing water for dry season growing. But even here, the water is drawn by hand and carried to the vegetables atop women's heads. By and large, women in Niumi continue to work laboriously over their rice fields, their vegetable gardens, their childrearing, and their food preparation.[34]

Of course, there have been changes for the better. Part of the reason the population is growing at such an astonishing clip—4.1 percent for the country since 1985, meaning its population has doubled over the past twenty years and The Gambia is now one of Africa's most densely populated countries—is related to greater longevity and lower rates of child mortality. Life expectancy at birth is about forty-two years, up from thirty-two in 1960; the mortality rate of children under five is 241 per 1,000, down from 375 per 1,000 in 1960.[35] Access to more modern health care and maternity care is better in Niumi than it ever has been. In 1988, amid considerable fanfare, President Jawara laid the foundation stone for a £300,000 health center in Essau, funded by a grant from the British Overseas Development Administration. That remains the major medical facility in Niumi, though there is an officially designated Minor Health Center in Kuntair and a dispensary at Madina Bafuloto.[36]

Greater access to education and improved health care are probably the most promising aspects of people's lives in Niumi in the mid-1990s. Otherwise, the outlook is not bright. In 1995 nearly one-third of Gambian imports consisted of food. As the country's trade fell off, it became necessary for the government to cut the annual budget by 23 percent, with some of the cuts coming in health care and education. Already the United Nations Development Program, which publishes a Human Development Index based on longevity, knowledge, and living standards, had The Gambia ranked second from the last, 159 out of the world's 160 nations.[37] This ranking included the 30 percent of the country's population around the capital city, where longevity, knowledge, and living standards are each considerably higher than in Niumi. There is not much doubt that the widespread change that has come to the region since independence has not brought ways of living that are noticeably improved.

The Military Takeover and Its Aftermath

A final blow to the Gambian economy, and thus indirectly to people in Niumi, was the bloodless overthrow of the government on July 22, 1994, by elements in the country's small military and the subsequent establishment of an Armed Forces Provisional Ruling Council to head the government. Former President Jawara was whisked off on an American naval vessel that happened to be in the river's mouth, and The Gambia's twenty-nine years of elected government was at an end. In reaction to the military takeover, Western nations suspended aid, banks prohibited further loans, and several European nations so effectively discouraged vacationers from visiting the country that the tourist trade, which had employed 6,000 Gambians and had been helping to prop up the staggering economy, fell by 75 percent. Gambia's economy spiraled downward, forcing the government—still burdened with imports five times greater than exports, a civil service drawing off a quarter of the national budget, and a foreign debt requiring interest payments equaling 35 percent of the annual budget—to raise taxes and reduce spending on some social services.[38]

What is ironic is that the government's overthrow had little direct effect on people in Niumi. Most of them awoke on July 23 without knowing that the country's government was different, and most could look around a year later and not recognize significant change in their lives. That people suffered from the weakening of the economy was nothing new. Their lives had changed gradually since independence with the decline in peanut production, the general decreasing reliance on agriculture, the slowly increasing access to health care and education, the pull of economic activities in the country's capital, and more. But in 1996, as in 1965 (when The Gambia became independent) or 1897 (when the British took formal control of Niumi), the region's existence on the periphery of a world-spanning economic system played a far larger role in how people lived than the makeup and character of their government. Elections could come and go; so could military coups, African Development Bank-sponsored studies, tourist-beckoning festivals, oil-exploration teams from The Netherlands, or, frankly, American academics with all the best feelings and intentions toward the people. What remain are poverty, ignorance, and ill-health—not just in relation to the world's core nations but in relation to almost everyone else—and not much prospect for change over the long haul.

Notes

1. Discussion of the celebrations at independence is in Berkeley Rice, *Enter Gambia: The Birth of an Improbable Nation* (Boston: Houghton Mifflin, 1967), ch. 2, a book that Gambians detest for its condescending tone. Rice was one of the few Western journalists on hand for the occasion.

2. Rice, *Enter Gambia*, 60.

3. Discussion of global events of the last half-century follows arguments in L.S. Stavrianos, *Lifelines from Our Past: A New World History* (Armonk, N.Y.: M.E. Sharpe, 1989), esp. 132–46.

4. International Bank for Reconstruction and Development, *Charter*.

5. The 1970 and 1980 figures are from L.S. Stavrianos, *Global Rift: The Third World Comes of Age* (New York: Morrow, 1981), 472. The 1990 figure is based on "World Bank Warns of Third World Debt," *New York Times*, December 16, 1991, D2. As of December 1991 the World Bank calculated Third World debt to be $1.3 trillion.

6. "Matchet's Diary," *West Africa* 2486 (January 20, 1965): 195.

7. "Grappling with the Gambia's Problems," *West Africa* 2563 (July 16, 1966): 791.

8. "A Bank in Disarray," *West Africa* 3630 (April 6, 1987): 658–61; "One-half of Gambia's Population Affected by Drought," *West Africa* 2703 (March 22, 1969): 339.

9. "The Gambia: Debt Exploitation," *West Africa* 3678 (February 12, 1988): 249–50.

10. "Stocktaking in Bathurst," *West Africa* 2699 (July 27, 1968): 864.

11. Christine Jones and Steven C. Radelet, "The Groundnut Sector," in *Economic Recovery in The Gambia: Insights for Adjustment in Sub-Saharan Africa*, ed. Malcolm F. McPherson and Steven C. Radelet (Cambridge: Harvard Institute for International Development, 1995), 207–8; Tijan M. Sallah, "Economics and Politics in The Gambia," *Journal of Modern African Studies* 28 (1990): 625.

12. Discussion of the economic plan and its effects is based on Steven Radelet, "Reform without Revolt: The Political Economy of Economic Reform in The Gambia," *World Development* 20 (1992): 1087–99; McPherson and Radelet, eds., *Economic Recovery in The Gambia*, chs. 1 and 2; and *Economic Management: Sector Adjustment Loan (SECAL)* (Banjul: Government of The Gambia, 1994), 18–21.

13. "Bank in Disarray," 661.

14. Jones and Radelet, "The Groundnut Sector," 207.

15. *Basic Needs in The Gambia* (Washington, D.C.: World Bank, 1981), I.

16. "The Gambia: Debt Exploitation," 249–50; Radelet, "Reform without Revolt," 1089–90.

17. Jones and Radelet, "The Groundnut Sector," 208.

18. *Country Profile: The Gambia; Mauritania* (London: Economist Intelligence Unit, 1995–96), 12, 21.

19. Susan Katz Miller, "Gambia Weathers Senegal Split," *Christian Science Monitor*, July 19, 1990, 8; *Economic Management (SECAL)*, 19–20; Peter Da Costa, "The Squeeze on The Gambia," *Africa Report* 39 (March/April 1994): 16–17.

20. Alex Haley, *Roots: The Saga of an American Family* (Garden City, N.Y.: Doubleday, 1976); Donald R. Wright, "Uprooting Kunta Kinte: On the Perils of Relying on

Encyclopedic Informants," *History in Africa: A Journal of Method* 8 (1981): 205–17; David A. Gerber, "Haley's *Roots* and Our Own: An Inquiry into the Nature of a Popular Phenomenon," *Journal of Ethnic Studies* 5 (1977): 87–88.

21. One version of Haley's story is in *Roots*, chs. 118–120.

22. Ibid., 579.

23. Ibid., 584.

24. Stephen Buckley, "From 'Roots' to Riches?" *Washington Post*, May 19, 1995, A27; Alex Haley, "Return to the Land of *Roots*," *GEO* 3 (November 1981): 104–22.

25. Buckley, "From 'Roots' to Riches?"

26. Figures cited are for the entire North Bank Division, which includes the former state of Baddibu with Niumi. Data for Niumi are not significantly different. They are in *1993 Household Economic Survey Report: The Gambia* (Banjul: Central Statistics Department, Ministry of Finance and Economic Affairs, 1994), ch. 3.

27. Much of this discussion on change related to farming in Niumi is based on Kathleen M. Baker, "Traditional Farming Practices and Environmental Decline, with Special Reference to The Gambia," in *Agricultural Change, Environment and Economy: Essays in Honour of W.B. Morgan*, ed. Keith Hoggart (London: Mansell, 1992), 180–202. Half of the villages Baker studied in 1990 and 1991 are in Niumi.

28. *Round Table Conference: Strategy for Poverty Alleviation* (Banjul: Government of The Gambia, 1994), 19.

29. Figures extrapolated from *1993 Household Economic Survey Report*, 54–55.

30. *Round Table Conference*, 1, 17–19; Baker, "Traditional Farming Practices," 191–93.

31. Baker, "Traditional Farming Practices," 185–86.

32. Ibid., 193.

33. Quoted in Judith Carney, "Struggles over Land and Crops in an Irrigated Rice Scheme: The Gambia," in *Agriculture, Women, and Land*, ed. Jean Davidson (Boulder, Colo.: Westview Press, 1988), 59–78.

34. Baker, "Traditional Farming Practices," 197–200.

35. *1993 Household Economic Survey Report*, 4–5; *Human Development Report 1991*, 123, 127.

36. "Face-to-Face with Farmers," *West Africa* 3719 (1988): 2186; *Health Sector Requirement Studies, Phase II Report* (Banjul: The Republic of The Gambia Ministry of Health, Social Welfare and Women's Affairs, 1995), ch. 4.

37. *Human Development Report 1991*, 121.

38. "In Gambia, New Coup Follows Old Pattern," *New York Times*, August 28, 1994, I, 4; *Country Profile*, 21; Steven C. Radelet and Malcolm F. McPherson, "Epilogue: The July 1994 Coup d'État," in McPherson and Radelet, eds., *Economic Recovery in The Gambia*, 311–17. In an election on September 26, 1996, Col. Yahya Jammeh, who led the 1994 coup and headed the Armed Forces Provisional Ruling Council, won and became The Gambia's new president.

EPILOGUE

Manneh wants millet; the rice is finished.
—Binta Manneh, cooking her father's dinner, 1996

The last time I was in Niumi was March 1996. I had traveled to The Gambia primarily for final reading in the National Archives for this book and to see for myself how the country was getting along almost two years after the overthrow of its elected government. The coup and the subsequent decline of trade and tourism were supposedly devastating to the Gambian economy, but that was not apparent in and around the capital. A grand airport terminal was under construction; taxis and buses clattered along a four-lane, divided highway between Banjul and its teeming bedroom communities; and trade along the capital's main streets seemed brisk as ever. Young men in shorts and thongs pushed and tugged flat carts loaded with commodities from Japan, Luxembourg, and Sri Lanka. Syrians in flowery shirts with pencils behind their ears strode among shipping cartons, barking orders. Bolts of colored cloth were everywhere. Across from the city market, slick money changers in sunglasses, tapping tiny electronic calculators, vied for space on the sidewalk with street vendors hawking cigarettes, kola nuts, bananas, peeled oranges, and fried cakes. Nearby, a line formed at the telephone that connected directly to an AT&T operator.

I picked a bright Saturday morning to cross the river to Niumi. I had enlisted a research officer with the National Council for Arts and Culture, Moro Komah, to accompany me. He was going to be posted to Niumi during the month of the Roots Heritage Festival and he wanted to feel things out. I was anxious and nostalgic. I had been back several times since I had spent nine months there in 1975, but I knew that almost nothing would be the same. The old ferry terminals were gone, replaced by new, more efficient facilities with wharfs and gangplanks that adjusted for the tide. I remembered the countless times I had been carried piggyback across several yards of water to get off the boat on the Niumi side of the river. Fortunate, now, were those who could avoid such activity. The ferries were different from the old chuggers too. One wore the name *Niumi* in bold, blue capital letters. I liked its looks.

As with everything in The Gambia on this trip, my first and most lasting impression was of the crowd. The village of Barra had been a sleepy little place. I once took the boat over, walked the desolate stretch down to the ruins of Fort Bullen, and had no company but the gulls banking in the sea breeze. Not today. It was an absolute crush getting off the ferry and passing through the wide gate leading to the chaos of the parking lot. Barra is a teeming small city of maybe 10,000. I wondered how many of its residents are former peanut farmers from Niumi villages a few miles distant. The re-export trade seemed alive and well too. I thought I heard French spoken as frequently as English. Scores of traders' stalls surrounded the terminal, and down the road was the thriving market that must be thirty times the size of the one I used to wander through. Within a few feet of the ferry terminal I saw children's underwear sewn in China, Sony Walkmen, watches with famous European names that may have been authentic, tall bottles of Fanta Orange, and Levi's, fake-Levi's, and Levi's imitations. The most popular T-shirt was a red mesh with "Chicago Bulls" on the front and Michael Jordan's number "23" on the back. They were heavy nylon—nice quality. Shirts of various colors with America's other Michael—Jackson—ran a close second. We had to fight our way through a rank of aggressive young money changers waving fistfuls of currency. Everyone was selling CFA francs. One young man offered to buy pounds, French francs, marks, krona, or dollars.

"What if we had yen?" I asked Komah.

"We could get it changed," he answered.

Eventually we made our way over to one side of the lot, where stood the line of gray Peugeot pickups that take passengers off the main road toward Niumi's agricultural villages. Cobbled together, leaking fluids, rattling at idle, the vehicles made up a sorry fleet. As Komah stopped to smoke, I crawled into the covered back end of the vehicle filling to leave and sat between a Muslim man saying his beads and a woman holding a protesting chicken by its feet, upside down. Neither paid me the slightest attention. Before we left, two strong men hoisted massive bags of rice onto the top of the vehicle. They carried Chinese writing. One hundred yards up the road the driver pulled in beside a low, dark dwelling; his assistant walked in, returned with half a plastic Clorox bottle containing oil, and filled the crankcase.

Once under way and through Essau, I found out why the Peugeots were so lame. The road into the heart of old Niumi has a red-orange, packed dirt surface that makes winter-ravaged, pothole-filled streets in New York City seem like glass by comparison. No road ever needed grading more. I thought the fillings in my teeth were loosened and my spine compressed several inches from six miles in a metal seat on that road. Even the chicken was shaken into silence after a few hundred yards.

What did I notice in the ride besides many more houses, many more people, and several more gasoline stations (with petrol at about $3.50 a gallon)? A sign that informed Gambians of the danger of AIDS, with a dancing condom and a "Know-Your-Partner" message; a brand new, handsome secondary school that opened in 1995, the first ever on The Gambia's north bank; and a stark tower for the telephone service that connected Gambia with the world. I could have direct-dialed any of dozens of countries from a spot not a few hundred yards from where Niumi's *Soninke* warriors stood their ground, behind a stockade, against the forces of Islamic reform some 130 years before. Times had indeed changed.

But once I got where I was going, things were not so different from what I remembered. I stopped first at the village of Bunyadu, hoping to find one of my best informants from my original research, a man named Jerre Manneh. We walked up a sandy street patrolled by skinny goats to the dwelling of the village head and found him lying on the floor, sick with something apparently serious and unable to get up. He simply waved us toward Manneh's compound, a conglomeration of buildings back up our path.

We found Manneh at home, resting, at about 11:30 A.M. He came out barefooted, wearing off-white pants with faded green checks and a light-colored shirt buttoned unevenly. He had an ugly sore on one shin that tincture of mercurochrome was not healing. Manneh lives with several of his daughters, each of whom has less than a complete elementary education. The youngest left school last year. He said school fees were expensive. Each daughter is married; their husbands are off somewhere. Several grandchildren were tottering about; one daughter was nursing an infant across the room; another was in the detached kitchen, cooking Manneh his afternoon meal—a millet stew—because the rice was "finished."

Manneh boards a handful of his brothers' male children, young men who cannot find work, but who have had enough schooling and taste of city life around Banjul to know they do not want to farm. They sit around the compound idly. One came around to check me out:

"You know 'Pa'; you must be a good man," he allowed.

Manneh says he feeds eleven males each day. (He seems not to count the women, who eat after the men are done.) Manneh still tries to farm, but he is not good at it any longer and does not have much help. Of his nine children, only three were sons, he lamented, and they all are gone from Bunyadu. One is a policeman, one a sergeant in "The Marine," and the third completed Standard Four in school a year ago, dropped out, and is living near Banjul without a job. Three married daughters and two grandsons in their teens are there to help in the fields. Last year's crops were not good: Manneh said he produced less than a ton of peanuts, which netted him about 200 dalasies—$20. All of that went to pay the daughter's school fees and buy a few clothes. The policeman son sent him 150 dalasies for his taxes. It seemed apparent that if The Gambia's annual per capita income is 2,600 dalasies, then Manneh was not keeping up.

Manneh's life had much in common with other men in twentieth-century Niumi. He was born in Bunyadu in 1922, 106 years after his great-great-grandfather, Niumi *mansa* Kolimanka Manneh, "sold" Banjul Island to the English for use as the settlement of Bathurst. He had a grandfather who lived in Jatako, in the northern, Atlantic coastal part of Niumi, where he spent time as a child, learning to fish and listening to the stories of his proud ancestors who once ruled. His father, less full of stories, was a Bunyadu farmer, who grew peanuts and food crops.

When Manneh was eleven his father died, and an uncle living in Bakau, across the river near Cape St. Mary's, took him in and saw that he went to school. Manneh went through Standard Three in Denham School in Bakau, but the uncle who was looking after him died and the man's brothers brought him back to Bunyadu. There he studied the Qur'an and farmed for several years. In 1938, when he was sixteen, he had a chance to return to Bakau for more school, but he admits that his mind was not on his studies—he was old for Standard Four—and he made low marks. So in 1939 he left school, returned to Bakau, and took up farming and fishing.

Shortly after World War II broke out he was forced to join one of the Gambia Regiments of the West African Frontier Force. "The District Commissioners told the Seyfus [Chiefs], the Seyfus told the Alkalis [Village Heads]: 'Bring in your young men,' " he recalled.

Manneh was one of the young men. His voice took on an angry tone as he spoke about "fighting to save British ground, not ours; bad pay; no compensation on release. . . ." And it was not just the soldiers who suffered, he added: "They took so many there weren't enough men back home to farm. People in Bunyadu here went hungry."

Manneh became a telephone linesman for the signal corps and was one of the fortunate ones getting to stay home through the war. He knew many soldiers who went to Burma with the Gambia Regiment. A few were killed there. He remembers consorting with troops from Ghana and Nigeria at his duty post in Bakau. He remembers his boss, too, a British major, telling him, "you are a strong-headed man." Manneh apparently did not take orders well. After seven years (ages seventeen and twenty-four), he mustered out.

His telephone experience enabled him to join the Gambian civil service, where for the next eleven years he worked as a linesman in the Banjul-Bakau region. They do not seem to be particularly exciting years in his memory. But in the late 1950s he got caught up in the political excitement as the British began "Gambianization" of the government. Political parties were forming, elections were coming; Manneh tendered his resignation from public service, joined the People's Progressive Party (PPP), and in 1960 stood for election to parliament from his original home district, Lower Niumi. He was defeated then, he says bitterly, and again in 1962, by a member of the Sonko lineage of Essau. "In the old days we Mannehs were *mansa* just like the Sonkos, but when the British came the Sonkos became chiefs—just because the whites found Maranta Sonko ruling then in Essau. It was our turn after the Sonkos, but we never got the chance. Over half a century the Sonkos built up their authority in Niumi at the expense of the rest of us. I did not have a chance in the election running against the man who had been the chief and whose father had been the chief."

So, his political wings clipped, Manneh commenced to farm from his native home in Bunyadu, and he has done so ever since. In the late 1960s he stood for municipal election—to the Kerewan Area Council—and won. Eventually he became deputy chairman of the council and believes from that post he was effective in getting more elementary schools built in Niumi, getting the Gambian government to pay for a larger percentage of secondary school fees for qualifying Niumi students, and organizing farmers' cooperatives to market peanuts.

Manneh is unimpressed with improvements to people's lives since independence. He does not look back fondly on the colonial period: "No one wants to be ruled by someone else," he said, "but things were cheap before independence and people were not so hungry then, even though we did our farming with the most traditional tools. Today we grow less rice and coos [millet], we grow more groundnuts. We have to buy rice from someplace else. The price of rice goes up every year—150, 175, 200 dalasies a bag. Who makes the money from this? It is the money that has supported our government's corruption!"

"We have had thirty years of nothing," he continued, his voice rising. "Look at the secondary schools. Thirty years ago, we had two government secondary schools—Banjul High School and the school at Georgetown. How many were there until last year? Two! And our roads! There is only one road in this country: the Gambia River. Did you like the road you came here on?"

"No," I admitted.

"That is the main road going all the way up the north bank of the river. They tear apart the vehicles. No one cares about our roads!"

"What are the biggest problems that remain for people in Bunyadu?" I asked.

"Agricultural technology," was his quick answer. "We are farmers. Many women especially work with traditional methods. They have to plow in the rains and cannot do it so well. Thus they can only farm small areas. We have no tractors. You should see us plowing. '. . .

"Education is the other problem, but that is more promising. For very long we were disadvantaged. Students from Bunyadu who qualified for secondary school had to go live in Banjul, where they had no place to lodge and it was very expensive. The education we got just wasn't very good. Now we have the new secondary school—you passed it in Essau."

Manneh is outspokenly favorable of the "soldiers coup" that overthrew the government in 1994 and of the Armed Forces Provisional Ruling Council that has been in charge ever since. I thought I recognized some good things the military government had done—arrested corrupt officials, built schools, pared down the bloated government bureaucracy. But the military council was not moving as swiftly as promised toward democracy, it was tightening measures against the country's press, and it was spending Manneh's tax dalasies and millions more on construction of Arch 22, being erected across the main road leading into the capital to commemorate the July 22 military takeover. As Arch 22 was going up, government money for social services was being reduced. I thought the arch a bad symbol and its construction a bad omen for the future.

But Manneh was adamant: "Corruption was everywhere. It was everywhere! And it was my party, the PPP! President, ministers, MPs, all of them were corrupt. They took our money. As soon as anyone from Niumi got elected, he moved to Banjul and got rich. But now Jammeh [Col. Yahya Jammeh, the coup leader and chairman of the AFPRC] is doing things for the people, like the school . . . and the salt bunds. You know, between here and the river, salt got in the rice fields so the women couldn't grow much rice. Government has built bunds to block the saltwater, from here all the way up to Baddibu. Our women can now have a good rice harvest."

"Do you not want to have elections again?" I asked.

"They are an unavoidable circumstance," he answered. He wants Jammeh to stay in power. He does not care how.

"Do you think next year will be better for you?" I asked.

"Oh yes," he answered without thinking.

The afternoon meal was still simmering. The Manneh compound went through three bags of rice a month for several months. They are now eating up the millet that he grew. None of them like millet as well as rice. The meal his daughter was tending did not look like much. A few bitter tomatoes adorned the meager stew. Unlike every previous occasion, we were not invited to stay for dinner.

"I used to fish," Manneh said, wistfully. "I was a good fisherman, but I'm too old to do that now."

"Is there enough millet to last until the next harvest?" I asked.

"Oh yes," he said again, "Oh yes."

I caught Komah's eyes. We had looked around, inside and out. Neither of us was convinced.

After photographs and good-byes, we walked the mile and a half up the road to the neighboring village of Berending. There was no breeze whatsoever and it was hot in a way one never experiences in upstate New York, a thick, pervasive heat that seems unrelated to the sun. Fields were cleared but not yet planted. Everything had that reddish, dusty cast that so much of West Africa gets during the dry season. One vehicle clattered by and left us walking in dust for a quarter of a mile. I was perspiring and the dust clung to my shirt in a dirty orange film.

I wanted to stop in Berending to look up Alhaji Karamo Njie, the Imam (Muslim religious leader) of the town, whose warm hospitality I once had enjoyed for the better part of a week. Berending is bigger than Bunyadu and much larger than I remembered it. There were young boys, seemingly of that difficult junior high school age, lolling about in the shade of massive silk-cotton trees, listening to West Indian music on boom boxes, talking things over. They regarded Komah and me suspiciously. We convinced a small boy to walk us to the Imam's place. Njie was off at a naming ceremony, one of his wives said, but he would return soon. She offered us a drink of well water in a fat tin cup that had lost its handle and invited us to sit inside. Outside the compound stood a good-sized blue tractor that looked like a Ford and a blocky white Peugeot. Inside were a king-sized bed, two wooden chairs, a table, and on the floor in a corner a partially dismantled, gasoline-powered grinding machine of some sort. It looked like it had been there, in the same state, for a long time.

When Njie entered, he did not recognize me—perhaps because I have aged, of course, but also because his eyes are diseased and he cannot see much at all. He wore a full, ankle-length tan robe, yellow slippers, and the purple-and-gold headpiece that signifies he has completed the pilgrimage to Mecca. I thought he seemed pleased when he learned who I was.

Following a long exchange of pleasantries, I asked about men I had interviewed some years back: little Landing Nima Sonko, the hard-working farmer who had spent hours giving me impressions of his family's history?

"I am sorry; he is deceased; Allah be praised."

"Bakai Sonko?" He was the tall, good-natured lorry driver, who laughed about having wives scattered in villages along his route?

"Ah, your memory is good. I am sorry; he has died also. Allah be praised."

"Jerre Samateh, down the road at Tubab Kolong?"—the man who showed me where a British cannonball had passed through a village tree during one of those nineteenth-century "wars of pacification."

"Allah lost a good man in that one, a very religious man. He died not long after your visit."

These had not all been old men. Their deaths drove home what it means to live in a country where the life expectancy at birth is forty-two years.

"How is life for the Imam?" I inquired.

"Everything is fine; crops have been good. Allah looks over us."

After some time, I asked the Imam if he knew anyone in Berending who had served with the Gambia Regiment in World War II. After hearing of Manneh's experience, I was eager to know more. Njie summoned one of the half-dozen children staring at us through the open door, sent him off, and within minutes an old man stood blocking the sunlight from the doorway. This was Lamin Sowe, the oldest man in Berending—ninety-five, he says. He is tall, large-faced, strong-boned. He wore a long white robe and a light blue wrap on his head. He is an imposing figure, especially when he is walking briskly, bent forward, with a thick walking stick that he does not seem to need.

The Imam offered Sowe a seat on the bed, but he preferred the floor. He spoke for half an hour about his Berending youth, his growth into a willful young man, and his misfortune, early in 1941, of being "captured by some of the commissioner's guards and forced to enlist in the West African Frontier Force" while walking along a rural stretch of road.

"Forced?" I asked, naively.

"Forced!" he thundered. A district chief had sent the guards to look for young men to meet a recruiting quota set by the British and they brought in Sowe. It must have taken several of them, I thought.

Because of his size and commanding presence, he was made a sergeant in the 2nd Gambia Regiment (Service Number 25401). He learned to march at Bakau and then shipped off, first to Bombay and then to a place with a name that sounded like "Kingdom Come." It was there, he said, that he learned to shoot. Sowe then took ten minutes to recite from memory the various places his unit marched in India and Burma. It was a long list. They fought fairly continuously and, according to Sowe, "shot many people." The people were shooting back, of course, and Sowe was one of those injured. At one point he rose, pulled up his gown, and revealed scar tissue on his left calf and from beside his left knee up his thigh, the result of a mortar attack.

"Was anyone from the regiment from Berending killed?" I asked.

"No," he said. "Five men in the regiment were from Berending. Some were wounded, but none killed." All together, though, 288 from the Gambian Regiment were killed in the Burma campaign.

Although promised compensation as a wounded veteran, Sowe never got any. He returned with a strip of medals, but received nothing when he mustered out in 1948, a subject that still makes him an angry man. Once back in Berending he commenced farming, growing peanuts and millet, and took up art, becoming a decorator of calabash containers and mortars.

Still, Sowe seems fair minded in his assessment of colonial rule. "It brought us peace," he says. "Before then, we were constantly fighting with one another, riding horses, capturing people; it was dangerous to live around here and try to farm. But all that ended when the whites took over."

But there was a down side that sticks in his memory: "They were rude and they made us work for them a lot. They came to the village and just rounded up a bunch of men and made us go off and clear the road or carry loads on our heads for the commissioners, who were traveling around."

"No pay for the work?" I asked.

He just chuffed.

The coming of independence was a good thing for people with an education, he thinks, because they knew what it meant and could take advantage of opportunities. Most of the people in Niumi could not, however, so it did not make much difference. "Chiefs were still chiefs," he said. "I guess there weren't any white commissioners any more."

Sowe is busy these days with two projects. He grows mangos from seed and transplants them into orchards. He proudly revealed mango seedlings growing in coffee cans behind his house, hundreds of them, making me think of him as Niumi's Johnny Appleseed for mangos. The work to which he puts less time but more emotional fervor is in his position with the Gambia Legion of the British Commonwealth Ex-Services League. He travels among the villages of Niumi, gathering names of Gambian veterans and their wives, all of which he forwards to the head of the Gambia Legion, Sam Silla, who works tirelessly, Sowe says, for veterans' rights and lost compensation. He is hopeful that, any day now, Silla will be successful so that he and the remaining Gambian veterans will receive their due.

When our talking was over I asked Sowe if I could snap his photograph. He assented, but not before going in and pinning on his medals. The war was the biggest thing in his life.

The trip back to Barra late that day was easy. After we had walked a mile up the road, Komah flagged down a huge truck hauling peanuts. He knew the driver, and so we got a lift right to the ferry terminal. The crowd at the gate was suffocating, but once I reached the boat's upper level there was a cooling breeze. We bought a cool drink—a sweet Kool-Aid-like mixture in a long plastic tube—took a seat on a wooden chest containing life preservers, and leaned back against the railing. Soon the boat shuddered and we were under way. I watched Barra and Essau, farther in the distance, shrink away. Around us bobbed one-man fishing canoes, whose occupants loathed the ferries and swore as we passed closer to their lines than they wished.

On the way back across the river, lulled into drowsiness by the setting sun and the steady throb of the ferry's diesels, I began thinking once more about Niumi's long history. Darkest Africa? Remote? Isolated? Hardly, I thought. Niumi had been part of a larger world, of one or another fairly elaborate world system, for a thousand years and more. Its people had been relying on products from elsewhere, often a long way off; its leaders had been living off the long-distance trade of commodities; and its culture had been changing because of influences from afar, into the distant past. I did not know for how long people living on the lower Gambia's north bank had been shipping products up and down the river and along the adjacent Atlantic coast, but I was certain Niumi's political and cultural ties to the Mali Empire—the ones I had heard about so often in regional oral traditions—were no more important to its history than its ties into the Sudanic and trans-Saharan economy, which *griots* never mentioned. That was its link to the massive world system of the Old World. It was via traders across these routes that Niumi was connected to the cultural world system of Islam, one of the most influential factors in the daily lives of Niumi residents over recent centuries.

My thoughts on the Islamic element troubled me. Muslim traders had been frequenting Niumi since the eleventh or twelfth centuries, and there were Muslim merchants and advisers with Niumi's ruler when the first Portuguese sailed into the Gambia River in the fifteenth century. Islam probably had benefited people in the state at various times in the past. In the nineteenth century it was influential Muslims who led the uprisings against the domineering ruling lineages; in the twentieth century Islam was an important cultural force that helped give Niumi's residents a sense of self-worth, in the eyes of Allah and His servants on earth, when European rules and customs were making them think otherwise. But in the face of the situation in the middle and late twentieth century, I was not so sure Islam was altogether a beneficial force. The resignation before "Allah's will" seemed to be working to keep people from asking the right questions about their plight. So many solid Niumi farmers saw Allah's hand in their poverty, hunger, illness, and short lives, and in the lack of sufficient medical care and educational facilities, whereas I was spending many of my waking hours considering how such things were the result of the hand of global humanity. Was it Allah's will that people like Jerre Manneh work hard and live poorly, or was it that Manneh was on the wrong end of a global economic system that limited his options? Was their perspective skewed, or was mine?

But I was digressing from my thoughts on Niumi's historical patterns. Without severing its ties to the inland savannas, the desert, and the world system of the Old World with its shifting core so far away, Niumi became involved in the expanding Atlantic complex. Between the mid-fifteenth and the early nineteenth century, the commerce associated with the Atlantic plantation system wrapped all around the little Gambian state and made it a focal point—to varying degrees at different times—of connections between West Africa's Sudanic economy and, via floating links, the European-managed, American-centered production system. Slaves were the commodity of much modern historical focus in the grand economic complex, but for Niumi the trade brought a host of necessary and optional commodities for the subsistence and pleasure of its people.

As I reflected more on the Atlantic system and Niumi's relationship with it, it was not clear to me that the standard world-systems model fit the situation. Before Europe industrialized, in the era of commercial capitalism, the division of labor was not so evident. I could recognize western Europe as the system's core—wealth and resources flowed to the core and people there, proper commercial capitalists that they were, used their wealth to build more. But wealth and resources came to Niumi, also. People there simply used the wealth to amass a different kind of capital—human and social capital, it seemed. They acquired additional working dependents and built and solidified what was most important to them for the sake of security and prestige: reciprocity-bound relationships of kinship.

The most important change in Niumi's modern existence, the process of events that placed Niumi on the periphery of the modern world system, occurred in the first half of the nineteenth century. I was more and more convinced of this. It was then that relationships changed most completely: when Europeans quickly appeared much more powerful—not only by having more effective weapons, but by being able to marshal troops and resources from an increasingly broad area of the world; when Europeans became remarkably efficient producers of consumable merchandise at reasonable prices; and, most specifically, when Niumi's population became producers of a staple commodity in demand in the system's core and eager consumers of more of the inexpensive goods that Europeans could bring. Niumi's peanut revolution was a revolution in its population's relationship with the expanding world system. After mid-century, people in Niumi were fully engaged on the system's periphery, and mired there, dependent on the relationship for much of what they needed and wanted. From then on, in terms of how they lived and their general level of well-being, who ruled them—whether it was one of the traditional ruling lineages, British colonial officials, Gambian politicians, or young military officers—mattered less than elements inherent in the world system—world commodity prices, interruptions of the international flow of goods, or political actions that affected these things. Through the colonial period and the time since Gambian independence in 1965, world economic fluctuations, global warring, epidemics, improved technologies, advances in health care—all would affect people's lives in Niumi by degrees or alter conditions over the short run, but would not change the basis of their existence. And in this Niumi was not alone. It seemed to be a fact of life across about two-thirds of the globe.

We were approaching Banjul. People were beginning to move toward the ferry's prow. I was still thinking how all this history was weighing heavily on the shoulders of Jerre Manneh. Like so many others, he is still trying to make it growing peanuts to sell in Belgium so he can purchase rice grown in China. He knows he will not have any extra cash for flashlight batteries from Japan, or tinned milk from the United Kingdom, or matches from France, or, Allah knows, one of those Chicago Bulls T-shirts (cut and sewn in Sri Lanka of cloth woven in Hong Kong). His options are remarkably limited, and so are those of his children and grandchildren.

This makes Manneh's faith in the future all the more surprising. "The new government cares about people!" he said. "Things are going to get better!"

As I thought about my visit to Manneh's compound just a few hours earlier—of his skinny frame and sore leg, of the empty rice bags from Taiwan and the pathetic millet and bitter-tomato stew that was to be his daily meal, of the scrawny goats and chickens that licked and pecked about us, of the unemployed young men and the hard-working young women and the runny-nosed little kids—I had my doubts. I really had my doubts.

BIBLIOGRAPHY

Unpublished Sources

Archives and Libraries

Archives Nationales de France, Paris
    Colonies: Sénégal et Côte Occidentale d'Afrique, B_4
    Marine: Service General, C_6
Archives Nationales de Sénégal, Dakar
    Albreda, 13_G
Bodleian Library, Oxford
    Rawlinson Manuscripts, C745–7
Public Record Office, Kew Gardens
    Colonial Office Series, CO*
    87: Gambia, General Correspondence
    90: Blue Books
    267: Sierra Leone, General Correspondence
    Treasury Series, T
    70: African Companies
The Gambia National Archives, Banjul
    All documents at present identified with the prefix CSO*

Dissertations and Manuscripts

Colvin, Lucie G. "Interstate Relations in Precolonial Senegambia." Paper presented at the annual meeting of the African Studies Association, Syracuse, N.Y., 1973.
Hunter, Thomas C. "The Development of an Islamic Tradition of Learning among the Jahanke of West Africa." Ph.D. dissertation, University of Chicago, 1977.
Steadman, Sharon R. "Isolation vs. Interaction: Prehistoric Cilicia and Its Role in the Near Eastern World System." Ph.D. dissertation, University of California at Berkeley, 1994.
Tejada, Philip. "The Ñiuminka." Unpublished paper, Indiana University, c. 1980.
Wright, Donald R. "Niumi: The History of a Western Mandinka State through the Eighteenth Century." Ph.D. dissertation, Indiana University, 1976.

Oral Interviews

Fati, Afang Seku. Interview in Aljamdu, Upper Niumi District, The Gambia, December 14, 1974.

---

*A number of documents in the CO Series are duplicated in The Gambia National Archives. I cite the source I used.

Jammeh, Landing. Interview in Brikama, Kombo Central District, The Gambia, December 13, 1974.
Manneh, Jerre. Interview in Bunyadu, Lower Niumi District, The Gambia, March 16, 1996.
Sowe, Lamin. Interview in Berending, Lower Niumi District, The Gambia, March 16, 1996.

Published Sources

Newspapers and Periodicals

Africa Report, March/April 1994.
Christian Science Monitor, July 19, 1990.
New York Times, March 31, August 24, 1976; December 16, 1991; August 28, 1994; February 29, 1996.
Wall Street Journal, December 13, 1993.
West Africa, January 20, 1965; July 16, 1966; July 27, 1968; March 22, 1969; April 6, 1987; February 12, 1988.

Books and Articles

Abu-Lughod, Janet L. *Before European Hegemony: The World System A.D. 1250–1350*. New York: Oxford University Press, 1989.
————. *The World System in the Thirteenth Century: Dead-End or Precursor?* Washington, D.C.: American Historical Association, 1993.
Adas, Michael P. *"High" Imperialism and the "New" History*. Washington, D.C.: American Historical Association, 1995.
————. *Machines as the Measure of Men: Science, Technology, and Ideologies of Western Dominance*. Ithaca: Cornell University Press, 1989.
Alford, Terry. *The Fortunate Slave*. New York: Oxford University Press, 1977.
Almada, Andre Alvares de. *Tratado breve dos Rios de Guiné*, trans. P.E.H. Hair. 2 vols. Liverpool: University of Liverpool. 1984.
Alpern, Sidney B. "The European Introduction of Crops into West Africa in Precolonial Times." *History in Africa: A Journal of Method* 19 (1992): 13–43.
————. "What Europeans Got for Their Slaves: A Master List of European Trade Goods." *History in Africa: A Journal of Method* 22 (1995): 5–43.
Anonymous [Col. George A.K. d'Arcy]. "Gambia Colony and the Civil War." *Colburn's United Service Magazine* 419–20 (1863): 236–58, 401–18, 498–508.
Anstey, Roger. *The Atlantic Slave Trade and British Abolition, 1760–1810*. Cambridge: Cambridge University Press, 1975.
Austen, Ralph. *African Economic History*. Portsmouth, N.H.: Heinemann, 1987.
Azurara, Gomes Eanes de. *The Chronicle of the Discovery and Conquest of Guinea*, ed. C.R. Beazley and E. Prestage. 2 vols. London: Hakluyt Society, 1896–99.
Baker, Kathleen M. "Traditional Farming Practices and Environmental Decline, with Special Reference to The Gambia." In Hoggart 1992, 180–202.
Barrett, Hazel R. *The Marketing of Foodstuffs in The Gambia, 1400–1980*. Aldershot: Avebury, 1988.
————. *Le royaume du Waalo: Le Sénégal avant la conquête*. Paris: François Maspero, 1972.

————. "Senegambia from the Sixteenth to the Eighteenth Century: Evolution of the Wolof, Sereer, and 'Tukulor.' " In *General History of Africa*, vol. 5, *Africa from the Sixteenth to the Eighteenth Century*, ed. B.A. Ogot, 262–99. Paris: UNESCO, 1992.

Basic Needs in The Gambia. Washington, D.C.: World Bank, 1981.

Blake, J.W. *Europeans in West Africa, 1450–1560.* 2 vols. London: Hakluyt Society, 1942.

Boulègue, Jean. *Le grand Jolof (xiiie-xvie siècle).* Paris: Diffusion Karthala, 1987.

————. *Les Luso-Africains en Sénégambie, xvie-xixe siècle.* Lisbon: Instituto de Investiga, cao Cientifica Tropical, 1989.

Bovill, E.W. *The Golden Trade of the Moors.* 2nd ed. London: Oxford University Press, 1968.

Braudel, Fernand. *Civilisation and Capitalism, 15th–18th Century*, vol. 3, *The Perspective of the World.* New York: Harper & Row, 1994.

Brooks, George E. *Landlords and Strangers: Ecology, Society, and Trade in Western Africa, 1000–1530.* Boulder, Colo.: Westview Press, 1993.

————. "Kola Nuts and State-Building: Upper Guinea Coast and Senegambia, 15th–17th Centuries." In Boston University African Studies Center Working Papers. No. 38. Boston: Boston University African Studies Center, 1980.

————. "Peanuts and Colonialism: Consequences of the Commercialization of Peanuts in West Africa, 1830–1870." *Journal of African History* 16 (1975): 29–54.

Bühnen, Stephan. "Place Names as an Historical Source: An Introduction with Examples from Southern Senegambia and Germany." *History in Africa: A Journal of Method* 19 (1992): 1–57.

Cadamosto, Alvise da. "The Voyages of Cadamosto." In *The Voyages of Cadamosto and Other Documents in Western Africa in the Second Half of the Fifteenth Century*, ed. G.R. Crone, 1–84. London: Hakluyt Society, 1937.

Carney, Judith. "Struggles over Land and Crops in an Irrigated Rice Scheme: The Gambia." In *Agriculture, Women, and Land*, ed. Jean Davidson, 59–78. Boulder, Colo.: Westview Press, 1988.

Chaudhuri, K.N. *Asia before Europe: Economy and Civilisation in the Indian Ocean from the Rise of Islam to 1750.* Cambridge: Cambridge University Press, 1990.

————. *Trade and Civilisation in the Indian Ocean: An Economic History from the Rise of Islam to 1750.* Cambridge: Cambridge University Press, 1985.

Clarke, Peter B. *West Africa and Islam: A Study of Religious Development from the 8th to the 20th Century.* London: Edward Arnold, 1982.

Cohen, Abner. "Cultural Strategies in the Organization of Trade Diasporas." In *The Development of Indigenous Trade and Markets in West Africa*, ed. Claude Meillassoux, 266–84. Oxford: Oxford University Press, 1971.

Conrad, David C., and Barbara E. Frank. "*Nyamakalaya*: Contradiction and Ambiguity in Mande Society." In *Status and Identity in West Africa: Nyamakalaw of Mande*, ed. David C. Conrad and Barbara E. Frank, 1–23. Bloomington: Indiana University Press, 1995.

Country Profile: The Gambia; Mauritania. London: Economist Intelligence Unit, 1995–96.

Crosby, Alfred W. *Germs, Seeds, & Animals: Studies in Ecological History.* Armonk, N.Y.: M.E. Sharpe, 1994.

————. "The Potato Connection." *World History Bulletin* 12 (1996): 1–5.

Crowder, Michael. *Colonial West Africa: Selected Essays.* London: Frank Cass, 1978.

————. "The First World War and Its Consequences." In *General History of Africa*, vol. 7, *Africa under Colonial Domination, 1880–1935*, ed. A. Adu Boahen, 283–311. Paris: UNESCO. 1985.

Cultru, Prosper. *Premier Voyage de Sieur de la Courbe fait à la coste d'Afrique en 1685.* Paris: Emile Larose, 1913.

Curtin, Philip D. "The Abolition of the Slave Trade from Senegambia." In *The Abolition of the Slave Trade: Origins and Effects in Europe, Africa, and the Americas,* ed. David Eltis and James Walvin. Madison: University of Wisconsin Press, 1981.

―――. *The Atlantic Slave Trade: A Census.* Madison: University of Wisconsin Press, 1969.

―――. *Cross-Cultural Trade in World History.* Cambridge: Cambridge University Press, 1984.

―――. *Death by Migration: Europe's Encounter with the Tropical World in the Nineteenth Century.* Cambridge: Cambridge University Press, 1995.

―――. *Economic Change in Precolonial Africa: Senegambia in the Era of the Slave Trade.* Madison: University of Wisconsin Press, 1975.

―――. "Epidemiology and the Slave Trade," *Political Science Quarterly* 83 (1968): 190–216.

―――. "Jihad in West Africa: Early Phases and Inter-Relations in Mauritania and Senegal." *Journal of African History* 12 (1971): 11–24.

―――. *The Rise and Fall of the Plantation Complex.* Cambridge: Cambridge University Press, 1989.

―――. "The Slave Trade and the Atlantic Basin: Intercontinental Perspectives." In *Key Issues in the Afro-American Experience.* 2 vols. Ed. Nathan I. Huggins, Martin Kilson, and Daniel M. Fox, 1:74–93. New York: Harcourt Brace Jovanovich, 1971.

―――. *The Tropical Atlantic in the Age of the Slave Trade.* Washington, D.C.: American Historical Association, 1991.

Davidson, Basil. *Black Mother: Africa and the Atlantic Slave Trade.* Rev. ed. Harmondsworth, UK: Penguin, 1980.

Demanet, Abbé. *Nouvelle histoire de l'Afrique françoise.* 2 vols. Paris: Duchesne, 1767.

Dey, Jennie. "Gambian Women: Unequal Partners in Rice Development Projects." *Journal of Development Studies* 17 (1981): 109–122.

Dorjahn, V.R., and Christopher Fyfe. "Landlord and Stranger: Change in Tenancy Relations in Sierra Leone." *Journal of African History* 3 (1962): 391–97.

Durand, J.B.L. *A Voyage to Senegal.* London: Printed for Richard Phillips, 1806.

Eaton, Richard M. *Islamic History as Global History.* Washington, D.C.: American Historical Association, 1990.

Echenberg, Myron. *Colonial Conscripts: The* Tirailleurs Sénégalais *in French West Africa, 1857–1960.* Portsmouth, N.H.: Heinemann, 1991.

Economic Management: Sector Adjustment Loan (SECAL). Banjul: Government of The Gambia, 1994.

Elbl, Ivana. "Cross-Cultural Trade and Diplomacy: Portuguese Relations with West Africa, 1441–1521." *Journal of World History* 3 (1992): 165–204.

―――. "The Horse in Fifteenth-Century Senegambia." *International Journal of African Historical Studies* 24 (1991): 85–110.

Fage, J.D. *On the Nature of African History.* Birmingham: Birmingham University Press, 1965.

Fernandes, Valentim. *Description de la côte occidentale d'Afrique (Sénégal au Cap de Monte, Archipels),* ed. and trans. Theodore Monod et al. Bissau: Centro de Estudos da Guiné Portuguesa, 1951.

Frank, Andre Gunder, and Barry K. Gillis, eds. *The World System: Five Hundred Years or Five Thousand?* New York: Routledge, 1993.

Froelich, J.D. "Essai sur les causes et méthods de l'Islamisation de l'Afrique de l'Ouest du xie au xxe siècle." In *Islam in Tropical Africa*, ed. I.M. Lewis, 160–73. London: Oxford University Press, 1966.

Froger, François. *Relation d'un voyage . . . aux côtes d'Afrique*. Amsterdam: Chez les Heritiers d'Antoine Shelte, 1702.

Gailey, Harry A. *A History of the Gambia*. New York: Praeger, 1965.

Gerber, David A. "Haley's *Roots* and Our Own: An Inquiry into the Nature of a Popular Phenomenon." *Journal of Ethnic Studies* 5 (1977).

Giraud, Jean. *L'or du Bambouk: une dynamique de civilisation ouest-africaine: du royaume de Gabou à la Casamance*. Geneva: Georg Editeur, 1992.

Gomes, Diogo. "The Voyages of Diogo Gomes." In *The Voyages of Cadamosto and Other Documents in Western Africa in the Second Half of the Fifteenth Century*, ed. G.R. Crone, 91–99. London: Hakluyt Society, 1937.

Goody, Jack. "The Impact of Islamic Writing on the Oral Cultures of West Africa." *Cahiers d'Etudes Africaines* 11 (1971): 455–66.

———. *Technology, Tradition, and the State in Africa*. London: Oxford University Press, 1971.

Gray, John M. *A History of the Gambia*. London: Frank Cass, 1940.

Green, Kathryn L. "Dyula and Sonongui Roles in the Islamization of the Region of Kong." In *Rural and Urban Islam in West Africa*, ed. Nehemia Levtzion and Humphrey J. Fisher, 97–117. Boulder: Lynn Rienner, 1987.

Haley, Alex. "Return to the Land of *Roots*." *GEO* 3 (1981): 104–22.

———. *Roots: The Saga of an American Family*. Garden City, N.Y.: Doubleday, 1976.

Harlan, J.R., J.J.J. de Wet, and A.B.L. Stemler, eds. *Origins of African Plant Domestication*. The Hague: Mouton, 1976.

Hatton. P.H.S. "The Gambia, the Colonial Office, and the Opening Months of the First World War." *Journal of African History* 7 (1966): 123–31.

Headrick, Daniel P. *The Tools of Empire: Technology and European Imperialism in the Nineteenth Century*. New York: Oxford University Press, 1981.

Health Sector Requirement Studies, Phase II Report. Banjul: The Republic of The Gambia Ministry of Health, Social Welfare and Women's Affairs, 1995.

Hodder, B.W. "Indigenous Cloth Trade and Markets in Africa." In *Textiles in Africa*, ed. Dale Idiens and K.G. Ponting, 203–10. London: Pasold Research Fund, 1980.

Hogendorn, Jan S. "Economic Initiative and African Cash Farming: Pre-Colonial Origins of Early Colonial Developments." In *Colonialism in Africa, 1870–1914*, vol. 4, *The Economics of Colonialism*, ed. Peter Duignan and L.H. Gann, 283–328. Cambridge: Cambridge University Press, 1975.

Hoggart, Keith, ed. *Agricultural Change, Environment and Economy: Essays in Honour of W.B. Morgan*. London: Mansell, 1992.

———. "The 'Vent-for-Surplus' Model and African Cash Agriculture to 1914." *Savanna* 5 (1976): 15–28.

Household Economic Survey Report, 1993: The Gambia. Banjul: Central Statistics Department, Ministry of Finance and Economic Affairs, 1994.

Human Development Report 1991. New York: Oxford University Press for the United Nations Development Program, 1991.

Inikori, J.E. "The Import of Firearms into West Africa, 1750–1807: A Quantitative Analysis." *Journal of African History* 18 (1977): 339–68.

Jobson, Richard. *The Golden Trade*. London: Dawsons of Pall Mall, 1623.

Johnson, Marion. "Cloth as Money: The Cloth Strip Currencies of Africa." In *Textiles in Africa*, ed. Dale Idiens and K.G. Ponting, 193–202. London: Pasold Research Fund, 1980.

Jones, Christine, and Steven C. Radelet. "The Groundnut Sector." In *Economic Recovery in The Gambia*, ed. McPherson and Radelet 1995, 205–17.

Kea, Ray E. "Firearms and Warfare on the Gold and Slave Coasts from the Sixteenth to the Nineteenth Centuries." *Journal of African History* 12 (1971): 185–213.

Klein, Martin A. "The Demography of Slavery in the Western Sudan in the Late Nineteenth Century." In *African Population and Capitalism: Historical Perspectives*, ed. Joel Gregory and Dennis Cordell, 50–62. Boulder, Colo.: Westview Press, 1987.

———. *Islam and Imperialism in Senegal: Sine-Saloum, 1847–1914*. Stanford: Stanford University Press, 1968.

———. "Social and Economic Factors in the Muslim Revolution in Senegambia." *Journal of African History* 13 (1972): 419–41.

———. "Women in Slavery in the Western Sudan." In *Women and Slavery in Africa*, ed. Claire C. Robertson and Martin A. Klein, 67–92. Madison: University of Wisconsin Press, 1983.

Labat, Jean-Baptiste, *Nouvelle rélation de l'Afrique occidentale*. 5 vols. Paris: Chez Guilaume Cavalier, 1728.

Lafont, F. "Le Gandoul et les Niominkas." *Bulletin du comité des études historiques et scientifiques de l'Afrique occidentale française* 21 (1938): 385–458.

Langley, J. Ayodele. *Pan-Africanism and Nationalism in West Africa, 1900–1945: A Study in Ideology and Social Classes*. Oxford: Clarendon Press, 1973.

Law, Robin. *The Horse in West Africa: The Role of the Horse in the Societies of Pre-colonial West Africa*. Oxford: Oxford University Press. 1980.

———. "Slaves, Trade, and Taxes: The Material Basis of Political Power in Precolonial West Africa." *Research in Economic Anthropology* 1 (1978): 37–52.

Levtzion, Nehemia. *Ancient Ghana and Mali*. London: Methuen, 1973.

———. "The Eighteenth Century: Background to the Islamic Revolutions in West Africa." In *Eighteenth-Century Renewal and Reform in Islam*, ed. Nehemia Levtzion and John O. Voll, 21–38. Syracuse: Syracuse University Press, 1987.

———. *Islam in West Africa: Religion, Society and Politics to 1800*. Aldershot: Variorum, 1994.

———. "Patterns of Islamization in West Africa." In *Conversion to Islam*, ed. Nehemia Levtzion, 206–17. New York: Holmes & Meier, 1979.

———. "The Sahara and the Sudan from the Arab Conquest of the Maghrib to the Rise of the Almoravids." In *The Cambridge History of Africa*, vol. 2, *From c. 500 B.C. to c. A.D. 1500*, ed. J.D. Fage. Cambridge: Cambridge University Press, 1978, 637–84.

Lo, Jung-Pang. "The Decline of the Early Ming Navy," *Oriens Extrêmus* 5 (1958): 149–68.

———. "The Emergence of China as a Sea Power during the Late Sung and Early Yuan Periods." *Far Eastern Quarterly* 14 (1955): 489–503.

Louis, William Roger. *Imperialism at Bay: The United States and the Decolonization of the British Empire, 1941–1945*. New York: Oxford University Press, 1978.

Lovejoy, Paul. *Transformations in Slavery: A History of Slavery in Africa*. Cambridge: Cambridge University Press, 1983.

Lugard, Lord. *The Dual Mandate in British Tropical Africa*. London: Blackwood and Sons, 1922.

McNeill, William H. *Plagues and Peoples*. Garden City, N.J.: Anchor Books, 1976.

———. "The Rise of the West after Twenty-Five Years." *Journal of World History* 1 (1990): 1–21.

McPherson, Malcolm F., and Steven C. Radelet, eds. *Economic Recovery in The Gambia: Insights for Adjustment in Sub-Saharan Africa*. Cambridge: Harvard Institute for International Development, 1995.

Mané, Mamadou. "Contribution à l'histoire du Kaabu, des origines au xix siècle," *Bulletin de l'Institut Fondamental d'Afrique Noire,* Series B 40 (1978): 87–159.

Mark, Peter. "Constructing Identity: Sixteenth- and Seventeenth-Century Architecture in the Gambia-Geba Region and the Articulation of Luso-African Ethnicity," *History in Africa: A Journal of Method* 22 (1995): 307–27.

Martin, S.M. "The Long Depression: West African Export Producers and the World Economy, 1914–1945." In *The Economies of Africa and Asia in the Inter-war Depression,* ed. Ian Brown, 74–94. New York: Routledge, 1989.

Mbaeyi, Paul. *British Military and Naval Forces in West African History, 1807–1874.* New York: Nok, 1978.

Meillassoux, Claude. *The Anthropology of Slavery: The Womb of Iron and Gold,* trans. Alide Dasnois. Chicago: University of Chicago Press, 1986.

Meirs, Suzanne, and Igor Kopytoff, eds. *Slavery in Africa: Historical and Anthropological Perspectives.* Madison: University of Wisconsin Press, 1977.

Moore, Francis. *Travels into the Inland Parts of Africa.* London: Edward Cave, 1738.

Munro, J. Forbes. *Africa and the International Economy: An Introduction to the Modern Economic History of Africa South of the Sahara.* Totowa, N.J.: Rowman and Littlefield, 1976.

Nicholson, Sharon E. "Climatic Variations in the Sahel and Other African Regions during the Past Five Centuries." *Journal of Arid Environments* 1 (1978): 3–24.

O'Brien, Donal Cruise. "Toward an 'Islamic Policy' in French West Africa, 1854–1914." *Journal of African History* 8 (1967): 303–16.

Oliver, Roland. *The African Experience: Major Themes in African History from Earliest Times to the Present.* London: Weidenfeld & Nicholson, 1991.

Pales, Leon. *Les sels alimentaires: sels minéraux, problème des sels alimentaires en AOF.* Dakar: Direction Général de la Santé Publique, 1950.

Park, Mungo. *Travels in the Interior of Africa.* London: Cassell, 1887.

Pélissier, Paul. *Les paysans du Sénégal: Les civilisations agraires du Cayor à la Casamance.* Paris: Imprimerie Fabrèque, 1966.

Phillips, William D., Jr., and Carla Rahn Phillips. *The Worlds of Christopher Columbus.* Cambridge: Cambridge University Press, 1992.

Quinn, Charlotte A. "Maba Diakhou and the Gambian *Jihad,* 1850–1890." In *Studies in West African Islamic History,* vol. 1, *The Cultivators of Islam,* ed. John Ralph Willis, 233–58. London: Frank Cass, 1979.

————. *Mandingo Kingdoms of the Senegambia: Traditionalism, Islam, and European Expansion.* Evanston: Northwestern University Press, 1977.

Radelet, Stephen C. "Reform without Revolt: The Political Economy of Economic Reform in The Gambia." *World Development* 20 (1992): 1087–99.

————. "Epilogue: The July 1994 Coup d'État." In McPherson and Radelet, 1995, 311–17.

Ragin, Charles, and Daniel Chirot. "The World System of Immanuel Wallerstein: Sociology and Politics as History." In *Vision and Method in Historical Sociology,* ed. Theda Skocpol, 276–312. Cambridge: Cambridge University Press, 1984.

Rice, Berkeley. *Enter Gambia: The Birth of an Improbable Nation.* Boston: Houghton Mifflin, 1967.

Robinson, David. "Abdul Qadir and Shaykh Umar: A Continuing Tradition of Islamic Leadership in Futa Toro." *International Journal of Africa Historical Studies* 6 (1973): 286–303.

————. *The Holy War of Umar Tal: The Western Sudan in the mid-Nineteenth Century.* Oxford: Clarendon Press, 1985.

Rodney, Walter. *A History of the Upper Guinea Coast, 1545–1800.* Oxford: Oxford University Press, 1970.

————. *How Europe Underdeveloped Africa.* London: Bogle-l'Ouverture, 1972.

Round Table Conference: Strategy for Poverty Alleviation. Banjul: The Government of The Gambia, 1994.

Russell Wood, A.J.R. *World on the Move: The Portuguese in Africa, Asia, and America, 1415–1808.* New York: St Martin's Press, 1992.

Sallah, Tijan M. "Economics and Politics in The Gambia." *Journal of Modern African Studies* 28 (1990): 621–48.

Sanneh, Lamin O. *The Jahanke: The History of an Islamic Clerical People of the Senegambia.* London: Oxford University Press, 1979.

Sapir, Olga Linares de. "Shell-Middens of Lower Casamance and Diola Protohistory." *West African Journal of Archaeology* 1 (1971): 23–54.

Searing, James F. *West African Slavery and Atlantic Commerce: The Senegal River Valley, 1700–1860.* Cambridge: Cambridge University Press, 1993.

Shaffer, Lynda N. "Southernization." *Journal of World History* 5 (1994): 1–21.

Shannon, Thomas Richard. *An Introduction to the World-System Perspective.* Boulder, Colo.: Westview Press, 1989.

Sidibe, B.K. *A Brief History of Kaabu and Fuladu, 1300–1930: A Narrative Based on Some Oral Traditions of the Senegambia.* Banjul: Oral History and Antiquities Division, 1974.

Smil, Vaclav. *Energy in World History.* Boulder, Colo.: Westview Press, 1994.

Spindel, Carol. *In the Shadow of the Sacred Grove.* New York: Vintage. 1989.

Stavrianos, L.S. *Global Rift: The Third World Comes of Age.* New York: Morrow, 1981.

————. *Lifelines from Our Past: A New World History.* Armonk, N.Y.: M.E. Sharpe, 1989.

Stearns, Peter. *Interpreting the Industrial Revolution.* Washington, D.C.: American Historical Association, 1991.

Swindell, Ken. "African Food Imports and Agricultural Development: Peanut Basins and Rice Bowls in The Gambia, 1843–1933." In Hoggart 1992, 159–79.

————. "Serawoollies, Tillibunkas and Strange Farmers: The Development of Migrant Groundnut Farming along the Gambia River, 1848–1895." *Journal of African History* 21 (1980): 93–104.

Tamari, Tal. "The Development of Caste Systems in West Africa." *Journal of African History* 32 (1991): 221–50.

Thornton, John. *Africa and Africans in the Making of the Atlantic World, 1400–1680.* New York: Cambridge University Press, 1992.

————. "Precolonial African Industry and the Atlantic Trade, 1500–1800." *African Economic History* 19 (1990): 1–54.

Tuden, Arthur, and Leonard Plotnicov, *Social Stratification in Africa.* New York: Free Press, 1970.

Voll, John O. "Islam as a Special World System." *Journal of World History* 5 (1994): 213–26.

Wallerstein, Immanuel. "Africa and the World-Economy." In *General History of Africa,* vol. 6, *Africa in the Nineteenth Century until the 1880s,* ed. J.F. Ade Ajayi, 23–39. Paris: UNESCO, 1989.

————. *The Modern World-System: Capitalist Agriculture and the Origins of the European World-Economy in the Sixteenth Century.* New York: Academic Press, 1974.

————. *The Modern World-System II: Mercantilism and the Consolidation of the European World-Economy.* New York: Academic Press, 1980.

————. *The Modern World-System III: The Second Era of Great Expansion of the Capitalist World-Economy.* San Diego: Academic Press, 1988.

Watson, Andrew. *Agricultural Innovation in the Early Islamic World: The Diffusion of*

Crops and Farming Techniques, 700–1100. Cambridge: Cambridge University Press, 1983.

Webb, James L.A. *Desert Frontier: Ecological and Economic Change along the Western Sahel, 1600–1850.* Madison: University of Wisconsin Press, 1995.

Wilkinson, David. "Core, Peripheries, and Civilization." In *Core/Periphery Relations in Precapitalist Worlds,* ed. C. Chase-Dunn and T. Hall, 113–66. Boulder, Colo.: Westview Press, 1991.

Willis, John Ralph. "Introduction: Reflections on the Diffusion of Islam in West Africa." In *Studies in West African Islamic History,* vol. 1, *The Cultivators of Islam,* ed. John Ralph Willis, 1–39. London: Frank Cass, 1979.

Wolff, Eric R. *Europe and the People without History.* Berkeley: University of California Press, 1982.

World Tables 1995. Baltimore: Johns Hopkins University Press, 1995.

Wright, Donald R. *The Early History of Niumi: Settlement and Foundation of a Mandinka State on the Gambia River.* Athens, Ohio: Ohio University Center for International Studies, 1977.

———. "The Epic of Kelefa Saane as a Guide to the Nature of Precolonial Senegambian Society—and Vice Versa." *History in Africa: A Journal of Method* 14 (1987): 307–27.

———. *Oral Traditions from The Gambia.* 2 vols. Athens, Ohio: Ohio University Center for International Studies, 1979, 1980.

———. "Uprooting Kunta Kinte: On the Perils of Relying on Encyclopedic Informants." *History in Africa: A Journal of Method* 8 (1981): 205–17.

INDEX

Donald R. Wright is a Distinguished Teaching Professor of History at the State University of New York, College at Cortland, where he has been on the faculty since 1976. He holds M.A. and Ph.D. degrees in history from Indiana University and a B.A. from DePauw University. He has received Fulbright-Hays, NEH, and SUNY fellowships for research in Africa. His previous books include two on early African American history and a two-volume collection of oral traditions from The Gambia.